FOR ACCOUNTING

Excel® & Access®

Glenn Owen

Allan Hancock College

University of California
at Santa Barbara

THOMSON

SOUTH-WESTERN

Australia · Canada · Mexico · Singapore · Spain · United Kingdom · United States

Excel and Access for Accounting
Glenn Owen

Editor-in-Chief:
Jack Calhoun

Team Leader:
Melissa Acuña

Acquisitions Editor:
Sharon Oblinger

Developmental Editor:
Erin E. McGraw

Marketing Manager:
Mignon Tucker

Senior Production Editor:
Kara ZumBahlen

Production Coordinator:
Jodi Morris

Manufacturing Coordinator:
Doug Wilke

Compositor:
DPS Assoicates, Inc.

Printer:
QuebecorWorld, Dubuque

Design Project Manager:
Rik Moore

Internal Designer:
Imbue Design

Cover Designer:
Rik Moore

Cover Photo:
PhotoDisc, Inc.

Library of Congress Cataloging-
in-Publication Data
Owen, Glenn
Excel and Access for accounting /
Glenn Owen.
p. cm.
Includes index.
ISBN 0-324-06857-3 (Text and CD)
ISBN 0-324-18212-0 (CD only)
ISBN 0-324-18277-5 (Text only)
1. Microsoft Excel (Computer file)
2. Access (Computer file)
3. Accounting—Computer programs.
4. Small business—Accounting—
Computer programs. 5. Small
business—Finance—Computer
programs. 6. Financial statements—
Computer programs. I. Title.

HF5679.O945 2002
657'.0285'5369—dc21   2001057715

Brief Contents

Contents

vi   **Contents**

What if you could integrate two critical business software programs into your classroom without using confusing and complicated manuals? What if your students could use these programs to reinforce basic accounting concepts in an interactive case setting? What if you could do both without spending a fortune and a vast amount of time preparing examples, cases, and illustrations? *Excel and Access for Accounting* by Glenn Owen is a textbook that fulfills and expands upon all three of these "what ifs."

WHY IS THIS TEXTBOOK NEEDED?

Many accounting educators are looking for ways to incorporate more business software into their accounting curriculum without displacing basic accounting instruction. They have tried to accomplish this by creating a stand-alone computer-based course, a lab component course, or by adding business computer software to their regular accounting curriculum. Current texts in this field are very generic in nature, spending little if any time on accounting-specific issues. Those that do address accounting issues address only worksheet or database issues, but not both. Some texts that have a worksheet focus deliver a wide array of financial and managerial topics but lack a natural case flow. Some with a database focus emphasize the creation of accounting systems but do not address how databases are used to support the accounting function.

Moreover, employers expect today's college student to be computer literate in commercial accounting, worksheet, and database software. The demand for this type of training is growing daily as more and more businesses employ business software to solve real-world problems.

Instructors often want to incorporate business software into the first course, but are reluctant to invest the time and effort necessary to accomplish this goal. Existing materials are often "preparer" driven in that they focus on the creation of worksheets and databases without addressing the effective use of these tools. Students are often discouraged in their use of computers because of the complicated and confusing manuals that concentrate on using the software without any business or accounting context.

This text responds to all of those needs. It provides a self-paced, step-by-step environment in which the students use a worksheet (Excel®) and a database (Access®) to solve real accounting and business problems.

The text is designed to reinforce the concepts students learn in their first accounting courses and to show how worksheets and databases can help users make better and more informed business decisions.

WHAT ARE THE GOALS OF THIS TEXTBOOK?

This textbook takes a user perspective by illustrating how worksheets and databases are both used and created. Both Excel and Access are user-friendly, with extensive help features and helpful toolbars to aid in accessing commonly used functions. The textbook uses a proven and successful pedagogy to demonstrate both software programs' features and elicit student interaction.

The textbook's first goal is to help students apply the accounting concepts they've learned to real-world problems, aided by the use of a worksheet and/or database. The content complements the first course in accounting and therefore should either be used as a supplement to that course or as the primary textbook in a stand-alone course which follows the first course in accounting. Some instructors have found use of this textbook and the *QuickBooks for Accounting* textbook an ideal match for a "Computers in Accounting" stand-alone course.

The second goal is motivate students to become more familiar with and more at ease using a worksheet and/or database to solve accounting and business problems. Using this software application in an accounting context maintains student interest and provides additional incentive for pursuing an accounting degree or emphasis.

The third goal of this text is to reduce the administrative burdens of accounting faculty by providing a self-paced environment for their students to learn how important software applications are used in business. Accounting faculty must now manage different learning styles of students and teach accounting concepts and practice techniques. The task of integrating computer applications into the classroom as well will be made simpler with the use of this text.

WHAT ARE THE KEY FEATURES OF THIS TEXTBOOK?

Following is a list of the key features of this book:

- The chapters incorporate a continuing, interesting, realistic case— Coast Jewelers, Inc.—that helps students apply Excel and Access features.

- A tested, proven, step-by-step methodology keeps students on track. Students enter data, analyze information, and make decisions all within the context of the case. The text constantly guides students, letting them know where they are in the course of completing their accounting tasks.

- Numerous screen shots include callouts that direct students' attention to what they should look at on the screen. On almost every page in the book, you will find examples of how steps, screen shots, and callouts work together.

- **trouble?** paragraphs anticipate the mistakes that students are likely to make or problems they are likely to encounter, and help students recover and continue with the chapter. This feature facilitates independent learning and frees the instructor to focus on accounting concepts rather than on computer skills.

- The end-of-chapter material begins with questions intended to test students' recall of what they learned in the chapter.

- Chapter Assignments follow the Questions and provide students additional hands-on practice with Excel and Access skills.

- A continuing Case Problem—Kelly's Boutique, a retail store—concludes each chapter. This case has approximately the same scope as the Coast Jewelers chapter case.

- The Instructor's Package contains an Instructor's Manual, including solutions to end-of-chapter materials, a test bank, and a CD with student files and completed assignment files.

USING THIS TEXT EFFECTIVELY

Before you begin, note that this textbook assumes you are familiar with the basics of Windows 98 or Windows 2000: how to control windows, how to choose menu commands, how to complete dialog boxes, and how to select directories, drives, and files. If you do not understand these concepts, please consult your instructor.

The best way to work through this textbook is to carefully read the text and complete the numbered steps, which appear on a shaded background, as you work at your computer. Read each step carefully and completely before you try it.

As you work, compare your screen with the figures in the chapter to verify your results. You can use Excel 2000 and Access 2000 with either Windows 98, 2000, or ME. The screen shots you see in this book were captured in a Windows 98 environment. If you are using Windows 2000 or ME, you might see some minor differences between your screen and the screens in this book. Any significant differences that result from using the different operating systems with Excel or Access will be explained.

Don't worry about making mistakes—that is part of the learning process. The **trouble?** paragraphs identify common problems and explain how to correct them or get back on track. Follow the suggestions *only* if you are having the specific problem described.

After you complete a chapter, you can answer the Questions, Assignments, and Case Problem found at the end of each chapter. They are carefully structured so that you will review what you have learned and then apply your knowledge to new situations. Feel free to page back through the text to clarify how to accomplish each task.

YOUR STUDENT CD

To complete the chapter and exercises in this book, you must have a Student CD. The Student CD contains some practice files you need for the chapters, the Assignments, and the Case Problem. Your instructor or lab manager may provide you with a Student CD, your instructor may require you to make your own Student CD, or you may be asked to use the disk that accompanies this text. See your instructor for specific details. In any case, this text will assume you have a Student CD that contains the above-mentioned practice files. Before you begin each chapter, copy the files from the chapter folder on the Student CD to your hard drive.

EXCEL AND ACCESS VERSIONS

The text and related data files created for this text were constructed using Excel 2000 and Access 2000 Series Release 1. To check your version and release number select About Microsoft Excel or About Microsoft Access from the Help menu. All references to Excel and Access throughout the rest of this textbook refer to Excel 2000 or Access 2000.

Microsoft has recently released Office XP, in which new versions of the Excel and Access applications are included. These are now referred to as Excel 2002 and Access 2002. This book can be used with the updated versions of each application. Data files will be read with no difficulty; however, some screen shots and steps will be different in the new versions. If you use the text with the new versions of Excel and/or Access, be aware of these potential differences.

EXCEL AND ACCESS OPTIONS

Excel and Access have many options that can be altered by the user. In a lab environment, or in an environment where different people use the same computer, these options may have been altered from the default settings set when the software was first installed. Using the Tools menu, you should select Options and compare the settings on your computer with those used in the creation of this text. Differences in these options will most certainly lead to confusion in the interpretation of this text. For example, the Excel settings listed on the Edit tab of the Options window should show that the check box "Move selection after Enter" is checked. If it is not checked, pressing the Enter key will not move the active cell. Each tab of the Excel Options window is shown in Figures P.1 through P.8 for comparison.

FIGURE P.1

*View Tab of the
Options Window*

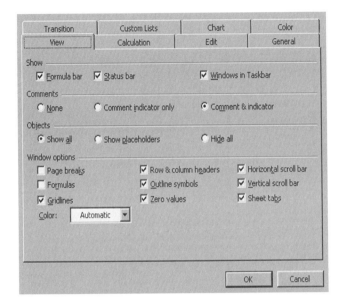

FIGURE P.3

*Edit Tab of the
Options Window*

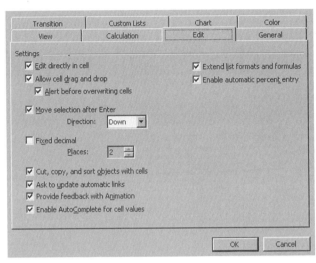

FIGURE P.2

*Calculation Tab of the
Options Window*

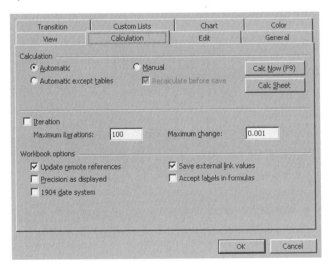

FIGURE P.4

*General Tab of the
Options Window*

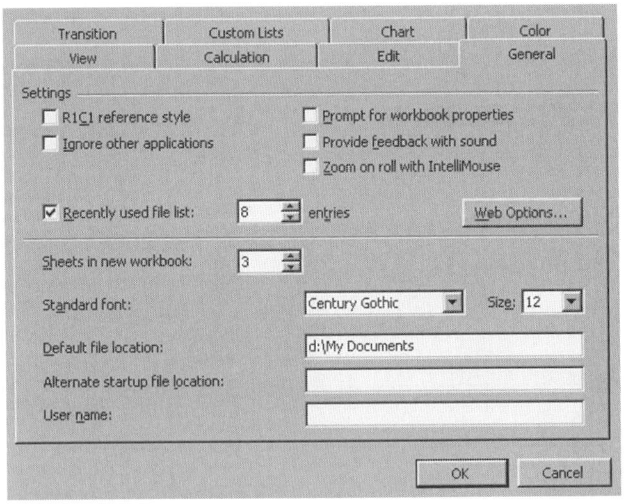

FIGURE P.5

Transition Tab of the Options Window

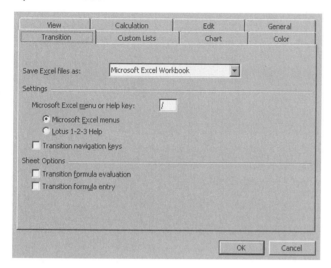

FIGURE P.7

Chart Tab of the Options Window

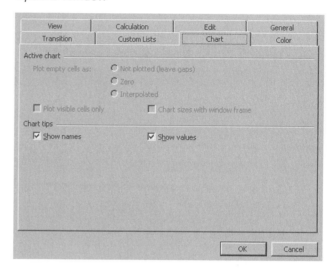

FIGURE P.6

Custom Lists Tab of the Options Window

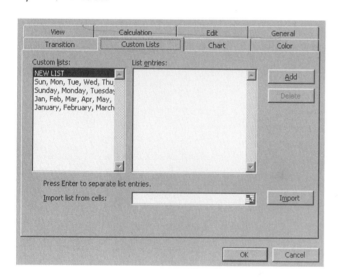

FIGURE P.8

Color Tab of the Options Window

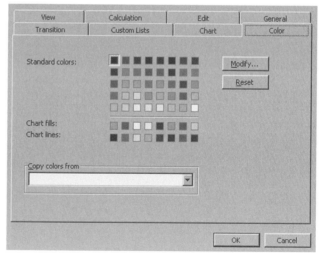

In Access, the settings listed on the Keyboard tab of the Options window should show that the "Move after enter" section has the "Next field" option button selected. If it is *not* selected, and the "Next record" option *is* selected, pressing the Enter key will move the focus to the next record instead of the next field. Each tab of the Access Options window is shown for comparison in Figures P.9 through P.16.

FIGURE P.9

View Tab of the Options Window

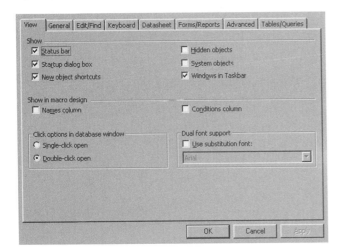

FIGURE P.10

General Tab of the Options Window

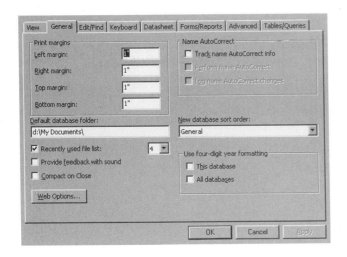

FIGURE P.11

Edit/Find Tab of the Options Window

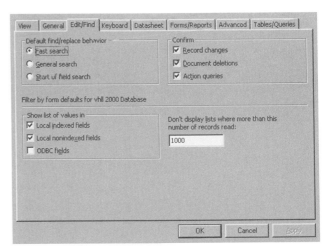

FIGURE P.12

Keyboard Tab of the Options Window

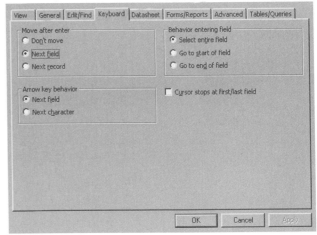

FIGURE P.13

*Datasheet Tab of the
Options Window*

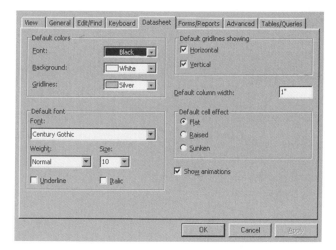

FIGURE P.15

*Advanced Tab of the
Options Window*

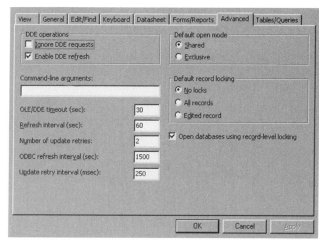

FIGURE P.14

*Forms/Report Tab of the
Options Window*

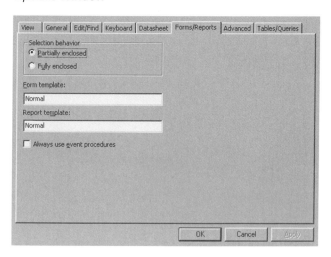

FIGURE P.16

*Tables/Queries Tab of the
Options Window*

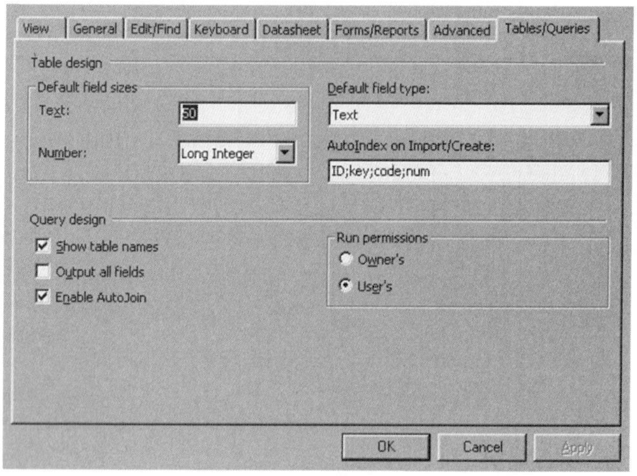

ABOUT THE AUTHOR

Glenn Owen is a tenured faculty member of Allan Hancock College's Accounting and Business Department where he lectures on accounting and information systems. In addition, he is a lecturer at the University of California at Santa Barbara, where he has been teaching accounting and information systems courses since 1980. His professional experience includes five years at Deloitte & Touche CPA and seven years as vice-president of finance positions at Westpac Resources, Inc. and ExperTelligence, Inc. He is active in the American Accounting Association, and he has authored many Internet-related books and accounting course supplements. He is the author of the popular *QuickBooks for Accounting* text and teaches both regular and distance-learning (Internet-based) financial and managerial accounting courses. His innovative teaching style emphasizes the decision-maker's perspective and encourages students to think creatively. His graduate studies in educational psychology and 28 years of business experience combine for a balanced blend of theory and practice.

part 1

Excel for Accounting

Excel Tour

In this chapter you will learn:

- **Excel basics**

- **Excel's help system**

- **How to work with files**

- **How to enter information into a worksheet**

- **How to use formulas more extensively**

- **How to manipulate data and structure worksheets**

- **How to print a worksheet**

CASE: COAST JEWELERS, INC.

Nathan Peters and Meagan Lopez own Coast Jewelers, Inc. located in Santa Barbara, California. They've been in business for five years and have developed a number of repeat customers. As is typical in the beach-side resort town, they also cater to the tourists who flock to the community each summer. They specialize in diamond jewelry manufacturing and sales, both retail and wholesale, and are eager to expand their customer base and their supplier pool. Their local C.P.A., Kyle Ski, has suggested hiring a local college student to help them computerize their operations. He suggests they use QuickBooks to keep their accounting records but also encourages them to use a worksheet software application to help them analyze their business situation and support their accounting operations. Nathan, excited to get started, places an ad in the local college paper.

As an accounting student at the local college, you've become fairly adept at using computers to complete homework assignments but you're eager to broaden your horizons. You'd like to combine your accounting and computer skills with some practical experience. Lucky for you an ad in the college paper for part-time computer and accounting help falls on your desk one afternoon. After an intense interview and background check, you're hired!

Your initial meeting with Nathan, Meagan, and Kyle reveals some unfamiliarity with the software application Kyle has suggested you use. Kyle has agreed to coach you through the basic use of the worksheet program after Nathan and Meagan reluctantly agree to pay his fees. They're hoping of course that you can learn the worksheet application quickly and help them use it to further their business expansion.

First off, Kyle introduces you to Excel, a powerful worksheet application he has been using since the mid-eighties. Kyle explains that this most recent incarnation of Excel is far more than a simple calculation program.

EXCEL BASICS

In this section you will become familiar with the Excel window, its toolbars, layout, and functions.

What is Excel?

You have used worksheets in your accounting courses and ask Kyle if Excel is just an electronic version of that same worksheet. He explains that in essence you are correct. In your basic accounting courses a worksheet might have been used to adjust a trial balance for accrual accounting and to separate balance sheet and income statement accounts. In that case, each column represented debits or credits for the trial balance, adjustments, and adjusted trial balance amounts. Excel can automate that task and others by automatically adding columns and performing complex math functions.

Excel is, however, much more than an expensive calculator. Built-in functions can help you produce financial statements, reports and analyses, depreciation schedules, loan amortization schedules, cash flow budgets, and even a cost-volume-profit analysis complete with charts for better visualizations. Excel also has the ability to help you prepare web pages and a whole lot more.

First, you must learn to start Excel, become familiar with the Excel window, and use Excel's built-in help system.

Starting Excel

To begin, Kyle asks you if you're familiar with starting programs in Windows 98. While Nathan and Meagan admit to very little knowledge of computers, you offer to demonstrate. First you explain that some of the company's computer equipment uses the Windows 95 operating system while the one you are most familiar with uses Windows 98. In either case, you explain that starting Excel is the same.

To start Excel:

1 Click the **Start** button.

2 Select the Office 2000 menu and look down the list for Excel. An example of what you might see is shown in Figure 1.1.

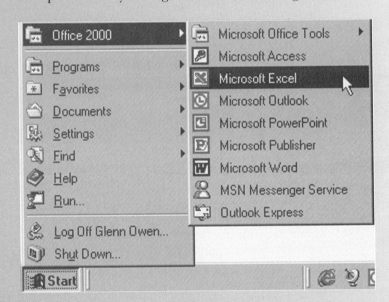

FIGURE 1.1

Starting Excel

3 Once you've located the Excel program, click and release the Excel icon or name.

trouble? Your start menu may be completely different from that shown above. See your instructor or lab manual to identify the location of the Excel shortcut needed to start the program.

Now that you've started Excel, you can begin to learn how to use it.

The Excel Window

Excel always opens a blank worksheet when first started as shown in Figure 1.2. Kyle describes that a **worksheet** is a grid of rows and columns into which you enter data. A **workbook**, on the other hand, is an Excel document or file that contains as many worksheets or charts as you wish.

Nathan notices that his screen looks different from Kyle's. Kyle explains that the menus and toolbars used in Excel can be customized. Thus, those shown in the figure might not match those on your screen. By default, Excel displays two toolbars: the Standard toolbar and the Formatting toolbar. By holding your mouse pointer over any tool, you can see a screen tip explaining the tool.

If the Standard and Formatting toolbars are not visible on your screen, right-click the toolbar area and check the Standard and Formatting check boxes. Uncheck any other toolbars.

The menu bar, shown at the top of the Excel window, is dynamic, not static, in that it changes based upon the user's activity. It adjusts the display of menu items to make your favorite commands more accessible. Meagan complains that this is too confusing, as her menus will be changing every time she uses the program. She shows Kyle how the View menu at first shows just a few menu items and after a few seconds, shows more. Kyle notes that this is progress.

FIGURE 1.2

The Excel Window

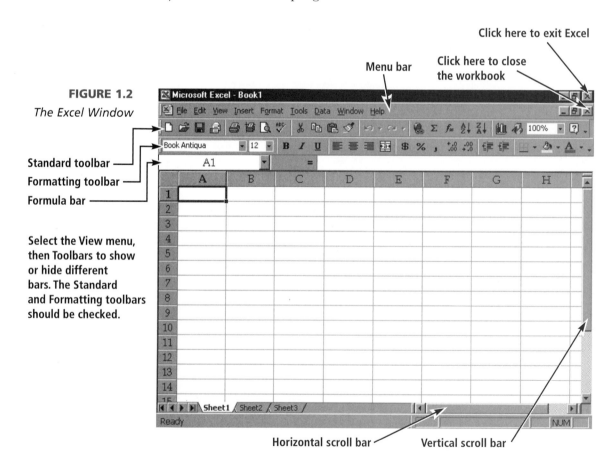

To explore the worksheet window:

1 Click the **View** menu and notice the double down-arrow at the bottom of the menu.

2 Continue to hold the mouse pointer over the View menu for about five seconds and notice how the menu expands. (Alternatively, you could have clicked the double down-arrow to expand the menu quicker.)

3 Click somewhere else on the worksheet to de-select the View menu.

4 Hold the mouse pointer over the first button on the Standard toolbar, which should look like a piece of paper. Note the screen tip that appears indicating that this button, if clicked, will create a new workbook. Move the mouse pointer over other buttons to view their screen tips.

5 Click the arrow in the vertical scroll bar once to scroll one row at a time.

6 Click above or below the scroll box in the vertical scroll bar to scroll up or down one window at a time.

7 Click the arrow in the horizontal scroll bar once to scroll one column at a time.

8 Click to the left or right of the scroll box in the horizontal scroll bar to scroll left or right one window at a time.

9 Drag the scroll box in either the vertical or horizontal scroll bar to move quickly over a large worksheet.

"That wasn't so bad," claims Nathan. Kyle cautions you, Nathan, and Meagan to have patience. The help system he's about to explain will save you time and energy down the road.

The Help System

Excel has a built-in help system to assist you in your learning experience. For example, new Excel users often want to use keyboard shortcuts to expedite their use of the program. Kyle offers to demonstrate how Excel's help system can point out some of those keyboard shortcuts.

To use the help system to identify keyboard shortcuts:

1 Click **Help** on the menu bar, then click **Microsoft Excel Help**. (Alternatively, you can press the **F1** key.)

2 Move both the vertical and horizontal scroll boxes of the Microsoft Excel Help window to the top and left respectively.

3 Click once on the **Getting Help** topic to collapse the sub items. Now your screen should look like Figure 1.3.

Click the + sign to expand the sub items under
Using Shortcut Keys

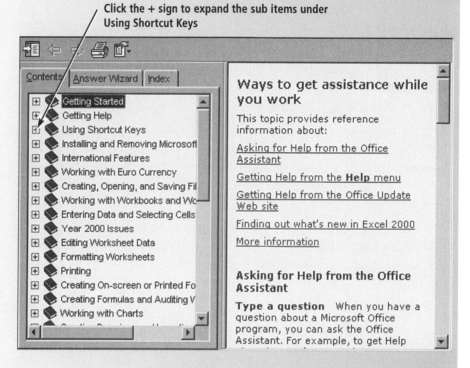

4 Click the + sign next to Using Shortcut Keys then click **Keyboard shortcuts**. The window to the right of the help table of contents should now display Keyboard Shortcuts and ask, "Which keys do you want to use?"

5 Click **keys for moving and scrolling in a worksheet or workbook**.

6 Scroll down this list of keyboard shortcuts noting how to use the arrow keys, Home key, Page Down, Page Up, and End key.

7 Close the Microsoft Excel Help window (by clicking in the close window **X** in the upper right corner of the Help window), then test your newfound knowledge of shortcut keys by moving around the Excel window using each key.

You can use the help system anytime Excel is open to learn new techniques or remember how to do something you thought you already knew! Now you are ready to work with existing Excel documents or files.

WORKING WITH FILES

To effectively use Excel as a business tool you must understand how to open existing files and save them or save new files for later use. In this section you will learn how to do both.

Opening Files

This text provides many Excel workbooks that are used to start a text example, a lab assignment, or case. The files are either on a disk provided with the text or provided by your instructor. If you are uncertain, please see your instructor.

Kyle has created a basic trial balance on a worksheet for you to experiment with. He suggests you open the file by using either the File menu or the Open tool on the Standard toolbar.

To open an existing workbook file:

1 Click **File**, then **Open** from Excel's menu bar or click the **Open** tool on the Standard toolbar.

2 Double-click the filename **ch1-01.xls** to reveal a file, which should look like Figure 1.4.

trouble? The Open window may not list the Excel files you need for this text. There may be several reasons for this. Make sure the Look in: text box in the Open window refers to the location in which these files are kept. In some instances this might be a chapter directory on the CD drive. In other cases it might be the network drive on which your instructor has placed the files.

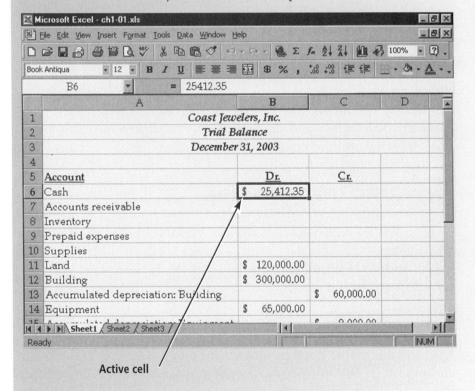

FIGURE 1.4

The Trial Balance

Active cell

The most difficult part of opening files is remembering where you've saved them. Keeping a consistent pattern of file storage is key to proper computer application usage.

Saving Files

When you create a file from scratch or modify an existing file, it is important that you save the file in a safe location. If you are working in a lab environment your best alternative is to save files to a 3½" floppy disk or some other type of removable storage. This way you can transport the file to another computer for further modification.

Kyle suggests you save the trial balance file under a different name so that changes made later on do not overwrite the original file.

To save a workbook file:

1 With the trial balance file still open (ch1-01.xls), click **File**, then click **Save**. Alternatively you can click the Save tool, which looks like a little diskette on the Standard toolbar. This saves any changes you might have made to the file (we didn't make any changes yet) to the existing file name (ch1-01.xls).

2 To save the workbook under a different file name, click **File**, then **Save As**.
trouble? If you accidentally select Save instead of Save As, the file will be saved with the old name and any changes you've made will be written over the old file. Be careful as there is no Undo command for file changes such as this.

3 In the File name: text box of the Save As window, type the new file name **ch1-01a.xls**, then click **Save**.

Meagan comments that the trial balance opened above doesn't look complete. Kyle agrees and suggests that the next step in your learning process include how to enter information.

ENTERING INFORMATION

To complete the trial balance it will be necessary to enter additional text and numbers. The basic data entry container for Excel is a cell. Each cell has an address determined by its location on the worksheet grid. The column number and row number determine the address.

Entering Data

Kyle explains that to put data into a cell, you must first select the cell by clicking on it. As you type, the data is also automatically entered into the formula bar. Text entries into cells are often referred to as *labels*, while numbers or formula entries are referred to as *values*.

To enter data into the worksheet:

1 Click cell **B7**, type **84245.25**, then press the **Enter** key. Note how the number is automatically formatted for you. More on this later. Note also that the active cell is now one row lower at cell B8.

2 Type **125351.45** in cell B8, then press the **Enter** key.

3 Click cell **C20**, type **1527515.65**, then press the **Enter** key. Note that the cell value may show several # signs. If this happens, you need to fix this by resizing the column width. More about this later.

4 Click cell **A26**, type the label **Total**, then press the **Enter** key. We'll format this cell later.

5 Continue to fill in the remaining empty cells so that your worksheet looks like that shown in Figure 1.5.

FIGURE 1.5

Almost Completed Trial Balance

	A	B	C
1	*Coast Jewelers, Inc.*		
2	*Trial Balance*		
3	*December 31, 2003*		
4			
5	**Account**	**Dr.**	**Cr.**
6	Cash	$ 25,412.35	
7	Accounts receivable	84,245.25	
8	Inventory	125,351.45	
9	Prepaid expenses	15,624.45	
10	Supplies	10,245.15	
11	Land	120,000.00	
12	Building	300,000.00	
13	Accumulated depreciation: Building		$ 60,000.00
14	Equipment	65,000.00	
15	Accumulated depreciation: Equipment		$ 8,000.00
16	Accounts payable		$ 75,182.10
17	Long-term debt		$400,000.00
18	Common stock		$ 10,000.00
19	Retained earnings		$ 15,000.00
20	Sales revenue		########
21	Cost of goods sold	993,900.30	
22	Advertising expense	54,215.45	
23	Depreciation expense	16,000.00	
24	Payroll expense	240,451.45	
25	Utilities	45,251.90	
26	Total		

Sheet1 / Sheet2 / Sheet3 /

The # signs indicate the column width is too small to show the number

You have now entered both values and labels into your worksheet. Before moving on, save your work to the existing file named ch1-01a.xls. Now you can make changes to the data already entered.

Changing Column Width and Row Height

Perhaps now is a good time to fix that sales number on the trial balance as Kyle suggests. The problem occurred when a number entered in cell C20 was wider than the column permitted. The result was a cell filled with # signs. To fix it, Kyle explains, all you have to do is resize column C. However, for uniformity, resize both column B and C.

To change the column width and row height of a worksheet:

1 Place the mouse pointer between column C and column D at the top of the columns so that the mouse pointer cursor changes into a line with two arrows pointing left and right.

2 Click and hold the mouse button down to reveal the column width as being Width: 12.63 (106 pixels).

3 While still holding the mouse button down drag the column width to the right until the width is 13.00 (109 pixels).

4 To resize both column B and C point the mouse pointer to the **B** of column B and click once. (This selects the entire column B.)

5 Now click and drag from the **B** of column B to the **C** of column C. (This selects both columns B and C.)

6 With both columns selected, place the mouse pointer between column B and column C at the top of the columns so that the mouse pointer cursor changes into a line with two arrows pointing left and right.

7 Click and drag the column width to the right until the width is 13.00 (109 pixels). Both columns should now be the same width 13.00 (109 pixels).

8 To resize the height of row 4, click between rows 4 and 5 at the far left of the worksheet until the mouse pointer cursor changes into a line with two arrows pointing up and down.

9 While still holding the mouse button down drag the row height down until the height is 21.00 (28 pixels).

"If you are like me," Kyle admits, "you will find yourself making a few mistakes along the way."

Editing Data

Nathan agrees and wants to know about correcting errors. He claims he's not very good at typing and has made some mistakes when entering the information above. Kyle explains that you can always edit the information you enter into worksheet whether you've pressed the Enter key or not. Excel gives you two ways to edit data. You can either edit the formula bar, or edit data directly in the cell. For instance, the utilities expense number you entered in cell B25 above should have been 45251.09 not 45251.90. Also, prepaid expenses entered in cell B9 should have been 15625.26 not 15624.45.

To edit data in the worksheet:

1 Click once in cell **B25**, click in the formula bar on the far right of the number 45251.9. Now press the **Backspace** key once and type **09**, then press **Enter**. This is the formula edit process.

2 Scroll to the top of the worksheet, then double-click cell **B9**. Click and drag the mouse pointer over the number **4.45**, type **5.26**, then press **Enter**. This is the cell edit process.

Meagan says she prefers the formula edit process, although Nathan likes the cell edit process. You like both, depending on your mood. In either case, each process corrects errors and makes changes in the worksheet.

Controlling the Appearance of Data

You ask Kyle why the numbers on the trial balance are formatted with the $. He explains that initially he formatted both columns B and C to be in the currency format. Formatting does not change the text or numbers in the cell itself. Instead, formatting changes the way the text or numbers appear in the worksheet. To experiment, he suggests you remove the currency format from all but cells B6, C13, B26, and C26, as the top and bottom of a column of accounting numbers are usually formatted with the $. He further suggests you replace the format with a comma and cents format using the format painter.

To remove the $ format and replace it with a comma and cents format:

1 Click cell **B7**, then click the **Comma Style** tool (it looks like a comma) on the Format toolbar. Note how the number still has the comma and cents formatting from before but no longer contains the $.

2 With cell B7 still selected, click the **Format Painter** tool (it looks like a paintbrush) on the Standard toolbar. Note that cell B7 now has ants dancing around the border of the cell and that the mouse pointer has an added paintbrush.

3 Click and hold the mouse button over cell B8, drag down until you reach cell B25, then unclick the mouse. You have now painted the comma format across those cells.

4 Now repeat the same comma formatting for cells C15 to C25.

Kyle also explains that it is common practice to total the debit and credit columns of a trial balance and include a double underline under such totals. Because you are in the midst of formatting cells, he suggests you format the two total cells before you create a formula adding a column of cells.

To format the total cells with a double underline:

1 Click and highlight cells **B26** and **C26**, by clicking first in B26 and then dragging the mouse to C26 while holding down the mouse button.

2 Place the mouse pointer over the Borders tool located on the Format toolbar, specifically over the little arrow located on the right of the Borders tool. Click the arrow to reveal several border options.

3 Click the **Top and Double Bottom Border** tool to format the cells.

To finish the trial balance all you need now is a total for each column.

Entering Formulas and Using Functions

Formulas in Excel always begin with an equal sign (=). These formulas can use numbers; math symbols to add, subtract, multiply, or divide (+, –, *, /); cell references; and/or functions. Nathan asks if Excel has a calculator built in so you could add the column and then put the result in the total cell. Kyle explains that though that might work, later if your numbers change you would be required to re-add the column. Meagan asks if the best way to add a column of numbers then would be to add each cell. Kyle explains you could certainly do that by typing a formula like this: =B6+B7+B8 etc.

However, Kyle explains that Excel includes some functions that accomplish this task in a more efficient manner. The SUM function, for instance, will sum up specified series of cells.

"Hold on," you say. "Functions sound like programming and I'm just an accounting student who has no desire to learn computer programming."

"Don't panic!" Kyle advises. "Excel's functions are fairly simple. Each function reacts to certain arguments you provide. For instance, the SUM function is written as follows: =SUM(argument). The argument is a series of cell references you want summed. Let me show you how to add the sum function to your trial balance to add up the debit and credit columns."

To use the SUM function to add a column of numbers:

1 Type **=SUM(B6:B25)** in cell B26, then press **Enter**. The result of that function should be the amount $2,095,697.75.

2 Alternatively, you can enter the argument by clicking and dragging the mouse pointer over the cells to be added. Type **=SUM(** in cell C26. (Do not press the **Enter** key yet.)

3 Scroll to the top of the worksheet and click and hold the mouse pointer over cell C6.

4 Now drag the mouse pointer down the worksheet (keeping the mouse button down) until you reach cell C25.

5 Release the mouse button and press **Enter**.

Kyle explains that now you've entered a sum function to add up both the debit and credit columns using two different methods. In both cases the resulting formula is the same. You have simply used different methods to achieve the same goal. Plus, if you enter different data in the cells B6 to B25 or C6 to C25, the SUM function will automatically add them up. The now completed trial balance is shown in Figure 1.6.

FIGURE 1.6
Completed Trial Balance

	A	B	C	
1	Coast Jewelers, Inc.			
2	Trial Balance			
3	December 31, 2003			
4				
5	**Account**	**Dr.**	**Cr.**	
6	Cash	$ 25,412.35		
7	Accounts receivable	84,245.25		
8	Inventory	125,351.45		
9	Prepaid expenses	15,625.26		
10	Supplies	10,245.15		
11	Land	120,000.00		
12	Building	300,000.00		
13	Accumulated depreciation: Building		$ 60,000.00	
14	Equipment	65,000.00		
15	Accumulated depreciation: Equipment		$ 8,000.00	
16	Accounts payable		$ 75,182.10	
17	Long-term debt		$ 400,000.00	
18	Common stock		$ 10,000.00	
19	Retained earnings		$ 15,000.00	
20	Sales revenue		$1,527,515.65	
21	Cost of goods sold	993,900.30		
22	Advertising expense	54,215.45		
23	Depreciation expense	16,000.00		
24	Payroll expense	240,451.45		
25	Utilities	45,251.09		
26	Total	$2,095,697.75	$2,095,697.75	

|◄ ◄ ► ►|\ **Sheet1** / Sheet2 / Sheet3 /

MORE EXTENSIVE USE OF FORMULAS
· ·

Nathan comments that he envisions another use of this worksheet software. Weekly he prepares a watch sales worksheet by hand that identifies how many Citizen watches have been sold each week, their cost, markup, sales price, discount, and total sales. Kyle suggests that this might be a good opportunity to illustrate a more extensive use of formulas in Excel.

Entering and Editing Formulas

As explained earlier in this chapter, formulas in Excel always begin with an equal sign (=). These formulas can use numbers; math symbols to add, subtract, multiply, or divide (+, −, *, /); cell references; and/or functions.

Kyle prepares a worksheet with titles and headings similar to Nathan's hand-prepared worksheet and recommends that you, Nathan, and Meagan use it to prepare a weekly watch sales worksheet for the week of November 6, 2003. In it he includes the names of the four types of watches sold that week, the cost or price Coast paid for each watch, the usual markup on cost used to determine the price, the discount offered that week on each watch, and the quantity of each watch sold.

The price for each watch is based on the watch cost and markup percentage. For example, if a watch costs $100 and the markup is 50 percent, Coast sells the watch for $150 (the $100 cost plus a markup of 50 percent × $100, or $50).

The total column is the product of the price less discount times the number of watches sold. For example, if the price (as previously determined) was $150 but that week it was discounted 10 percent, the net price would be $135 (the selling price of $150 minus the $15 discount). If five watches were sold, the total would be $675 (5 × $135).

Kyle offers to walk you through the creation of formulas, use of references, and later, manipulating the data.

To enter and edit formulas for the weekly watch worksheet:

1 Click **File**, then **Open** from Excel's menu bar or click the **Open** tool on the Standard toolbar.

2 Double-click the filename **ch1-02.xls** to reveal a file that should look like Figure 1.7.

3 Click in cell **D6** where you will place the formula to calculate price.

4 Remember the formula for determining price is cost plus markup, thus you need to enter a formula that computes the markup and then adds it to the cost. Type the formula **=B6+(B6*C6)** into cell D6, then press **Enter**. Note that B6 is the location of the cost and C6 is the location of the markup percentage. Note also that the cell has been preformatted so that two decimal places are always shown.

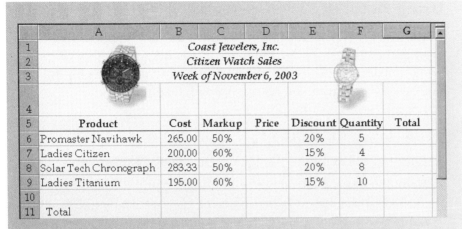

	A	B	C	D	E	F	G
1		*Coast Jewelers, Inc.*					
2		*Citizen Watch Sales*					
3		*Week of November 6, 2003*					
4							
5	Product	Cost	Markup	Price	Discount	Quantity	Total
6	Promaster Navihawk	265.00	50%		20%	5	
7	Ladies Citizen	200.00	60%		15%	4	
8	Solar Tech Chronograph	283.33	50%		20%	8	
9	Ladies Titanium	195.00	60%		15%	10	
10							
11	Total						

FIGURE 1.7

Partially Completed Weekly Watch Sales Worksheet

5 Click in cell **G6** where you will place the formula to calculate the total sales of the Promaster Navihawk.

6 Remember the formula for determining total sales is price less discount times the number sold, thus you need to enter a formula that computes the net price and then multiplies it by the number sold. Type the formula **=(D6−(D6*E6))*F6** into cell G6, then press **Enter**. Note that D6 is the location of the price, E6 is the location of the discount percentage, and F6 is the location of the number sold. Note also that the cell has been preformatted so that two decimal places are always shown.

"Hold on a minute," Meagan says. "All of those parentheses are confusing me."

Kyle explains that the formula required those parentheses to specify the order of calculation. The formula, (D6−**(**D6*E6**)**)*F6, requires the innermost set of parentheses to be calculated first (see bold parentheses). This is the calculation of the discount (the price times the discount percentage). The next set of parentheses in the formula, (D6−**(**D6*E6**)**)*F6, is acted on next. This is the calculation of the discounted price (price less discount). Lastly, the formula multiplies the newly calculated discounted price times the number sold to yield the total.

"Do we now have to type additional formulas for the other watches?" you ask.

"Thank goodness, no," Kyle explains. "Excel has an AutoFill feature that saves you the time and effort of reentering similar formulas."

MANIPULATING DATA AND STRUCTURING WORKSHEETS

The AutoFill feature is very handy whenever you need formulas or data replicated down or across a worksheet. Kyle explains that along with this feature, it will be important to also understand the concept of relative and absolute references.

Using AutoFill

In the Weekly Watch Sales worksheet you created formulas to calculate price and total sales for the Promaster Navihawk watch. Now you want to use a similar formula to calculate the price and total sales for the other watches. Kyle suggests you try the AutoFill feature yourself.

To use the AutoFill feature:

1 Click in cell **D6** on the Weekly Watch Sales worksheet.

2 Note that when selected the cell is outlined and that small square is located in the lower right corner of the cell. Click and hold the mouse button down so the mouse pointer is over that square. Then drag the frame down to cell D9 and release the mouse button.

3 Click in cell **G6**.

4 Click and hold the mouse button down so the mouse pointer is over the square in the lower right corner of the cell. Drag the frame down to cell G9 then release the mouse button.

"I see," you say. "By using the AutoFill feature we've copied the same formula down the worksheet."

"Not exactly," Kyle responds. "In fact, you've copied a similar formula down the worksheet, but it's not the same."

Kyle suggests that this is a good time to explain the worksheet concept of relative and absolute references.

Using Relative and Absolute References

The formula placed in cells D7, D8, and D9 after using the AutoFill feature is similar but not exactly like the formula you wrote in cell D6. If you look at the resulting formula created in cell D7 and compare it to the formula in cell D6 you will see relative referencing at work. Cell D6 contains the formula B6+(B6*C6). Cell D7 contains the formula B7+(B7*C7). In other words, using AutoFill changed the formula by increasing the row reference by one, from row 6 to row 7. This will continue to occur as Autofill moves down relative to the original formula. Once again, looking at cell D8, you see the formula B8+(B8*C8) and at cell D9 the formula B9+(B9*C9).

"Do you always want AutoFill to change the references?" Nathan asks.

"Not necessarily," Kyle answers.

Kyle points out that in this particular worksheet relative referencing works. One alternative situation, which would not require relative referencing, would be if the discount were some specific percentage for all sales. If you locate that percentage in one cell relative referencing would not work. He suggests you create a cell that specifies a discount percentage for that week, clear the discount part of the worksheet, and rewrite the total formula.

To use absolute references in the worksheet:

1 Before making the following changes, click **File**, then **Save As** to save the Excel file.

2 Name the file **ch1-02a.xls**, then click **Save**. You will now make changes to the file to illustrate absolute references.

3 Type **Discount %** in cell A13. This is a label for the value you will place in cell B13. Press the **Tab** key to move to the next cell.

4 Type **10%** in cell B13, then press the **Enter** key.

5 Select cells E5 through E9 by clicking in cell **E5**, then while holding down the **Shift** key, click cell **E9**. (This selects the five contiguous cells.) Alternatively, you could click in cell E5 and, while holding the mouse button down, drag the mouse pointer down to cell E9.

6 Right click the selected cells to reveal the Shortcut menu, then click **Clear Contents**. This removes values and text previously shown at E5 through E9.

7 Change the formula at G6 to **(D6–(D6*B13))*F6**. This requires replacing the cell reference E6 with the cell reference B13. This can be done by placing the cursor in the formula to the right of the E6 reference, backspacing twice, typing **B13**, then pressing the **Enter** key. Alternatively, you could have double-clicked **E6** and then placed the mouse pointer over cell B13, clicked once, then pressed the **Enter** key.

8 Using AutoFill, replicate the formula in cell G6 down to G9. This, however, causes a problem because of relative referencing. Note that the formula in G7 now contains a reference to B14 instead of the discount specified in B13. What we should have done is changed the B13 reference from a relative reference to an absolute reference.

9 Change the formula at G6 to **(D6–(D6*$B$13))*F6** by placing the $ in front of the B and the 13. The addition of the $ freezes the reference to an absolute cell, regardless of where the cell may be copied to or automatically filled using AutoFill. After you have edited the formula, press the **Enter** key.

10 Using AutoFill, replicate the modified formula in cell G6 down to G9. Your worksheet should now look like Figure 1.8 on the following page.

"So what happens if I change the discount from 10 percent to 13 percent?" Nathan asks. Kyle demonstrates that the new formula creates new totals as a different discount percentage is entered into cell B13. He suggests you try some alternative percentages to see the effects on the total column. When you are finished experimenting, return the discount to 10 percent.

FIGURE 1.8

*Modified Weekly Watch
Sales Worksheet*

	A	B	C	D	E	F	G
1			Coast Jewelers, Inc.				
2			Citizen Watch Sales				
3			Week of November 6, 2003				
4							
5	Product	Cost	Markup	Price	Quantity	Total	
6	Promaster Navihawk	265.00	50%	397.50	5	1,788.75	
7	Ladies Citizen	200.00	60%	320.00	4	1,152.00	
8	Men's Citizen	300.00	50%	450.00	1	405.00	
9	Solar Tech Chronograph	283.33	50%	425.00	8	3,059.96	
10	Ladies Titanium	195.00	60%	312.00	10	2,808.00	
11	Total					9,213.71	
12							
13	Discount %	10%					

Sheet1 / Sheet2 / Sheet3

Ready   NUM

Inserting and Deleting Columns and Rows

To clean up the look of the worksheet, Kyle suggests you remove the old discount column and row 10, and add a formula to sum total sales for the week in cell F10.

In addition, Nathan wants to know how to add a row if a different watch is sold.

To insert and delete columns and rows from the worksheet:

1 Click the **8** in row 8 to select the entire row.

2 Right click the **8** in row 8 to reveal the Shortcut menu, then click **Insert** to add a new row.

3 Add the following watch sales information: product—**Men's Citizen**, cost—**$300**, markup—**50%**, quantity—**1**.

4 Use AutoFill to fill down the proper formulas for cells D8 and G8.

5 Click the **E** in column E to select the entire column.

6 Right click the **E** in column E to reveal the Shortcut menu, then click **Delete** to delete the column.
trouble? Excel has an Undo command, which allows you to reverse any number of actions you have executed on a worksheet. If you accidentally delete the wrong column or too many columns, click the Undo button on the Standard toolbar or choose Undo from the Edit menu.

7 Click the **11** in row 11 to select the entire row.

8 Right click the **11** in row 11 to reveal the Shortcut menu, then click **Delete** to delete the row.

9 Click cell **F11**. Previously you created a formula with a SUM function in the trial balance by typing the function name and cell references. Alternatively, you can use the AutoSum tool on the Standard toolbar.

10 Click the **AutoSum** tool on the Standard toolbar, then press **Enter**. Note how Excel's AutoSum feature automatically selects cells adjacent to cell F11 that it thinks contain data you want to sum. While this is a handy feature it doesn't always select the cell you want to sum. In this case it worked great!

11 To polish off your worksheet click cell **F11** again and format it with a **Top and Double Bottom Border** by using the Borders tool on the Format toolbar.

12 Click cell **A13**. Format the cell to make the label bold by clicking the **Bold** tool on the Format toolbar. Your completed worksheet should look like Figure 1.9.

FIGURE 1.9

Completed Weekly Watch Sales worksheet

	A	B	C	D	E	F	G
1		Coast Jewelers, Inc.					
2		Citizen Watch Sales					
3		Week of November 6, 2003					
4							
5	Product	Cost	Markup	Price	Quantity	Total	
6	Promaster Navihawk	265.00	50%	397.50	5	1,788.75	
7	Ladies Citizen	200.00	60%	320.00	4	1,152.00	
8	Men's Citizen	300.00	50%	450.00	1	405.00	
9	Solar Tech Chronograph	283.33	50%	425.00	8	3,059.96	
10	Ladies Titanium	195.00	60%	312.00	10	2,808.00	
11	Total					9,213.71	
12							
13	Discount %	10%					

Sheet1 / Sheet2 / Sheet3

Ready   NUM

13 Save your work by clicking the **Save** tool on the Standard toolbar. Note that the file is still called ch1-02a.xls.

Working with Multiple Worksheets

Meagan is pleased with the results of the completed Weekly Watch Sales worksheet but wishes the sales could be summarized in four-week increments. Kyle replies that the best way to handle that would be to use multiple worksheets. You can create a worksheet for every week and a summary sheet for every four-week period.

At the bottom of the worksheet in Figure 1.9 you can see three tabs labeling each worksheet: Sheet1, Sheet2, and Sheet3. Kyle suggests you first re-label Sheet1 to November 6, indicating the beginning of the week. Then he suggests you copy the November 6 worksheet and create a November 13 worksheet, then again for November 20, and so on until four worksheets are completed.

To work with multiple worksheets:

1 Double-click the tab **Sheet1**, change the name of the worksheet to **November 6**, then press the **Enter** key.

2 Right-click the newly labeled tab **November 6** to reveal the Shortcut menu, then click **Move or Copy**.

3 Check the **Create a copy** checkbox, click **Sheet2**, then click **OK** in the Move or Copy window. A new worksheet labeled November 6 (2) appears in the workbook.

4 Double-click the tab **November 6 (2)**, change the name of the worksheet to **November 13**, then press the **Enter** key. You now have two identical worksheets.

5 Continue this process two additional times to create a total of four worksheets, the last two labeled **November 20** and **November 27**. To see all the worksheets you may have to shrink the scroll box on the bottom of the worksheet.

6 Place the mouse pointer just to the left of the arrow on the horizontal scroll box. Click and drag the mouse pointer to the right until all four weekly worksheet tabs are visible.

7 Change the title of each worksheet to reflect the new dates by editing cell **A3**. Click cell A3 on the worksheet November 13 and change the date to read November 13. Continue the same process for the last two worksheets. Remember, to change active worksheets click the title of each worksheet on the bottom tabs.

8 Change the number of watches sold for the week of November 13 (located in cells E6 to E10) to **3,2,7,1,4** respectively. Also change the discount percentage of cell B13 to **0%**.

9 Change the number of watches sold for the week of November 20 (located in cells E6 to E10) to **4,1,8,2,5** respectively. Also change the discount percentage of cell B13 to **5%**.

10 Change the number of watches sold for the week of November 27 (located in cells E6 to E10) to **3,6,7,4,8** respectively. Also change the discount percentage of cell B13 to **15%**.

11 You now have four worksheets with different sales information for each period. Your workbook should look like Figure 1.10.

12 Click **File**, then **Save As** to save the Excel file.

13 Name the file **ch1-02b.xls**, then click **Save**.

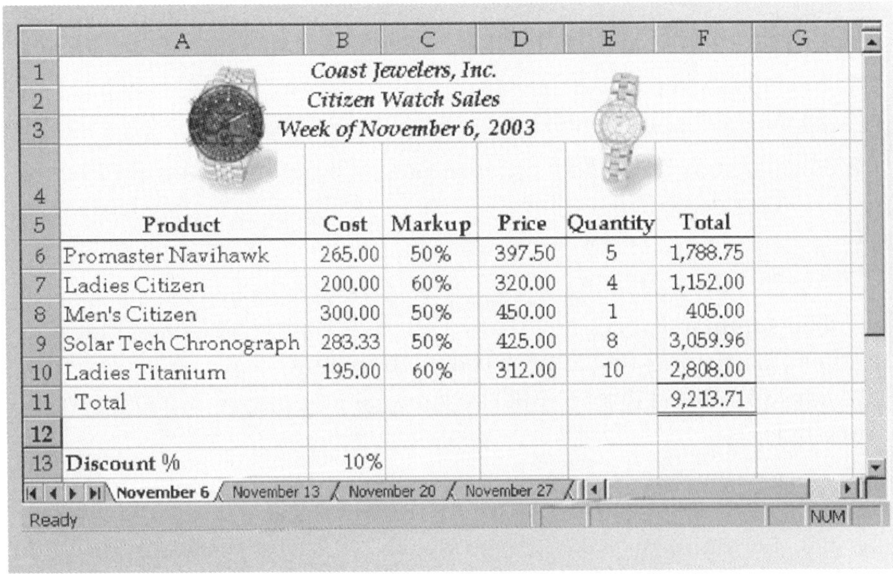

	A	B	C	D	E	F	G
1		*Coast Jewelers, Inc.*					
2		*Citizen Watch Sales*					
3		*Week of November 6, 2003*					
4							
5	**Product**	**Cost**	**Markup**	**Price**	**Quantity**	**Total**	
6	Promaster Navihawk	265.00	50%	397.50	5	1,788.75	
7	Ladies Citizen	200.00	60%	320.00	4	1,152.00	
8	Men's Citizen	300.00	50%	450.00	1	405.00	
9	Solar Tech Chronograph	283.33	50%	425.00	8	3,059.96	
10	Ladies Titanium	195.00	60%	312.00	10	2,808.00	
11	Total					9,213.71	
12							
13	**Discount %**	10%					

FIGURE 1.10

Watch Sales Worksheet for Week of 11/6.

Finally, a summary worksheet can be created that summarizes sales from each week. Kyle suggests you change the name of Sheet2 to Summary, move that worksheet to the front of the workbook, and set up a summary worksheet using the copy and paste features of Excel.

To set up a summary worksheet, double-click the tab **Sheet2**, change the name of the worksheet to **Summary** and press the **Enter** key.

1 Click and hold the mouse button down over the tab Summary, then drag the tab to the left-most part of the workbook, just to the left of the November 6 tab. Release the mouse button.

2 Activate the November 6 worksheet by clicking the **November 6** tab.

3 Select cells A1 to A3, right click the mouse to activate the Shortcut menu and click **Copy** to copy the worksheet title and pictures.

4 Activate the Summary worksheet, click in cell **A1**, right click the mouse button, and click **Paste** to paste the worksheet title and pictures.

5 Click cell **A3** and type **Summary**.

6 Resize the height of row **4** to **47** pixels.

7 Activate the November 6 worksheet.

8 Select cells A5 to A11, right click the mouse to activate the Shortcut menu and click **Copy** to copy the product title and names.

9 Activate the Summary worksheet, click in cell **A5**, right click the mouse button, and click **Paste** to paste the product title and names.

10 Resize column A to fit the product title and names (181 pixels).

11 In cells B5 to F5 type the various weekly dates: **Nov 6**, **Nov 13**, **Nov 20**, **Nov 27**, and **Total** respectively.

12 Format cells **B5 to F5** using the **Bold**, **Center**, and **Bottom Border** tools on the Format toolbar.

The summary worksheet you've set up is now ready for weekly data. Rather than typing the totals from each product for each week, Excel provides you the ability to link the summary worksheet with the weekly worksheets.

To link the summary worksheet to weekly worksheets:

1 Click in cell **B6** of the Summary worksheet.

2 Type = into cell B6.

3 Before pressing Enter, activate the November 6 worksheet and click in cell **F6**. This automatically enters the reference 'November 6'!F6 into the Summary worksheet cell B6. Now press **Enter**.

4 Use AutoFill to replicate the formula now entered in the Summary worksheet cell B6 down the worksheet to cell B10.

5 Click in cell **C6** of the Summary worksheet.

6 Type = into cell C6.

7 Before pressing Enter, activate the November 13 worksheet and click in cell **F6**. This automatically enters the reference 'November 13'!F6 into the Summary worksheet cell C6. Now press **Enter**.

8 Use AutoFill to replicate the formula now entered in the Summary worksheet cell C6 down the worksheet to cell C10.

9 Continue this process for November 20 and November 27.

10 Use the SUM function to total sales by product in cells F6 through F10 on the Summary worksheet.

11 Use the SUM function to total weekly sales in cells B11 through F11.

12 Format cells B11 to F11 with a Top and Double Bottom Border.

13 Increase the size of column F to remove the # signs in cell F11.

14 Reduce the size of the horizontal scroll box to reveal all worksheet tabs in your Watch Sales workbook. The completed summary worksheet should look like Figure 1.11.

15 Save your work again to ch1-02b.xls.

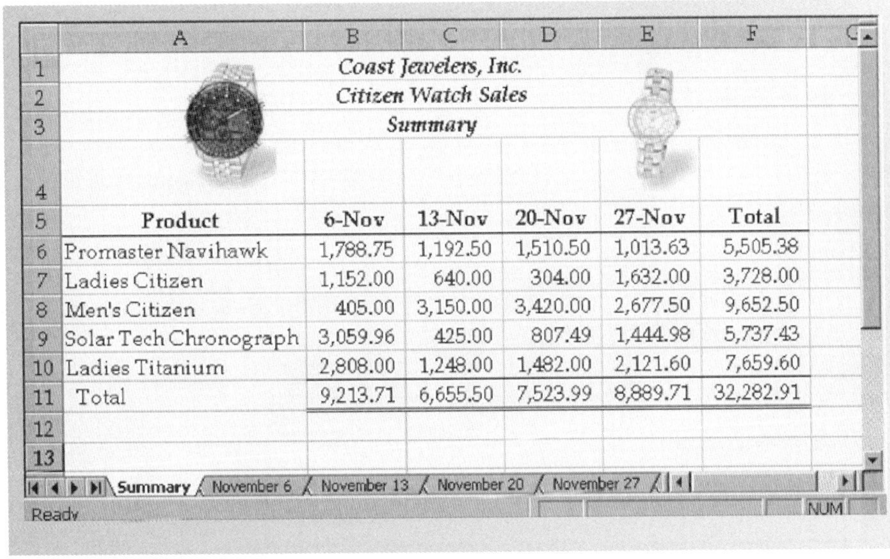

FIGURE 1.11
Completed Summary Worksheet

Using Headers and Footers

Often you will create multiple versions of a worksheet and, when they are printed, you won't know which version is which. Thus, it's important to include a date and time stamp on each worksheet. Kyle indicates that Excel has a built-in function that will not only date and time stamp your work but also indicate the file name on each worksheet when printed. Both of these functions can be placed in either a worksheet header or footer.

To use headers and footers in a worksheet:

1 Click the **View** menu, then click **Header and Footer....**

2 Click **Custom Header,** click inside the Right section text box, then click the **Date** tool which looks like a calendar with the numbers 7 and 8. This inserts &[Date] into the right section text box and will print the system date in the upper right corner of each worksheet. (The system date is the current date you are printing your worksheet.)

3 Click **OK** and note the current date in the Header preview box.

4 Click **Custom Footer,** click inside the Right section text box, then click the **File Name** tool which looks like a sheet with the Excel logo. This inserts &[File] into the right section text box and will print the worksheet file name in the lower right corner of each worksheet.

5 Click **OK** and note the file name (ch1-02b.xls) in the Footer preview box. The completed Page Setup window should look like Figure 1.12 on the following page.

6 Click **OK** to close the Page Setup window. More about the Page Setup window in a minute.

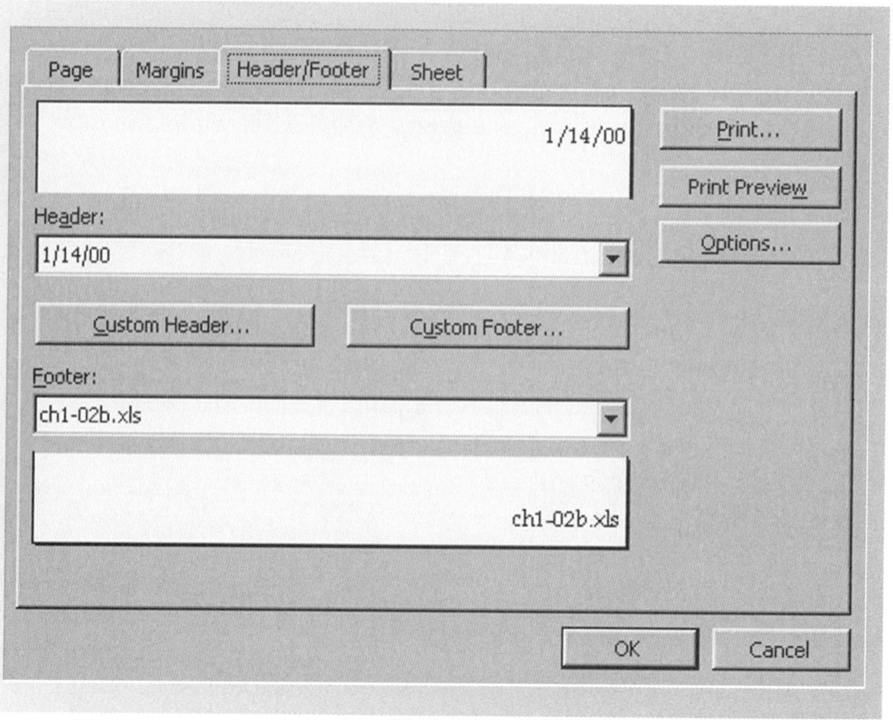

FIGURE 1.12
Entering Headers and Footers

PRINTING

· ·

Printing often requires three steps: editing the page setup, previewing the print job, and then finally printing the worksheet. Kyle suggests that to save paper, these three steps should always be performed.

Using Page Setup

Page Setup establishes the worksheet's page orientation and scaling, margin specifications, headers and footers (which were just addressed), and sheet provisions that include print area and print titles.

The Page section is the first tab, located on the far left of the Page Setup window. Here you can specify the page orientation (Portrait or Landscape). Kyle prefers the terms vertical and horizontal, which more accurately communicate the direction the worksheet will be printed on a standard 8½" by 11" piece of paper. If the worksheet is too big to print on just one sheet, the user can scale the printing by a percentage of its normal size or fit it to a specific number of pages wide and/or tall.

The Margin section is the second tab. Here you can modify the header and footer depth, as well as the top, bottom, right, and left margins. In addition, you can specify that the worksheet be centered on the page either horizontally, vertically, both, or neither.

The Sheet section allows you to restrict printing to a certain segment of the worksheet and to repeat titles at the top or left of the worksheet if your printing extends over more than one page. While editing worksheets Kyle likes to print his work in process and take it on the road, where he doesn't have a computer. In this case he prints the gridlines and row and column headings so he can write additional formulas by hand.

Kyle decides to modify the page setup for the summary worksheet by specifying a portrait orientation, centering the worksheet horizontally, with gridlines and row and column headings.

To edit the page setup of a worksheet:

1 Click the **File** menu, then **Page Setup** to reveal the Page Setup window.

2 Click the **Page** tab and **Portrait** orientation option button if it is not already selected.

3 Click the **Margins** tab and click the **horizontally** checkbox on the **Center on page** section.

4 Click the **Sheet** tab and click the **Gridlines** and **Row and column headings** checkboxes.

5 Do not close the Page Setup window.

Previewing the Print Job

Previewing the print job will save you lots of paper and headaches, Kyle explains. A print preview is available from either the Print window (see below) or Page Setup window. In addition to previewing the print job, the Print window also gives you the option of zooming in on the print job, modifying margins, viewing page breaks, and printing the job.

To preview a print job:

1 With the Page Setup window still open, click **Print Preview**.

2 Click **Zoom** to magnify the pending print job, then use the scroll bars to move around your view of the print job.

3 Click **Zoom** again to bring the view back to normal.

4 Again, do not close the Print Preview window.

Printing a Worksheet

As mentioned above, you can print from the Print Preview window or print directly from the worksheet. Kyle once again suggests that you always preview your work before printing, thus he suggests you get into the habit of printing from the Print Preview window. This action opens the same window you would see if you clicked Print from the File menu. If you had selected the Print tool on the Standard toolbar from the worksheet window, the Print window would not appear and the worksheet would be printed without further options.

The Print window allows you to select a printer (assuming more than one printer is connected to your computer or network). In addition, you can specify the print range (which pages to print), what you wish to print (the entire workbook, the active sheet(s), or a specific selection you've already highlighted on the worksheet), and/or how many copies you want printed.

Meagan suggests you print one copy of the entire workbook with the gridlines and row and column headings specified previously, and one copy of the summary worksheet without gridlines and row and column headings.

To print the workbook (Steps 1 and 2) and to print a summary worksheet without row and column headings (Steps 3 through 6):

1 From the Print Preview window, click **Print**.

2 In the Print window click the **Entire workbook** option button in the Print what section, then click **OK**.
trouble? You may have to specify which printer to print to in lab situations. Please see the lab consultant or your instructor for instructions. This should print five pages.

3 With the Summary worksheet active, click **File** then **Print**.

4 Click **Preview**, then **Setup**.

5 If necessary click the **Sheet** tab, uncheck the **Gridlines** and **Row and column headings** checkboxes in the Print section, then click **OK**.

6 From the Print Preview window, click **Print**. This should print the Summary page without gridlines and row and column headings. See Figure 1.13.

FIGURE 1.13

Printed Summary Worksheet

Coast Jewelers, Inc.
Citizen Watch Sales
Summary

Product	6-Nov	13-Nov	20-Nov	27-Nov	Total
Promaster Navihawk	1,788.75	1,192.50	1,510.50	1,013.63	5,505.38
Ladies Citizen	1,152.00	640.00	304.00	1,632.00	3,728.00
Men's Citizen	405.00	3,150.00	3,420.00	2,677.50	9,652.50
Solar Tech Chronograph	3,059.96	425.00	807.49	1,444.98	5,737.43
Ladies Titanium	2,808.00	1,248.00	1,482.00	2,121.60	7,659.60
Total	9,213.71	6,655.50	7,523.99	8,889.71	32,282.91

7 Save your work.

Nathan notices that when the workbook was printed in total, only the Summary worksheet had a header and footer. Kyle explains that because you had set up the header and footer for the Summary worksheet only, headers and footers for the remaining worksheets would not be expected.

Printing and Viewing Formulas

"Is there any way to look at a worksheet and see all the formulas in the worksheet without clicking on each cell?" Nathan asks.

"Yes," Kyle replies. "Not only can you view the underlying formulas but often you'll want to print them for later analysis."

Kyle offers to demonstrate this Excel feature and suggests that whenever you print a worksheet with formulas that you also include gridlines and row and column headings for easy reference.

To view and print formulas in a worksheet:

1 While holding the **Ctrl** key down, press the ` key (located just above the Tab key). This reveals all cells as formulas, a feature known as the formula view. Note that when you press these keys the columns become larger.

2 While holding the **Ctrl** key down, press the ` key again and the worksheet reverts back to values, also known as the value view. Note again that when you press these keys the columns become smaller.

3 Switch to the formula view once again. (While holding the **Ctrl** key down, press the` key).

4 Resize each column so that all formulas are viewable. (This will require some columns to be widened and some to be narrowed.)

5 Preview the print job. (Note that printing this worksheet requires two pages as specified in the lower left corner of the print preview window.)

6 Click **Setup** in the Preview window, then click the **Page** tab and change the page orientation to **Landscape**. (This will tell the printer to print the worksheet horizontally instead of vertically.)

7 Click **OK** in the Page Setup window. (Note that even with changing the page orientation, printing may require two pages.)

8 Click **Setup** again and change the Scaling to **Fit to 1 page wide by 1 page tall**.

9 Click the **Sheet** tab and check the **Gridlines** and **Row and column headings** checkboxes so that the worksheet, when printed, can help you decipher the formulas.

10 Click **OK** in the Page Setup window. (Note that now the printing requires only one page as specified again in the lower left corner of the Print Preview window.) Your window should look like Figure 1.14, with the exception of the date located in the right header.

11 Click **Print** in the Print Preview window.

12 Click **OK** in the Print window.

13 Close the worksheet but do not save changes.

FIGURE 1.14 *Formula View*

CoastJewelers, Inc.
Citizen Watch Sales
Summary

Product	36836	36843	36850	36857	Total
Promaster Navihawk	='November 6'!F6	='November 13'!F6:F10	='November 20'!F6	='November 27'!F6	=SUM(B6:E6)
Ladies Citizen	='November 6'!F7	='November 13'!F7:F11	='November 20'!F7	='November 27'!F7	=SUM(B7:E7)
Men's Citizen	='November 6'!F8	='November 13'!F8:F12	='November 20'!F8	='November 27'!F8	=SUM(B8:E8)
Solar Tech Chronograph	='November 6'!F9	='November 13'!F9:F13	='November 20'!F9	='November 27'!F9	=SUM(B9:E9)
Ladies Titanium	='November 6'!F10	='November 13'!F10:F14	='November 20'!F10	='November 27'!F10	=SUM(B10:E10)
Total	=SUM(B6:B10)	=SUM(C6:C10)	=SUM(D6:D10)	=SUM(E6:E10)	=SUM(F6:F10)

Kyle explains that printing the formula view is an effective way of examining your worksheet logic and correcting any errors. It also allows you to view the formula logic away from the computer when one is not available.

"That's a lot to grasp in one sitting," you complain.

"Oh there's a lot more to come, but let's take a break and start again tomorrow," Kyle says.

END NOTE

The three of you are somewhat overwhelmed by the capabilities of Excel but are pleased with what you've accomplished. You've learned some basics about Excel's help system, how to work with files, and how to enter information into a worksheet, use formulas, manipulate data, structure a worksheet, and print worksheets in both value and formula views.

In the next chapter you will learn how to use Excel to create financial statements.

practice

Chapter 1 Questions

1 Explain the difference between a worksheet and a workbook.

2 Explain how Excel's menus are dynamic and not static.

3 Explain how one would move about an Excel worksheet with the vertical and horizontal scroll bars.

4 Describe the two methods of accessing Excel's help system.

5 Explain why the Open window may not list the Excel files you need.

6 Explain how information is entered into an Excel worksheet.

7 Identify the difference between labels and values.

8 What does it mean when a cell or cells in a worksheet include a series of # signs?

9 Explain the process for changing column width or row height.

10 Explain the difference between the formula edit process and the cell edit process.

11 What does the Format Painter tool do?

12 How are formulas written in Excel?

13 Explain the arguments used in the SUM function.

14 Explain the importance of parentheses in formulas.

15 How does the AutoFill feature of Excel help the worksheet user?

16 Why would you want to use absolute references instead of relative references?

17 How do you change a relative reference to an absolute reference?

18 Describe the procedure used to insert a column or row into a worksheet.

19 How do you change the name of a sheet in a workbook?

20 What is the recommended procedure for printing a workbook or worksheet?

Chapter 1 Assignments

1 *Create Coast Jewelers' trial balance for March 31, 2003*

You are to create Coast's trial balance in a format identical to that created for December 31, 2003 in this chapter. Include a debit and credit column, totals for each column, and appropriate labels and formatting. Save the file as ch1-03.xls. Print the completed trial balance (values view and formula view) with your name and date printed in the worksheet lower left footer and file name in the lower right footer. An alphabetical listing of account information as of March 31, 2003 follows:

Accounts payable	85,124.25
Accounts receivable	95,125.15
Accumulated depreciation: Building	60,000.00
Accumulated depreciation: Equipment	8,000.00
Advertising expense	15,874.24
Building	315,000.00
Cash	28,335.14
Common stock	10,000.00
Cost of goods sold	275,135.54
Depreciation expense: Equipment	70,000.00
Inventory	130,541.87
Land	120,000.00
Long-term debt	380,000.00
Payroll expense	65,152.87
Prepaid expenses	10,544.27
Retained earnings	192,697.36
Sales revenue	410,325.17
Supplies	8,888.78
Utilities	11,548.92

2 ***Modify Coast Jewelers' Diamond Ring Sales Worksheet***

For this assignment use Ch1-04.xls. Add appropriate formulas to the existing Diamond Ring Sales worksheet to calculate price, total sales for each ring for the week, and total sales for all rings. Complete this worksheet in a manner consistent with the Watch Sales worksheet completed in this chapter. Prior to entering your formulas the worksheet should look like Figure 1.15. Print the value and formula view worksheets.

FIGURE 1.15
Partially Completed Diamond Ring Sales Worksheet

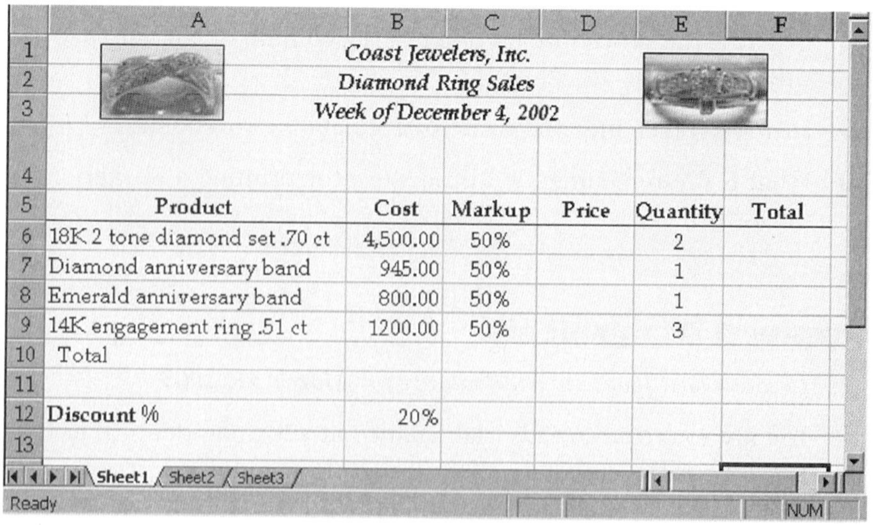

	A	B	C	D	E	F
1		*Coast Jewelers, Inc.*				
2		*Diamond Ring Sales*				
3		*Week of December 4, 2002*				
4						
5	**Product**	**Cost**	**Markup**	**Price**	**Quantity**	**Total**
6	18K 2 tone diamond set .70 ct	4,500.00	50%		2	
7	Diamond anniversary band	945.00	50%		1	
8	Emerald anniversary band	800.00	50%		1	
9	14K engagement ring .51 ct	1200.00	50%		3	
10	Total					
11						
12	**Discount %**	20%				
13						

Sheet1 / Sheet2 / Sheet3

Ready NUM

Chapter 1 Case Problem: Kelly's Boutique

Kelly's Boutique, located in Pewaukee, Wisconsin, sells a unique combination of books and women's shoes. Customers love to peruse her book inventory while trying on the latest in shoe fashions, often buying both books and shoes even though they came in to buy only one type of merchandise. Casey, Kelly's youngest son, a college student studying accounting, is home for the holidays and can't wait to help his mom come in from the dark ages and use computers in her business. Throughout this text Casey will make every attempt to bring his mom up to speed by teaching her the use of Excel and Access as they apply to her accounting and business needs.

To begin, Casey suggests that Kelly use a worksheet to make a list of her book inventory. She doesn't maintain a large inventory, but she does carry books that she thinks moms in the community might be interested in reading or buying as gifts for their children or friends.

1 Use the worksheet ch1-05.xls.

2 Format this worksheet exactly like Figure 1.16. This includes, but is not limited to, bold and italics formatting for the titles and bold and border formatting for the column names.

3 Add formulas for column E to compute the sales price as list price less the discount specified. (Test your results by comparison to Figure 1.16.)

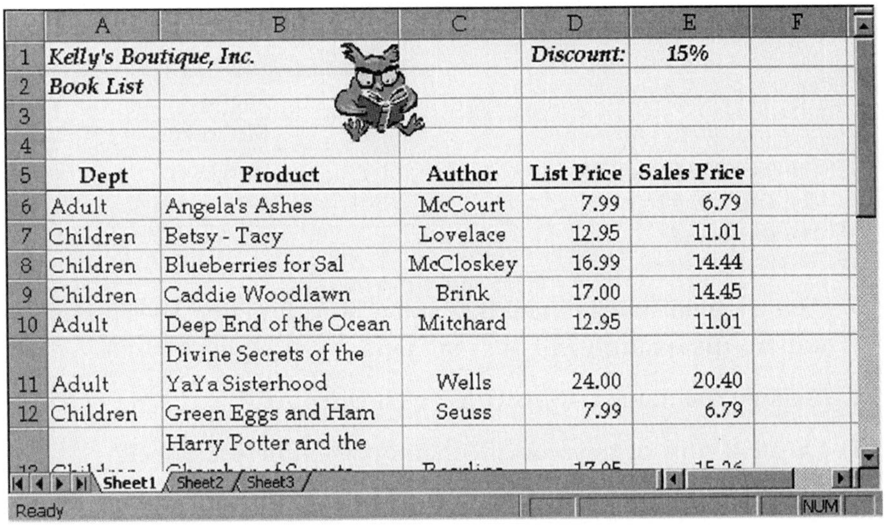

FIGURE 1.16

Partially Completed Book List

4 Add the following two books and related information to the list. (Be sure the list maintains its alphabetic organization by inserting rows in the correct place.)

Dept	Product	Author	List Price
Children	*Make Way for Ducklings*	McClosky	17.99
Adult	*Snow Falling on Cedars*	Guterson	21.95

5 Add a footer to the worksheet with your name and date on the left and the name of this file on the right.

6 Save this file as **ch1-05a.xls**.

7 Print the worksheet.

8 Insert a new column D with the title "On Hand" in bold, centered, and center justified.

9 Change the formatting of the column to no decimals.

10 Add the following on hand values to column D.

Product	Author	On Hand
Angela's Ashes	McCourt	5
Betsy – Tacy	Lovelace	2
Blueberries for Sal	McCloskey	2
Caddie Woodlawn	Brink	1
Deep End of the Ocean	Mitchard	4
Divine Secrets of the YaYa Sisterhood	Wells	3
Green Eggs and Ham	Seuss	1
Harry Potter and the Chamber of Secrets	Rowling	4
Harry Potter and the Prisoner of Azkaban	Rowling	3
Harry Potter and the Sorcerer's Stone	Rowling	2
Hop on Pop	Seuss	1
Horse Whisperer	Evans	2
Lentil	McCloskey	2
Make Way for Ducklings	McCloskey	2
Memoirs of a Geisha	Golden	4
Message in a Bottle	Sparks	2
One Morning in Maine	McCloskey	1
Snow Falling on Cedars	Guterson	2
The Cat in the Hat	Seuss	1
The Notebook	Sparks	3

11 Add a "Total" label in cell B27 and a SUM function in cell D27 to add up the quantity of books on hand.

12 Change the name of Sheet1 to "15% Discount."

13 Create a copy of this worksheet and place it before Sheet2.

14 Change the name of the newly created worksheet to "20% Discount."

15 Change the discount in cell F1 of this worksheet to 20 percent.

16 Save this file as **ch1-05b.xls**.

17 Print each worksheet in value view.

18 Print the 15% Discount worksheet in formula view, landscape orientation, scaling to fit to 1 page wide by 1 page tall, with gridlines and row and column headings.

chapter 2

Financial Statements

In this chapter you will learn:

- **How to prepare an income statement from a trial balance**

- **How to prepare a statement of retained earnings from a trial balance**

- **How to prepare a balance sheet from a trial balance**

CASE: COAST JEWELERS, INC.
. . . .

Back from a few days break you are eager to apply your newfound knowledge in Excel to the creation of financial statements.

Kyle explains that the trial balance, after period-end adjustments, is the key source of information for all financial statements. You remember that the order of financial statement preparation is critical because before you can calculate ending retained earnings for the balance sheet you must first create the statement of retained earnings. Before you can create the statement of retained earnings you must have already calculated net income, which means you must first prepare the income statement.

CREATING AN INCOME STATEMENT FROM A TRIAL BALANCE
. . . .

Kyle describes how each of the statements you will be preparing are just a reformatting and subtotaling of the trial balance, thus this is a great example of how Excel can be used repeatedly to prepare financial statements for different periods. Kyle tells you he has already prepared the trial balance for June 30, 2003 and instructs you to set up an income statement on a new worksheet in that workbook.

To setup an income statement:

1 Start Excel and open file ch2-01.xls.

2 Click the **Sheet2** tab and change the name of the worksheet to **Income Statement**.

3 To create a title for the income statement and properly format it, click cell **A1** on the Income Statement worksheet and type **Coast Jewelers, Inc.**, then press **Enter**.

4 Click cell **A2** and type **Income Statement**, then press **Enter**.

5 Click cell **A3** and type **For the 6 Months Ended June 30, 2003**, then press **Enter**.

6 Click and drag the mouse pointer over cells A1 through C1.

7 To center the title over the income statement, click the **Merge and Center** tool on the Format toolbar. This action merges cells A1, B1, and C1 and centers the text in cell A1 over all three.

8 Perform the same steps to merge and center the statement title and period for cell A2 and then cell A3.

9 Click and drag the mouse pointer over all three newly merged cells, then click both the **Bold** and **Italics** tools on the format menu.

10 Resize column A to 182 pixels.

11 Resize columns B and C to 105 pixels each.

12 In cells A5 through A16 type the labels exactly as shown in Figure 2.1. Be sure to bold and indent text as shown. Don't enter the valucs or formulas yet.

	A	B	C
1	Coast Jewelers, Inc.		
2	Income Statement		
3	For the 6 Months Ended June 30, 2003		
4			
5	Sales Revenue		$ 825,974.15
6	Less: Cost of Goods Sold		489,547.25
7	Gross Margin		336,426.90
8	Expenses:		
9	Advertising	$ 26,548.55	
10	Depreciation	22,000.00	
11	Interest	32,338.94	
12	Payroll	129,547.97	
13	Utilities	27,546.16	237,981.62
14	Net income before taxes		98,445.28
15	Income taxes		31,600.00
16	Net income		$ 66,845.28

FIGURE 2.1

Income Statement

Kyle wants to use the trial balance as the source for all three financial statements you are about to prepare. You will accomplish that by using multiple worksheets and referencing each statement back to the trial balance. In many cases the financial statements will contain subtotals or totals that depend on the references you make on each sheet. In any event, the beauty of using Excel to prepare these statements is that in later periods, when you have to create new statements, all you'll need is new trial balance amounts.

To enter formulas into the income statement:

1 Click cell **C5** and type =.

2 Click the **Trial Balance** sheet tab and click cell **C22**, then press **Enter**. This enters the formula ='Trial Balance'!C22 into cell C5 and moves the active cell to C6.

3 Once again type = (you should be in cell C6).

4 Click the **Trial Balance** sheet tab, click cell **B23**, then press **Enter**. This enters the formula ='Trial Balance'!B23 into cell C6 and moves the active cell to C7.

5 Cell C7 requires a formula to compute gross margin, which is sales revenue minus cost of goods sold. Type the formula **=C5–C6** into cell C7, then press **Enter**.

6 Use your knowledge of multiple worksheets from the steps above to enter formulas for cells B9 through B13, which make cell references to the appropriate cell on the Trial Balance worksheet.

7 Cell C13 requires a formula to compute total expenses. Though you can enter a formula that adds each cell, B9 + B10 + B11, etc., this is an ideal situation in which to use the SUM function. Click in cell **C13**.

8 Click the **AutoSum** tool on the Standard Toolbar (Σ, the sigma symbol). Alternatively, you can type the SUM function into the cell.

9 The AutoSum tool looks around the worksheet for number values contiguous to the cell it has been entered into. In this case it automatically selected cell B13 as its argument. Replace B13 by placing the mouse pointer over cell B9. Click and hold the mouse button then drag it down to cell B13.

> **trouble?** If you accidentally press the Enter key or move to another cell, simply click on cell C13 and edit the argument to the SUM function by selecting the cells specified in the argument and then point to the correct cells B9:B13.

10 Cell C14 requires a formula to compute net income before taxes, which is gross margin minus expenses. Type **=C7–C13** in cell C14.

11 Type **='Trial Balance'!B26** in cell C15, or better yet, make cell references to the appropriate cell on the Trial Balance worksheet.

12 Compute net income (net income before taxes minus income taxes) by typing **=C14–C15** into cell C16.

To complete the income statement you'll need to properly format the worksheet. In some cases you will need to format number cells with the comma format. In other cases it is necessary to format number cells with the currency format. Borders will also be necessary to indicate subtotals and totals. Finally, you should save your work and print an income statement.

To format the income statement:

1 Click cell **C5**, then click the **Currency Style** tool on the Formatting toolbar.

2 Click cell **C6**, then click the **Bottom Border** tool on the Formatting toolbar.

3 Click cell **B9**, then click the **Currency Style** tool on the Formatting toolbar.

4 Select cells B13 and C13, then click the **Bottom Border** tool on the Formatting toolbar.

5 Click cell **C16**, then click the **Currency Style** tool on the Formatting toolbar and click the **Top and Double Bottom Border** tool on the Formatting toolbar.

6 Save your work to ch2-01a.xls.

7 Click **View** then **Header and Footer** from the menu. Place your name and date in the left section of the footer and the filename in the right section of the footer.

8 Click **Print Preview** and click **Print** to make sure the worksheet will print the way you want and to print the income statement.

9 Save your work again to ch2-01a.xls.

Now that you've created the income statement from the trial balance it should be fairly easy to create the remaining two financial statements. Nathan volunteers to prepare the next statement in order.

CREATING STATEMENT OF RETAINED EARNINGS FROM A TRIAL BALANCE

You recall that the statement of retained earnings is an analysis of beginning and ending retained earnings. You explain to Nathan that two basic events cause a change in retained earnings: net income and dividends. You just completed the income statement and net income is specified on that worksheet and, although the company hasn't yet issued any dividends, the trial balance does contain a dividends account.

Nathan decides to repeat the effort shown him with the income statement. Thus, he first creates the statement of retained earnings structure (title and labels), followed by specific formulas, ending with formatting and printing.

To set up the statement of retained earnings:

1 Use the ch2-01a.xls file you saved earlier while creating the income statement.

2 Click the **Sheet3** tab and change the name of the worksheet to **Statement of Retained Earnings**.

3 To create a title for the statement and properly format it, click cell **A1** on the Statement of Retained Earnings worksheet and type **Coast Jewelers, Inc.**, then press **Enter**.

4 Click cell **A2** and type **Statement of Retained Earnings**, then press **Enter**.

5 Click cell **A3** and type **For the 6 Months Ended June 30, 2003**, then press **Enter**.

6 Click and drag the mouse pointer over cells A1 and B1.

7 To center the title over the income statement, click the **Merge and Center** tool on the Format toolbar. This action merges cells A1 and B1 and centers the text in cell A1 over both.

8 Perform the same steps to merge and center the statement title and period for cell A2 and then cell A3.

9 Click and drag the mouse pointer over both newly merged cells then click both the **Bold** and **Italics** tools on the Format menu.

10 Resize column A to 265 pixels.

11 Resize column B to 134 pixels.

12 In cells A5 through A8 type the labels exactly as shown in Figure 2.2 (be sure to indent as shown). Don't enter the values or formulas yet.

FIGURE 2.2

Statement of Retained Earnings

	A	B
1	*Coast Jewelers, Inc.*	
2	*Statement of Retained Earnings*	
3	*For the 6 Months Ended June 30, 2003*	
4		
5	Beginning Retained Earnings	$ 192,697.36
6	Add: Net Income	66,845.28
7	Subtract: Dividends	-
8	Ending Retained Earnings	$ 259,542.64

Nathan thinks he's getting the hang of this but doesn't always get the accounting parts. You explain that he shouldn't worry as long as you're around; you'll be able to explain the accounting basics. Once again it's time to enter formulas, specifically references to the income statement and trial balance.

To enter formulas into the statement of retained earnings:

1 Click cell **B5** and type =.

2 Click the **Trial Balance** sheet tab, then click cell **C20** (beginning retained earnings from the trial balance) and press **Enter**. This enters the formula ='Trial Balance'!C20 into cell B5 and moves the active cell to B6.

3 Once again type = (you should be in cell B6).

4 Click the **Income Statement** sheet tab, then click cell **C16** (net income from the income statement) and press **Enter**. This enters the formula ='Income Statement'!C16 into cell B6 and moves the active cell to B7.

5 Once again type = (you should be in cell B7).

6 Click the **Trial Balance** sheet tab, then click cell **B21** (dividends from the trial balance) and press **Enter**. This then enters the formula ='Trial Balance'!B21 into cell B7 and moves the active cell to B8.

7 Cell B8 requires a formula to compute ending retained earnings (beginning retained earnings + net income – dividends). Type the formula **=B5+B6–B7** into cell B8.

"It is beginning to look like a real set of financial statements," Nathan comments.

"Almost," Kyle responds. "All that is left is some formatting like before."

To format the statement of retained earnings:

1 Click cell **B5**, then click the **Currency Style** tool on the Formatting toolbar.

2 Note that when you referenced net income from the income statement above, Excel imported not only the value located at that cell but also the formatting. Click cell **B6**, then click the **Comma Style** tool on the Formatting toolbar.

3 Click cell **B8**, click the **Currency Style** tool on the Formatting toolbar, then click the **Top and Double Bottom Border** tool on the Formatting toolbar.

4 Save your work to ch2-01b.xls.

5 Click **View** then **Header and Footer** from the menu. Place your name and date in the left section of the footer and the filename in the right section of the footer.

6 Click **Print Preview**, then click **Print** to make sure the worksheet will print the way you want and to print the income statement.

7 Save your work again to ch2-01b.xls.

Meagan now volunteers for the final statement: the balance sheet. She notes that many of the accounts on the trial balance have yet to be referenced on the prior two statements. She assumes, correctly, that they must belong on the balance sheet.

CREATING A BALANCE SHEET FROM A TRIAL BALANCE

Now that ending retained earnings has been computed on the statement of retained earnings, the balance sheet can be prepared. In addition to using cell references to the trial balance and statement of retained earnings on the balance sheet, many subtotals and totals are used to calculate items such as current assets, current liabilities, etc.

Once again, Meagan will prepare the statement in three stages: structure (title and labels), specific cell references and formulas, and, finally, formatting and printing.

To set up a balance sheet:

1 Use the ch2-01b.xls file you saved earlier while creating the statement of retained earnings.

2 Right click the **Statement of Retained Earnings** tab and click **Insert...**, then click the **Worksheet** icon in the Insert window and click **OK** to insert a new worksheet into the workbook. (You have to do this as each workbook begins with only three blank sheets.)

3 Change the name of this worksheet to **Balance Sheet**.

4 Click the **Balance Sheet** tab, hold the mouse down, then drag the sheet just to the right of the **Statement of Retained Earnings** tab and release the mouse button. (This repositions the worksheet to the far right of all others.)

5 To create a title for the balance sheet and properly format it, click cell **A1** on the Balance Sheet worksheet and type **Coast Jewelers, Inc.**, then press **Enter**.

6 Click cell **A2** and type **Balance Sheet**, then press **Enter**.

7 Click cell **A3** and type **as of June 30, 2003**, then press **Enter**.

8 Click and drag the mouse pointer over cells A1 through C1.

9 To center the title over the balance sheet, click the **Merge and Center** tool on the Format toolbar. This action merges cells A1, B1, and C1 and centers the text in cell A1 over all three.

10 Perform the same steps to merge and center the statement title and period for cell A2 and then cell A3.

11 Click and drag the mouse pointer over all three newly merged cells then click both the **Bold** and **Italics** tools on the format menu.

12 Resize column A to 250 pixels.

13 Resize column B to 110 pixels.

14 Resize column C to 100 pixels.

15 Resize column D to 96 pixels.

16 In cells A5 through A28 type the labels exactly as shown in Figures 2.3 and 2.4 (with bold and indents). Don't enter the values or formulas yet.

Meagan likes the balance sheet layout and is now ready to enter cell references to the trial balance and statement of retained earnings. She also plans to create formulas to calculate subtotals and totals, remembering that the accounting equation (Assets = Liabilities + Stockholders' Equity) will be proven in this statement.

To enter formulas into the balance sheet:

1 Click cell **B7** and type **=**.

2 Click the **Trial Balance** sheet tab and click cell **B6** (cash from the trial balance), then press **Enter**. This enters the formula ='Trial Balance'!B6 into cell B7 and moves the active cell to B8.

FIGURE 2.3

*Asset Section of the
Balance Sheet*

	A	B	C	D
5	Assets			
6	Current Assets:			
7	Cash	$ 20,182.15		
8	Accounts Receivable	102,544.24		
9	Inventory	152,154.21		
10	Prepaid Expenses	15,241.75		
11	Supplies	6,578.24		$296,700.59
12	Property, Plant, and Equipment:			
13	Land	120,000.00		
14	Building	315,000.00		
15	Equipment	70,000.00	$505,000.00	
16	Less: Accumulated Depreciation		90,000.00	415,000.00
17	Total			$711,700.59

FIGURE 2.4

*Liabilities and Stockholders'
Equity Section of the
Balance Sheet*

	A	B	C	D
19	Liabilities and Stockholders' Equity			
20	Liabilities			
21	Current Liabilities:			
22	Accounts Payable	$ 84,005.70		
23	Payroll Liabilities	8,152.25	$ 92,157.95	
24	Long-Term Debt		350,000.00	$442,157.95
25	Stockholders' Equity			
26	Common Stock	10,000.00		
27	Retained Earnings	259,542.64		269,542.64
28	Total			$711,700.59

3 Once again type = (you should be in cell B8).

4 Click the **Trial Balance** sheet tab again and click cell **B7** (accounts receivable from the trial balance), then press **Enter**. This enters the formula ='Trial Balance'!B7 into cell B7 and moves the active cell to B9. Continue this process until all assets have been referenced. See Figure 2.3 to confirm the location and amounts for all assets.

5 To enter amounts for total accumulated depreciation click cell **C16** and type =.

6 Click the **Trial Balance** sheet tab, then click cell **C13**. Before pressing Enter, type + and click cell **C15**, then press **Enter**. This enters the formula ='Trial Balance'!C13+'Trial Balance'!C15 into cell C16 and effectively adds the two accumulated depreciation amounts together.

7 Calculate a subtotal for Current Assets by clicking cell **D11** and typing **=SUM(B7:B11)**, then press **Enter**.

8 Calculate a subtotal for Property Plant and Equipment by clicking cell **C15** and typing **=SUM(B13:B15)**, then press **Enter**.

9 Calculate a total for Net Property Plant and Equipment by clicking cell **D16** and typing **=C15-C16**, then press **Enter**.

10 Calculate a total for Assets by clicking cell **D17** and typing **=D11+D16**, then press **Enter**.

11 Check your work with Figure 2.3. Make any corrections necessary.

12 Click location of cell references and totals. Remember, however, that ending retained earnings on the balance sheet is not the retained earnings specified on the trial balance. Instead it is the amount shown in cell B8 on the Statement of Retained Earnings.

13 Compare your final balance sheet to Figures 2.3 and 2.4.

The balance sheet is taking form after Meagan has entered cell references and formulas. All that is left are cell number and border format changes.

To format the balance sheet:

1 Format the cells containing numbers with either the currency or comma formats to match Figures 2.3 and 2.4.

2 Format the cells with either the bottom or top and double bottom border tools to match Figures 2.3 and 2.4.

3 Save your work to ch2-01c.xls.

4 Click **View** then **Header and Footer** from the menu. Place your name and date in the left section of the footer and the filename in the right section of the footer.

5 Click **Print Preview**, then click **Print** to make sure the worksheet will print the way you want. Then print the balance sheet.

6 Save your work again to ch2-01c.xls.

Meagan is pleased with the final balance sheet and all other statements that she, Nathan, and you have created. She is concerned about the time and effort that went into the worksheet construction. Kyle explains that this worksheet has been constructed in a way that will facilitate its reuse every period that a financial statement is needed.

END NOTE

You've learned a few basics about Excel's cell referencing capabilities and multiple worksheet approach. In addition, you've utilized some of your accounting knowledge to link the financial statements together.

In the next chapter you will learn how to use Excel to perform financial statement analysis.

practice

Chapter 2 Questions

1 What is the purpose of the Merge and Center tool on the Format toolbar?

2 Describe the steps necessary to merge and center titles on a worksheet.

3 Describe the steps necessary to include a reference from another worksheet onto an active worksheet.

4 In what order must financial statements be prepared?

5 Describe the subtotals that are normally a part of the income statement.

6 Describe the subtotals that are normally a part of the statement of retained earnings.

7 Describe the subtotals that are normally a part of the balance sheet.

8 How is the statement of retained earnings linked to the income statement?

9 How is the balance sheet linked to the statement of retained earnings?

10 What should you always place in the footer of each worksheet?

Chapter 2 Assignments

1 *Create Coast Jewelers' financial statements for September 30, 2003*

You are to create Coast's financial statements as of September 30, 2003 from the trial balance information found on your student disk file ch2-02.xls.

a Follow the Chapter 2 examples for linking and formatting worksheets, then save the file as **ch2-02a.xls**.

b After placing your name, date, and filename in the footer to each worksheet, print the value and formula view worksheets that you create for the income statement, statement of retained earnings, and balance sheet.

c Save the file once again.

2 *Create Coast Jewelers' financial statements for December 31, 2003*

You are to create Coast's financial statements as of December 31, 2003.

a Use the ch2-02a.xls file that you created above.

b Update the trial balance based on the amounts in the table.

c Save the modified workbook as **ch2-02b.xls**.

d Update each financial statement's title to reflect the new time period.

e Print only the value view worksheets for the income statement, statement of changes in retained earnings, and balance sheet.

f Save the file once again.

Account	Dr	Cr.
Cash	$ 46,876.24	
Accounts receivable	105,365.25	
Inventory	160,895.44	
Prepaid expenses	9,524.98	
Supplies	7,508.54	
Land	120,000.00	
Building	315,000.00	
Accumulated depreciation: Building		$ 90,000.00
Equipment	70,000.00	
Accumulated depreciation: Equipment		22,000.00
Accounts payable		45,368.55
Payroll liabilities		2,458.65
Long-term debt		350,000.00
Common stock		10,000.00
Retained earnings		192,697.36
Dividends	12,000.00	
Sales revenue		1,768,997.24
Cost of goods sold	1,088,486.17	
Advertising expense	53,874.07	
Depreciation expense	44,000.00	
Income taxes	62,004.55	
Interest expense	64,987.33	
Payroll expense	265,124.55	
Utilities	55,874.68	
Total	$2,481,521.80	$2,481,521.80

Chapter 2 Case Problem: Kelly's Boutique

You are to create Kelly's Boutique's financial statements as of November 30, 2002 and as of December 31, 2002 from the trial balance information found on your student disk file ch2-03.xls. This company's fiscal year will end December 31, 2002.

1 Follow the Chapter 2 examples for linking and formatting worksheets in creating financial statements, then save the file as ch2-03a.xls. (Note: the accounts for Kelly's Boutique are different from those used for the Coast Jewelers, Inc. You are advised to create a new set of financial statements for these specific accounts.)

2 After placing your name, date, and filename in the footer of each worksheet, print the value and formula view worksheets that you create for the income statement, statement of retained earnings, and balance sheet.

3 Save the file once again.

4 Update the trial balance created above with balances as of December 31, 2002 shown below.

5 Save the modified workbook as ch2-03b.xls.

6 Update each financial statement's title to reflect the new time period.

7 Print only the value view worksheets for the income statement, statement of changes in retained earnings, and balance sheet.

8 Save the file once again.

Account	Dr	Cr
Cash	$ 10,100.51	
Accounts receivable	16,500.13	
Inventory	55,125.65	
Prepaid expenses	1,300.00	
Supplies	400.00	
Land	31,000.00	
Building	100,000.00	
Accumulated depreciation: Building		$ 20,000.00
Equipment	15,000.00	
Accumulated depreciation: Equipment		9,000.00
Accounts payable		6,200.00
Income taxes payable		2,200.00
Notes payable		82,000.00
Payroll liabilities		1,250.00
Mortgage payable		72,000.00
Common stock		1,000.00
Retained earnings		1,597.88
Dividends	1,500.00	
Sales revenue		360,196.00
Cost of goods sold	180,654.41	
Advertising expense	6,210.56	
Depreciation expense	9,000.00	
Interest expense	17,010.51	
Income taxes	1,800.00	
Payroll expense	97,042.11	
Supplies expense	5,600.00	
Utilities	7,200.00	
Total	$555,443.88	$555,443.88

3

Financial Statement Analysis

In this chapter you will learn:

- How to perform vertical financial analysis on a worksheet

- How to create a pie chart of expenses using the chart wizard

- How to perform horizontal financial analysis on a worksheet

- How to column chart horizontal financial data

- How to perform ratio analysis on a worksheet

CASE: COAST JEWELERS, INC.
. . . .

Now that financial statements have been prepared, Nathan and Meagan are ready to evaluate the company's performance, examine trends and relationships, and assess it's liquidity and solvency. Kyle suggests three forms of analysis that can provide information to Nathan and Meagan for business decision-making: vertical, horizontal, and ratio analysis.

You recall learning about these three methods of analysis while studying financial accounting. Kyle reminds you that Excel is a great tool for preparing these analyses and suggests that you take the lead in explaining the formulas used in creating these types of worksheets.

"Can Excel also help us prepare charts? We have to prepare some information for our bankers and they seem to prefer both numbers and charts," Nathan asks. "Most definitely!" Kyle answers. "We'll use Excel to look at the financial information we recently created, and compute vertical, horizontal, and ratio analyses as well as prepare charts to describe important relationships and trends."

VERTICAL ANALYSIS
. . . .

Vertical analysis, often referred to as component analysis, is used to express each item on a particular financial statement as a percentage of a single base amount. In an income statement the base is sales revenue. Each expense is expressed as a percentage of sales revenue.

To create a vertical analysis on an income statement:

1 Start Excel and open file ch3-01.xls.

2 Right click column **C** and click **Insert** to insert a new column.

3 Click in cell C4 and type "%" as a label to the new column.

4 Click in cell C5 and type the formula =B5/$B$5, then press **Enter**. (*Note:* use an absolute reference in the denominator so you can fill down the formula later.)

5 Click in cell C5 again and reformat the cell by clicking the % tool on the Formatting toolbar.

6 Resize column C to 61 pixels.

7 Fill down the formula in C5 to C16 by dragging the handle in the lower right corner of cell C5 to C16. (*Note:* this will also copy down the formatting from cell C5, removing border formats that you can fix later.)

8 Eliminate the formula from cell C8 by clicking the cell and pressing **Delete**, then **Enter**.

9 Add appropriate border formats to cells C6, C13, and C16.

10 Repeat Steps 3 to 9 in column E. Substitute E for C in all column references. Your worksheet should look like Figure 3.1.

	A	B	C	D	E
1	Coast Jewelers, Inc.				
2	Income Statement				
3	For the 6 Months Ended				
4		12/31/03	%	06/30/04	%
5	Sales Revenue	$ 850,511.65	100%	$ 825,974.15	100%
6	Less: Cost of Goods Sold	442,619.87	52%	489,547.25	59%
7	Gross Margin	407,891.78	48%	336,426.90	41%
8	Expenses:				
9	Advertising	20,654.21	2%	26,548.55	3%
10	Depreciation	22,000.00	3%	22,000.00	3%
11	Interest	40,846.24	5%	32,338.94	4%
12	Payroll	115,365.11	14%	129,547.97	16%
13	Utilities	23,541.25	3%	27,546.16	3%
14	Net income before taxes	185,484.97	22%	98,445.28	12%
15	Income taxes	65,218.98	8%	31,600.00	4%
16	Net income	$ 120,265.99	14%	$ 66,845.28	8%

FIGURE 3.1

Income Statement Vertical Analysis

11 Save your work to ch3-01a.xls.

12 Click **View** then **Header and Footer** from the menu. Place your name and date in the left section of the footer and the filename in the right section of the footer.

13 Click **Print Preview** and then **Print** to make sure the worksheet will print the way you want and to print the income statement.

14 Save your work again to ch3-01a.xls.

"Is the balance sheet used for vertical analysis as well?" Nathan asks. "Yes," you respond.

In a balance sheet the base is total assets. Each asset, liability, and equity component is expressed as a percentage of total assets.

To create a vertical analysis on a balance sheet:

1 Activate the balance sheet in the newly saved ch3-01a.xls file.

2 Right click column **C** and click **Insert** to insert a new column.

3 Click in cell C5 and type "%" as a label to the new column.

4 Click in cell C7 and type the formula **=B7/$B$17**, then press **Enter**. (*Note:* Once again use an absolute reference in the denominator so you can fill down the formula later.)

5 Click in cell C7 again and reformat the cell by clicking the % tool on the Formatting toolbar.

6 Resize column C to 61 pixels.

7 Fill down the formula in C7 to C17 by dragging the handle in the lower right corner of cell C7 to C17. (*Note:* This will also copy down the formatting from cell C7, removing border formats that you can fix later.)

8 Eliminate the formula from cell C12 by clicking the cell, and then pressing **Delete**, then **Enter**.

9 Add appropriate border formats to cell C17.

10 Repeat Steps 3 to 9 in column E. Substitute E for C in all column references. Part of your worksheet should look like Figure 3.2.

FIGURE 3.2

Balance Sheet Vertical Analysis

	A	B	C
1	Coast Jewelers, Inc.		
2	Balance Sheet		
3	as of		
4			
5	Assets	12/31/03	%
6	Current Assets:		
7	Cash	$ 25,412.35	4%
8	Accounts Receivable	84,245.25	12%
9	Inventory	125,351.45	18%
10	Prepaid Expenses	15,625.26	2%
11	Supplies	10,245.15	2%
12	Property, Plant, and Equipment:		
13	Land	120,000.00	18%
14	Building	300,000.00	44%
15	Equipment	65,000.00	10%
16	Less: Accumulated Depreciation	(68,000.00)	-10%
17	Total	$ 677,879.46	100%

11 Save your work to ch3-01a.xls.

12 Click **Print Preview** and then **Print** to make sure the worksheet will print the way you want and to print the balance sheet.

To complete the vertical analysis you offer to demonstrate Excel's charting capability by creating a pie chart of expenses for the six months ended December 31, 2003.

PIE CHARTS

"Excel's chart wizard makes creating a chart from a worksheet a breeze," you explain.

To create a pie chart of expenses:

1 Click on **Income Statement** tab and select cells A9 through B13.

2 Click the **Chart Wizard** tool on the Standard toolbar.

3 Select **Pie** from the list of Standard Chart types.

4 Click the picture of a pie chart with **3-D visual effect** from the Chart sub-type section of the Chart Wizard window (top row, middle chart).

5 Click **Next**, then click **Next** again to accept the default data range (='Income Statement'!$A$9:$B$13).

6 Type **Expenses for the Six Months Ended December 31, 2003** in the Chart Title edit box.

7 Click the **Legend** tab, select **Bottom** in the Placement section and click **Next**.

8 Click on **Data Labels**, select **Show percent**, and click **Next**.

9 In the Place chart section of the next window click the **As new sheet** option button and change the name of the sheet from Chart1 to **Expense Chart**, then click **Finish**. Your completed pie chart should look like Figure 3.3.

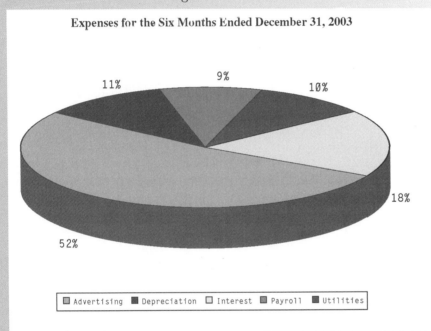

FIGURE 3.3
Pie Chart of Expenses

Expenses for the Six Months Ended December 31, 2003

□ Advertising ■ Depreciation □ Interest ■ Payroll ■ Utilities

10 Click **Print Preview** and then **Print** to make sure the worksheet will print the way you want and to print the income statement.

11 Save your work again to ch3-01a.xls.

You have now completed the vertical analysis with the exceptions of explaining or examining the percentages and chart in detail. Nathan and Meagan are eager to look these over more carefully but not until they see how horizontal and ratio analyses can be created in Excel.

HORIZONTAL ANALYSIS

Horizontal analysis examines trends over time. This can include comparisons of months, quarters, or years for both the income statement as well as the balance sheet. Income statements and balance sheets for two or more periods are compared side by side and a percentage increase or decrease is computed between periods.

"Isn't that what we just did in vertical analysis?" Meagan asks. "The percentages computed in vertical analysis are usually done for just one period, although they are often compared period to period," Kyle answers. "Remember, vertical analysis compares each statement element with a single base amount, such as sales or total assets. Horizontal analysis compares elements side by side with other periods."

To create a horizontal analysis on an income statement:

1 Start Excel and open file ch3-01.xls (This is the same file you opened for vertical analysis. It should still look the same as the changes you made were saved under another filename.)

2 Activate the Income Statement worksheet.

3 Click in cell D4 and type **% Change** as a label to the column.

4 Format cell D4 bold, center, bottom, and with a bottom border.

5 Click in cell D5 and type the formula **=(C5–B5)/B5**, then press **Enter**.

6 Format cell D5 as Percent Style by clicking cell **D5** and selecting the **Percent Style** tool on the Format toolbar.

7 Use the fill-down procedure to copy the formula from D5 to D16.

8 Delete the formula in cell D8.

9 Format cells D6 and D13 with a bottom border.

10 Format cell D16 with a top and double bottom border.

11 Resize column D to 96 pixels. Your completed income statement with horizontal analysis should look like Figure 3.4.

FIGURE 3.4

Income Statement with Horizontal Analysis

	A	B	C	D
1	Coast Jewelers, Inc.			
2	Income Statement			
3	For the 6 Months Ended			
4		12/31/03	06/30/04	% Change
5	Sales Revenue	$ 850,511.65	$ 825,974.15	-3%
6	Less: Cost of Goods Sold	442,619.87	489,547.25	11%
7	Gross Margin	407,891.78	336,426.90	-18%
8	Expenses:			
9	Advertising	20,654.21	26,548.55	29%
10	Depreciation	22,000.00	22,000.00	0%
11	Interest	40,846.24	32,338.94	-21%
12	Payroll	115,365.11	129,547.97	12%
13	Utilities	23,541.25	27,546.16	17%
14	Net income before taxes	185,484.97	98,445.28	-47%
15	Income taxes	65,218.98	31,600.00	-52%
16	Net income	$ 120,265.99	$ 66,845.28	-44%

12 Save your work to ch3-01b.xls.

13 Click **Print Preview** from the File menu, then click **Print** to make sure the worksheet will print the way you want and to print the income statement.

14 Save your work again as ch3-01b.xls.

"The trends reflected here are not very good," Nathan says. "The analysis reveals a decline in sales of 3 percent but an 11 percent increase in the costs of goods sold."

Kyle explains that the income statement analysis reveals operational and profitability performance and trends, and that the balance sheet reflects financial stability and solvency trends. The horizontal analysis on the balance sheet compares current balances for each asset, liability, and equity element with the same element in the prior period.

To create a horizontal analysis on a balance sheet:

1 Activate the Balance Sheet worksheet on the saved file Ch3-01b.xls.

2 Click in cell D5 and type **% Change** as a label to the column.

3 Format cell D5 bold, center, bottom, and with a bottom border.

4 Click in cell D7 and type the formula **=(C7–B7)/B7**, then press **Enter**.

5 Format cell D7 as Percent Style by clicking cell **D7** and selecting the Percent Style tool on the Format toolbar.

6 Use the fill-down procedure to copy the formula from D7 to D28.

7 Delete the formula in cells D12, D18–D21, D23, and D25.

8 Format cells D17 and D28 with a top and double bottom border.

9 Resize column D to 93 pixels. Your completed balance sheet with horizontal analysis should look like Figures 3.5 and 3.6.

	A	B	C	D
1	Coast Jewelers, Inc.			
2	Balance Sheet			
3	as of			
4				
5	Assets	12/31/03	06/30/04	% Change
6	Current Assets:			
7	Cash	$ 25,412.35	$ 20,182.15	-21%
8	Accounts Receivable	84,245.25	102,544.24	22%
9	Inventory	125,351.45	152,154.21	21%
10	Prepaid Expenses	15,625.26	15,241.75	-2%
11	Supplies	10,245.15	6,578.24	-36%
12	Property, Plant, and Equipment:			
13	Land	120,000.00	120,000.00	0%
14	Building	300,000.00	315,000.00	5%
15	Equipment	65,000.00	70,000.00	8%
16	Less: Accumulated Depreciation	(68,000.00)	(90,000.00)	32%
17	Total	$ 677,879.46	$ 711,700.59	5%

FIGURE 3.5

Balance Sheet Assets with Horizontal Analysis

	A	B	C	D
19	**Liabilities and Stockholders' Equity**			
20	Liabilities			
21	Current Liabilities:			
22	Accounts Payable	$ 75,182.10	$ 84,005.70	12%
23	Payroll Liabilities		8,152.25	
24	Long-Term Debt	400,000.00	350,000.00	-13%
25	Stockholders' Equity			
26	Common Stock	10,000.00	10,000.00	0%
27	Retained Earnings	192,697.36	259,542.64	35%
28	Total	$ 677,879.46	$ 711,700.59	5%
29				

FIGURE 3.6

Balance Sheet Liabilities and Equity with Horizontal Analysis

10 Save your work to ch3-01b.xls.

11 Click **Print Preview** from the File menu and then **Print** to make sure the worksheet will print the way you want and to print the income statement.

12 Save your work again as ch3-01b.xls.

"I'm a little concerned about the 22 percent growth in accounts receivable, the 21 percent growth in inventory, and the 21 percent decrease in cash," Meagan says. Kyle reminds her that she needs to remember that at the same time those events occurred, long-term debt decreased 13 percent and retained earnings increased 35 percent. "Excel can also provide some graphical evidence of these trends by creating column charts using the chart wizard," Kyle says.

COLUMN CHARTS

Previously you created a pie chart of expenses using Excel's Chart Wizard. Now it is time to create a column chart comparing expenses from one period to the next. The column chart you decide to create will illustrate expenses side-by-side for the two six-month periods ended December 31, 2003 and June 30, 2004.

To create a column chart comparing expenses:

1 Activate the Income Statement worksheet.

2 Select cells A9 through C13 (expenses for both periods).

3 Click the **Chart Wizard** tool.

4 Select Chart type: **Column**, then **Clustered column with a 3-D visual effect** from the Chart sub type section, then click **Next**.

5 Click the **Series** tab in the Chart Wizard window.

6 Select **Series1** from the Series section (see Figure 3.7).

7 Click in the far right of the Name edit box to reveal the Source Data – Name: window.

8 Click in cell B4 of the Income Statement worksheet, then press **Enter**.

9 Select **Series2** from the Series section (see Figure 3.7).

10 Click in the far right of the Name edit box to reveal the Source Data – Name: window.

11 Click in cell C4 of the Income Statement worksheet, and press **Enter**.

12 Click **Next** and select the **Titles** tab from the Chart Options window.

13 Type **Expense Comparison Between the Six Month Period Ended 12/31/03 and 6/30/04** in the Chart title: edit box.

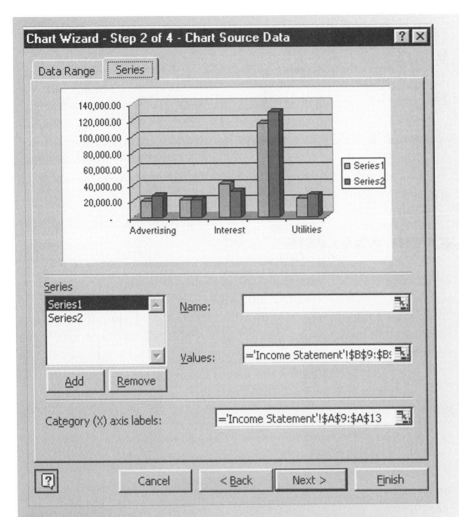

FIGURE 3.7
Chart Wizard Series Tab

14 Click **Next**, then click the **As new sheet** option button and change the name from Chart1 to **Expense Comparison** and click **Finish**. See Figure 3.8.

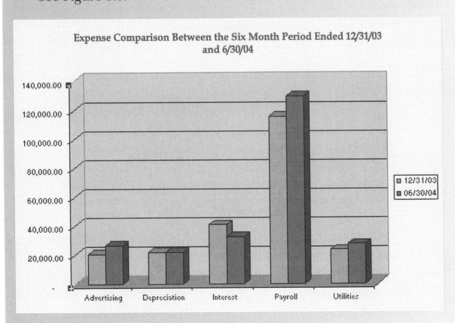

FIGURE 3.8
Completed Column Chart

15 Save your work to ch3-01b.xls again.

16 Click **Print Preview** from the File menu, then click **Print** to make sure the chart will print the way you want and print the chart.

17 Save your work again to ch3-01b.xls

"All of this is very interesting," says Nathan. "I'll bet there's more. Am I right?"

"Yes, we still have ratio analysis to complete our financial statement analyses portfolio," Kyle responds.

RATIO ANALYSIS

Kyle explains that several standard ratios are often used to assess a company's profitability, liquidity, and solvency. Profitability represents the company's ability to generate a profit to investors. Liquidity represents the company's ability to pay its bills currently. Solvency represents the company's ability to stay in business given its debt structure. A chart of each ratio's formula follows.

Profitability	
Return on owners' investment	Net income/Average stockholders' equity
Return on total investment	Net income before interest expense/Average total assets
Profit margin	Net income/Sales
Gross margin	Gross margin/Sales
Liquidity	
Current ratio	Current assets/Current liabilities
Quick ratio	Current assets less inventory/Current liabilities
Receivable turnover	Sales/Average accounts receivable
Inventory turnover	Cost of Goods Sold/Average inventory
Solvency	
Debt-to-equity	Total liabilities/Total equity
Liability	Total liabilities/Total assets

In Excel, each of these amounts is a part of a given financial statement or they can be computed. Therefore, you can create a new worksheet that has formulas referencing these amounts. Kyle suggests you create a new worksheet to compute these ratios.

To calculate the first financial ratio on a new worksheet:

1 Right-click the **Income Statement** tab of your workbook and click **Insert . . .** , then click **Worksheet**, then **OK** to insert a new worksheet.

2 Double-click the **Sheet1** tab and rename the worksheet **Ratio Analysis**.

3 Format the Ratio Analysis worksheet like Figure 3.9 with a heading and listing of ratios as shown. To format the date as June 2004, click cell **A3**. Go to Format, cleck **Cells**, click **Number** tab, and click **Custom** on the category list. Scroll through the list of options and choose **mmmm yyyy**.

	A	B
1	*Coast Jewelers, Inc.*	
2	*Ratio Analysis*	
3	*June 2004*	
4		
5	**Profitability**	
6	Return on owners' investment	
7	Return on total investment	
8	Profit margin	
9	Gross margin	
10	**Liquidity**	
11	Current ratio	
12	Quick ratio	
13	Receivable turnover	
14	Inventory turnover	
15	**Solvency**	
16	Debt-to-equity	
17	Liability	

FIGURE 3.9

Format for Ratio Analysis

4 Click in cell B6 and type the following =**'Income Statement' !C16/(('Balance Sheet'!B26+'Balance Sheet'!B27+'Balance Sheet' !C26+'Balance Sheet'!C27)/2)** to compute return on owners' investment.

5 Alternatively, you could utilize multiple worksheet referencing. Type = in cell B6, then activate the income statement worksheet and click cell **C16**.

6 Type **/((** (The forward slash or division symbol and two left parentheses. The parentheses once again help determine the all-important order of calculation.)

7 Activate the balance sheet worksheet and click cell **B26**.

8 Type **+**, then click cell **B27**.

9 Type **+**, then click cell **C26**.

10 Type **+**, then click cell **C27**.

11 Type **)/2)** to end the summation of equity accounts and divide the result by 2 to get an average.

12 Press **Enter** to end your formula.

13 Format cell B6 in a percent style.

trouble? If you choose to type the formula as written above and forget an apostrophe, exclamation point, or misspell a word, Excel will give you an error message and you'll have to debug your formula. Also, if you don't have the correct number of parentheses, Excel will give you an error message. Note that when you edit the formula, Excel changes the color of each set of parentheses so that you can clearly see which is which.

"The point and click method of cell referencing on multiple worksheets is sure easier than typing the references themselves." you comment. "Otherwise I would have to type all of those apostrophes and exclamation points. With my typing skills I would probably forget one of them and create an error in the formula."

"Good point," Kyle says. "Let's finish the profitability ratios next."

To enter remaining formulas for profitability analysis:

1 Click cell **B7** and type =.

2 Use the values at cells C16 and C11 on the income statement to compute the numerator of the return on total investment ratio.

3 Use the values at cells B17 and C17 on the balance sheet to add total assets, then divide the result by 2 to get an average.

4 Once your formula is typed press **Enter** to compute the ratio. Your formula should look like this: **=('Income Statement'!C16+'Income Statement'!C11)/(('Balance Sheet'!B17+'Balance Sheet'!C17)/2)**. Be careful to use the correct parentheses.

5 Format the cell in percent style.

6 In cell B8 use the values at cells C16 and C5 on the income statement to compute the profit margin. (Use the ratio chart, shown on the previous pages, to enter the appropriate formula.) Your formula should look like this: **='Income Statement'!C16/'Income Statement'!C5**.

7 Format the cell in percent style.

8 In cell B9 use the values at cells C7 and C5 on the income statement to compute the gross margin. (Use the ratio chart, shown on the previous pages, to enter the appropriate formula.) Your formula should look like this: **='Income Statement'!C7/'Income Statement'!C5**.

9 Format the cell in percent style.

10 Save your work as ch3-01c.xls.

Remember, the profitability ratios measure the company's ability to generate a profit to investors. In this case, Nathan and Meagan are fairly satisfied with their profitability in comparison to other companies of their size and type of business. They are eager to see if the liquidity ratios are equally as positive.

Kyle encourages you to continue with your ratio analysis.

To compute the liquidity ratios:

1 In cell B11 use the values in cells C7–C11 and C22–C23 on the balance sheet to compute the current ratio. (Use the ratio chart shown on the previous pages to enter the appropriate formula.) Your formula should look like this: **=SUM('Balance Sheet'!C7:C11) /SUM('Balance Sheet'!C22:C23)**.

2 Format the cell in comma style.

3 In cell B12 use the values in cells C7–C8 and C22–C23 on the balance sheet to compute the quick ratio. (Use the ratio chart shown on the previous pages to enter the appropriate formula.) Your formula should look like this: **=SUM('Balance Sheet'!C7:C8) /SUM('Balance Sheet'!C22:C23)**.

4 Format the cell in comma style.

5 In cell B13 use the values in cell C5 on the income statement and cells B8 and C8 on the balance sheet to compute the receivable turnover ratio. (Use the ratio chart shown on the previous pages to enter the appropriate formula.) Your formula should look like this: **='Income Statement'!C5/(('Balance Sheet'!B8+'Balance Sheet' !C8)/2)**.

6 Format the cell in comma style.

7 In cell B14 use the values in cell C6 on the income statement and cells B9 and C9 on the balance sheet to compute the inventory turnover ratio. (Use the ratio chart shown on the previous pages to enter the appropriate formula.) Your formula should look like this: **='Income Statement'!C6/(('Balance Sheet'!B9+'Balance Sheet' !C9)/2)**.

8 Format the cell in comma style.

9 Save your work again as ch3-01c.xls.

Remember, the liquidity ratios measure the company's ability to pay its bills currently. In this case, Nathan and Meagan are surprised at how good their current and quick ratios are. Usually, their current ratio is around 2:1, which is normal. The 3.22 current ratio and the 1.33 quick ratio indicate they have plenty of resources to meet their current liabilities. Receivable turnover is a little low given they have 30-day credit terms, although this is still a healthy report. Inventory turnover is a little slow at 3.53 but fairly common in their business. They are eager to see if the solvency ratios continue the trend.

To compute the solvency ratios:

1 In cell B16 use the values in cells C22–C24 and C26–C27 on the balance sheet to compute the debt to equity ratio. (Use the ratio chart shown on the previous pages to enter the appropriate formula.) Your formula should look like this: **=SUM('Balance Sheet' !C22:C24)/SUM('Balance Sheet'!C26:C27)**.

2 Format the cell in percent style.

3 In cell B17 use the values in cells C22–C24 and C17 on the balance sheet to compute the liability ratio. (Use the ratio chart shown on the previous pages to enter the appropriate formula.) Your formula should look like this: **=SUM('Balance Sheet'!C22:C24)/'Balance Sheet'!C17**.

4 Format the cell in percent style.

5 Save your work again as ch3.01c.xls. See Figure 3.10 for a completed ratio analysis.

FIGURE 3.10

Completed Ratio Analysis

	A	B
1	*Coast Jewelers, Inc.*	
2	*Ratio Analysis*	
3	*June 2004*	
4		
5	**Profitability**	
6	Return on owners' investment	28%
7	Return on total investment	14%
8	Profit margin	8%
9	Gross margin	41%
10	**Liquidity**	
11	Current ratio	3.22
12	Quick ratio	1.33
13	Receivable turnover	8.84
14	Inventory turnover	3.53
15	**Solvency**	
16	Debt-to-equity	164%
17	Liability	62%
18		

Now the news is not as good. It turns out the positive liquidity ratio information is somewhat offset by the solvency ratios that indicate that debt is 164 percent of equity. The company is financed heavily with debt that can lead to problems if the return on investment doesn't exceed the cost of the debt. The liability ratio reflects the same problem in that 62 percent of the company's assets are financed with debt versus equity. Nathan's business plan calls for a reduction in debt over the next several years as profits provide the cash necessary.

"This is great," Meagan says. "Although the solvency ratios are high, they do reflect our business plan and as long as we continue to generate profits and cash flow we should be able to improve the solvency ratios."

END NOTE

You've applied some of what you learned in the first two chapters to create a set of useful worksheets that identify trends and relationships. Plus you've created them in a reusable format for future periods.

In the next chapter you will learn how to use Excel to perform depreciation calculations and prepare depreciation schedules.

practice

chapter

3

Chapter 3 Questions

1 What is another term for vertical analysis?

2 What base amount is used for vertical analysis of an income statement?

3 What base amount is used for vertical analysis of a balance sheet?

4 What base amount is used for horizontal analysis of both income statements and balance sheets? Give an example.

5 What do profitability ratios represent?

6 What do liquidity ratios represent?

7 What do solvency ratios represent?

8 Why is the point and click method of cell referencing easier than typing in references into worksheet cells?

9 Which ratios are usually formatted as percentages?

10 Which ratios are usually formatted as numbers?

Chapter 3 Assignments

1 *Create Coast Jewelers' financial analysis for September 30, 2003*

You are to create Coast's financial analysis as of September 30, 2003 from the information found on your student disk file ch3-02.xls. This file contains five worksheets labeled Income Statement Vertical, Balance Sheet Vertical, Income Statement Horizontal, Balance Sheet Horizontal, and Ratios.

a Following the Chapter 3 examples, create:
  (1) Vertical analysis of both the income statement and balance sheet for September 2003 only.
  (2) Horizontal analysis of both the income statement and balance sheet. (*Note:* The horizontal analysis will compare June 30, 2003 with September 30, 2003.)
  (3) Pie chart of expenses as of June 30, 2003.
  (4) Column chart of expenses for June 30, 2003 and September 30, 2003.
  (5) Ratio analysis as of September 30, 2003.

b Save the file as **ch3-02a.xls**.

c After placing your name, date, and filename in the footer of each worksheet, print the value view worksheets you create for each of the above.

d Save the file once again.

2 *Create Coast Jewelers' financial analysis for December 31, 2002*

You are to create Coast's financial analyses as of December 31, 2002 from the information found on your student disk file ch3-03.xls. This file contains five worksheets labeled Income Statement Vertical, Balance Sheet Vertical, Income Statement Horizontal, Balance Sheet Horizontal, and Ratios.

  a Following the Chapter 3 examples, create:
    (1) Vertical analysis of both the income statement and balance sheet as of December 31, 2002 only.
    (2) Horizontal analysis of both the income statement and balance sheet. (*Note:* The horizontal analysis will compare September 30, 2003 with December 31, 2002.)
    (3) Pie chart of expenses as of September 30, 2003.
    (4) Column chart of expenses for September 30, 2003 and December 31, 2002.
    (5) Ratio analysis as of December 31, 2002.
  b Save the file as **ch3-03a.xls**.
  c After placing your name, date, and filename in the footer of each worksheet, print the value view worksheets you create for each of the above.
  d Save the file once again.

Chapter 3 Case Problem: Kelly's Boutique

You are to create Kelly's Boutique's financial analyses as of November 30, 2002 and as of December 31, 2002.

1 Following the Chapter 3 examples, use the student file ch 3-04.xls to create:
  a Vertical analysis of the balance sheet as of December 2002 only.
  b Vertical analysis of the income statement for the year ended December 2002.
  c Horizontal analysis of both the income statement and balance sheet. (*Note:* The horizontal analysis will compare November 30, 2002 with December 31, 2002.)
  d Pie chart of expenses as of November 30, 2002.
  e Column chart of expenses for November 30, 2002 and December 31, 2002.
  f Ratio analysis as of 1/1/02 and 12/31/02.

2 Save the file as **ch3-04a.xls**.

3 After placing your name, date, and file name in the footer of each worksheet, print the value view worksheets you create for each of the above.

4 Save the file once again.

Depreciation Calculations

In this chapter you will learn:

- How to calculate straight-line depreciation using Excel's built-in function

- How to use what-if analysis with the depreciation function

- How to create a depreciation summary for many assets

- How to calculate depreciation using double-declining balance and sum-of-the-years digits methods using Excel's built-in functions

- How to create charts to illustrate depreciation expense

CASE: COAST JEWELERS, INC.

Worksheets are used for more than financial statement preparation and analysis. For the accountant, worksheets can provide a very useful supporting schedule role. Nathan and Meagan want to make sure that you are fully trained on all aspects of Excel's use in accounting for their business.

PERFORMING DEPRECIATION CALCULATIONS

The financial statements you prepared and analyzed in the preceding chapters didn't just appear. They were created using the company's trial balance that was prepared from the accounts in the general ledger. Prior to financial statement preparation, accounts in the general ledger needed adjustment to properly present accrual accounting. One of those adjustments of course is the depreciation of a company's fixed assets.

You recall learning that depreciation is the allocation of a firm's investment in fixed assets in a systematic and rational manner. The easiest of several generally accepted methods of depreciating these assets is called the straight-line method.

"How can Excel help us with depreciation?" Nathan asks.

"Excel has some built-in functions that, when given the appropriate information, can calculate depreciation for you." Kyle responds.

"What about salvage value, useful life, etc.?" you ask. "Aren't those important factors in determining depreciation?"

"Indeed they are," Kyle says. "That's the appropriate information that I am referring to. To calculate depreciation the function needs information about the asset's cost, estimated salvage value, and economic useful life."

Kyle explains that Excel's built-in function to calculate straight-line depreciation is written as follows: **=SLN(Cost, Salvage Value, Useful life)**. SLN stands for straight-line depreciation. Inside the parentheses are three arguments separated by commas. The first argument identifies the asset's cost, the second its salvage value, the third its useful life. You can type the dollar cost, salvage value, and number of years into the function or you can point the function to the cell location where the cost, salvage value, and useful life is located. This second alternative is much more effective as the cell references can then be duplicated across several cells.

Kyle suggests that you use a template he's created to compute depreciation for one asset. You are up to the challenge and proceed with the task. The asset you'll depreciate, number 1001, Display Cases, was acquired January 1, 1999 for $15,000. It has no salvage value and has an economic useful life of five years.

To calculate depreciation using Excel's built-in function:

1 Start Excel and open file ch4-01.xls.

2 Make the Asset 1001 worksheet active. It should look like Figure 4.1 below. (*Note:* You'll use the summary worksheet later.)

	A	B	C
1	Coast Jewelers, Inc. Depreciation Schedule		
2			
3	Asset #		
4	Asset		
5	Date acquired		
6	Cost		
7	Depreciation method		
8	Salvage value		
9	Estimated useful life		
10			
11	Year	Depreciation Expense	Accumulated Depreciation
12	1999		
13	2000		
14	2001		
15	2002		
16	2003		

FIGURE 4.1

Depreciation Calculation Worksheet

3 Enter the appropriate information on the worksheet, such as the asset number, date acquired, depreciation method (use S/L for straight-line), salvage value, and estimated useful life.

4 Enter the formula **=SLN($B$6,$B$8,$B$9)** in cell B12. Then press the **Enter** key. B6 is the location of the asset's cost, B8 is the location of its salvage value, and B9 is the location of its useful life. (*Note:* Entering these references as absolute values using the $ will help later as we replicate the formula for each year.)

5 Fill the formula in cell B12 down to cells B13 through B16.

6 Enter the formula **=B12** into cell C12.

7 Enter the formula **=C12+B13** into cell C13 and fill this formula down to cells C14 through C16. These formulas create a running total of deprecation over the years. Your worksheet should now look like Figure 4.2.

8 Save your work to ch4-01a.xls.

Meagan offers to create another depreciation worksheet. The company purchased chairs on January 1, 1999 for $5,000. These assets were designated as asset #1002 and also had no salvage value and were estimated to have a five-year useful life.

FIGURE 4.2

*Completed Depreciation
Calculation Worksheet*

	A	B	C
1	Coast Jewelers, Inc. Depreciation Schedule		
2			
3	Asset #	1001	
4	Asset	Display Cases	
5	Date acquired	1/1/99	
6	Cost	$ 15,000.00	
7	Depreciation method	S/L	
8	Salvage value	$ -	
9	Estimated useful life	5	
10			
11	Year	Depreciation Expense	Accumulated Depreciation
12	1999	$3,000.00	$3,000.00
13	2000	$3,000.00	$6,000.00
14	2001	$3,000.00	$9,000.00
15	2002	$3,000.00	$12,000.00
16	2003	$3,000.00	$15,000.00

To create another deprecation worksheet:

1 Right-click the **Asset 1001** tab to reveal the Shortcut menu.

2 Click **Move or Copy**.

3 Check the **Create a Copy** checkbox, then click **OK**.

4 Change the name of the newly created worksheet to **Asset 1002**.

5 Enter the appropriate information on the worksheet, such as the asset number, date acquired, depreciation method (use S/L for straight-line), salvage value, and estimated useful life. Your completed worksheet should look like Figure 4.3.

FIGURE 4.3

*Depreciation Worksheet
for Asset 1002*

	A	B	C
1	Coast Jewelers, Inc. Depreciation Schedule		
2			
3	Asset #	1002	
4	Asset	Chairs	
5	Date acquired	1/1/99	
6	Cost	$ 5,000.00	
7	Depreciation method	S/L	
8	Salvage value	$ -	
9	Estimated useful life	5	
10			
11	Year	Depreciation Expense	Accumulated Depreciation
12	1999	$1,000.00	$1,000.00
13	2000	$1,000.00	$2,000.00
14	2001	$1,000.00	$3,000.00
15	2002	$1,000.00	$4,000.00
16	2003	$1,000.00	$5,000.00

6 Save your work to Ch4-01a.xls.

"How is using the SLN function and all the cell references different from using a calculator or just typing the values into the function?" Meagan asks. Kyle responds that Excel's power is in its sensitivity or what-if analysis capability, which he offers to illustrate next.

CONDUCTING WHAT-IF ANALYSIS WITH THE DEPRECIATION FUNCTION

What-if analysis helps you determine the consequences of changes in your assumptions or variables. For instance, what if Asset 1001 did have some salvage value. How would that change the depreciation calculation each year?

To utilize the what-if capabilities of Excel:

1 Activate the worksheet for Asset 1001.

2 Change the salvage value in your deprecation worksheet by entering **1000** into cell B8. Note the change in depreciation expense each period and the resulting change in accumulated depreciation.

3 Now change the cost of the asset from $15,000 to $20,000. Note the change in depreciation expense each period and the resulting change in accumulated depreciation.

4 Now change the cost back to $15,000 and the salvage value back to 0 and save again.

Kyle explains that the only thing missing is some way to collect similar asset cost, depreciation, and accumulated deprecation to support the financial statement.

CREATING A DEPRECIATION SUMMARY

A depreciation summary is designed to capture all the costs, depreciation, and accumulated depreciation from similar assets to facilitate preparation of financial statements on an annual basis. Kyle sketches out a worksheet design (shown in Figure 4.4) that he suggests could be used for this purpose.

	A	B	C	D	E	F	G	H	I	J
1	Coast Jewelers, Inc.									
2	Equipment Depreciation Summary									
3										
4	Asset	Date Acquired	Cost	Deprec. Method	1999 Deprec.	1999 Acc. Deprec.	2000 Deprec.	2000 Acc. Deprec.	2001 Deprec.	2001 Acc. Deprec.
5										
6										
7										
8										
9										
10	Total		$ -		$0	$0	$0	$0	$0	$0
11										

FIGURE 4.4

Depreciation Summary Worksheet

Using Excel, Kyle demonstrates how multiple worksheets can be summarized for this purpose.

To create a depreciation summary worksheet:

1 Activate the Summary worksheet. (*Note:* This worksheet is preformatted for you without formulas. Also note that your workbook should contain three worksheets: Summary, Asset 1001, and Asset 1002.)

2 In cell A5 enter the formula =**'Asset 1001'!B4**. (Remember from previous chapters that you can either type this formula or type = then click in the Asset 1001 worksheet at cell B4 and press Enter.)

3 Using either method, continue the same process to include the date acquired, cost, and depreciation method in cells B5, C5, and D5, respectively. Adjust column widths as needed and format without decimal places.

4 In cell E5 enter the formula =**'Asset 1001'!B12**. This enters the depreciation for 1999 on Asset 1001.

5 In cell F5 enter the formula =**'Asset 1001'!C12**. This enters the accumulated depreciation for Asset 1001 as of the end of 1999.

6 Continue the same process for cells G5, H5, I5, and J5 referencing depreciation and accumulated depreciation for years 2000 and 2001.

7 In cell A6 enter the formula =**'Asset 1002'!B4**. (Note that this is very similar to the formula used in cell A5 but now you are referencing a different asset, Asset 1002.)

8 Continue referencing formulas from Asset 1002 to the summary worksheet. Your completed worksheet should look like Figure 4.5.

FIGURE 4.5

Completed Depreciation Summary Worksheet

	A	B	C	D	E	F	G	H	I	J
1	Coast Jewelers, Inc.									
2	Equipment Depreciation Summary									
3										
4	Asset	Date Acquired	Cost	Deprec. Method	1999 Deprec.	1999 Acc. Deprec.	2000 Deprec.	2000 Acc. Deprec.	2001 Deprec.	2001 Acc. Deprec.
5	Display Cases	1/1/99	$ 15,000	S/L	$3,000	$3,000	$3,000	$6,000	$3,000	$9,000
6	Chairs	1/1/99	$ 5,000	S/L	$1,000	$1,000	$1,000	$2,000	$1,000	$3,000
7										
8										
9										
10										
11	Total		$ 20,000		$4,000	$4,000	$4,000	$8,000	$4,000	$12,000

9 Save your work again as ch4-01a.xls.

"Shouldn't these summary totals tie into the financial statements we created a while back?" Meagan asks. "Yes they should." Kyle explains. "The difference however is that we have one more asset to add—which we'll do later."

Kyle explains that while Coast Jewelers uses the straight-line method of depreciation, there are alternatives, such as declining balance and sum-of-the-years digits.

CALCULATING DEPRECIATION
USING OTHER METHODS

You inform Nathan and Meagan that though you are very familiar with the declining balance and sum-of-the-years digits methods, you've never used a worksheet to calculate depreciation.

Kyle explains how easy it is, given that you've already invested the time and energy creating the worksheet itself. He suggests you make a copy of one of the depreciation worksheets and just change the depreciation formula to include the new depreciation function.

To create a depreciation worksheet using the declining balance and sum-of-the-years digit methods:

1   Activate the Asset 1001 worksheet.

2   Right-click the **Asset 1001** tab, then click **Move or Copy**.

3   Click in the **Create a Copy** checkbox.

4   Change the To book: edit box to **(new book)**.

5   Click **OK**.

6   Change cell B7 to read **DDB** (for double declining balance)

7   Change cell B12 to read **=DDB($B$6,$B$8,$B$9,1)**. Once again the depreciation function DDB takes arguments located within the parentheses. The first three arguments are the same as the SLN function: cost, salvage value, and useful life. All three of these arguments have been set for absolute referencing so that later, when you copy them down the worksheet, they will continue to reference the appropriate cells. The fourth argument is the period for which the asset is being depreciated, such as the first, second, third, etc.

8   Change cell B13 to read **=DDB($B$6,$B$8,$B$9,2)**. Note that the only difference between B13 and B12 is the fourth argument.

9   Continue to place the DDB formula in cells B14, B15, and B16, changing only the last argument. This is best accomplished by filling down the formula and then going back to edit each individually. Upon completion your worksheet should look like Figure 4.6.

10   Save your work to ch4-01b.xls.

11   To modify this worksheet to reflect sum-of-the-years digits depreciation, type **SYD** in cell B7.

12   Change cell B12 to read **=SYD($B$6,$B$8,$B$9,1)**. Once again the depreciation function SYD takes arguments located within the parentheses. The first three arguments are the same as the SLN function: cost, salvage value, and useful life. All three of these arguments have been set for absolute referencing so that later, when you copy them down the worksheet, they will continue to reference the appropriate cells. The fourth argument is the period for which the asset is being depreciated, such as the first, second, third, etc.

FIGURE 4.6

Declining Balance Depreciation Worksheet

	A	B	C
1	Coast Jewelers, Inc. Depreciation Schedule		
2			
3	Asset #	1001	
4	Asset	Display Cases	
5	Date acquired	1/1/99	
6	Cost	$ 15,000.00	
7	Depreciation method	DDB	
8	Salvage value	$ -	
9	Estimated useful life	5	
10			
11	Year	Depreciation Expense	Accumulated Depreciation
12	2000	$6,000.00	$6,000.00
13	2001	$3,600.00	$9,600.00
14	2002	$2,160.00	$11,760.00
15	2003	$1,296.00	$13,056.00
16	2004	$777.60	$13,833.60

13 Change cell B13 to read **=SYD($B$6,$B$8,$B$9,2)**. Note that the only difference between B13 and B12 is the fourth argument.

14 Continue to place the SYD formula in cells B14, B15, and B16, changing only the last argument. This is best accomplished by filling down the formula and then going back to edit each individually. Upon completion your worksheet should look like Figure 4.7.

FIGURE 4.7

Sum-of-the-years Digits Depreciation Worksheet

	A	B	C
1	Coast Jewelers, Inc. Depreciation Schedule		
2			
3	Asset #	1001	
4	Asset	Display Cases	
5	Date acquired	1/1/99	
6	Cost	$ 15,000.00	
7	Depreciation method	SYD	
8	Salvage value		
9	Estimated useful life	5	
10			
11	Year	Depreciation Expense	Accumulated Depreciation
12	2000	$5,000.00	$5,000.00
13	2001	$4,000.00	$9,000.00
14	2002	$3,000.00	$12,000.00
15	2003	$2,000.00	$14,000.00
16	2004	$1,000.00	$15,000.00

15 Save your work to ch4-01c.xls.

"This makes calculating depreciation fairly easy!" you say. "That's the idea," Kyle responds.

Kyle points out that the charting feature you've previously used can also be used to help illustrate the effects of different depreciation methods.

CHARTING DEPRECIATION EXPENSE

You have created three files calculating depreciation expense for Asset 1001. Kyle states that by using the charting feature of Excel you can easily see the accounting impacts of the three different methods: straight-line, double-declining balance, and sum-of-the-years digits. First he suggests you create a simple chart illustrating the straight-line depreciation of Asset 1001.

To create a chart illustrating the straight-line depreciation of Asset 1001:

1 Open all three files: ch4-01a.xls, ch4-01b.xls, and ch4-01c.xls.

2 Make the Asset 1001 sheet in file ch4-01a.xls active.

3 Click and highlight cells B12 through B16 as shown in Figure 4.8.

FIGURE 4.8

Selected Cells in Sheet "Asset 1001"

	A	B	C
1	Coast Jewelers, Inc. Depreciation Schedule		
2			
3	Asset #	1001	
4	Asset	Display Cases	
5	Date acquired	1/1/99	
6	Cost	$ 15,000.00	
7	Depreciation method	S/L	
8	Salvage value	$ -	
9	Estimated useful life	5	
10			
11	Year	Depreciation Expense	Accumulated Depreciation
12	1999	$3,000.00	$3,000.00
13	2000	$3,000.00	$6,000.00
14	2001	$3,000.00	$9,000.00
15	2002	$3,000.00	$12,000.00
16	2003	$3,000.00	$15,000.00

4 Click the **Chart Wizard** button on the toolbar.

5 Select Chart type: Line and Chart sub-type: Line (located in the upper left corner of the window), then click **Next**.

6 Click the **Series** tab, then click the **Collapse Dialog** button located to the right of the Category (X) axis labels: edit box.

7 Click and highlight cells **A12** though **A16**, then press **Enter**.

8 Now change the Series name by typing **Straight-line Depreciation** in the Name: edit box, then click **Next**.

9 Click in the **Chart title:** edit box and change the title to **Depreciation Comparison**.

10 Click in the Category (X) axis: edit box and type **Year**.

11 Click in the Value (Y) axis: edit box and type **Amount**.

12 Click the **Gridlines** tab, then click in the **Major gridlines** checkbox to disable the gridlines.

13 Click the Legend tab, then click the **Bottom** placement option button.

14 Click **Next**, then click the **Place chart: As new sheet:** option button and change the name of the sheet to **Depreciation Comparison**, then click **Finish**. The resulting chart should look like Figure 4.9.

15 Save your work to ch4-01a.xls.

FIGURE 4.9

Straight-line Depreciation Chart

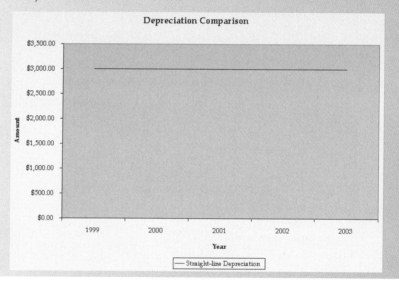

Kyle then explains to you the process of making the depreciation chart comparative. Once the original chart is created, all that is left is to add lines that depict depreciation based on the double-declining balance and sum-of-the-years digits methods.

Adding a new series of data to an existing chart is as simple as copying and pasting. First you select and copy the data to be included, then select the chart and paste the information. The chart will then update itself including axes values and display. Kyle suggests that you now add data from the double-declining and sum-of-the-years digits files that you saved before.

To create a chart illustrating the straight-line depreciation of Asset 1001:

1 Open all three files: ch4-01a.xls, ch4-01b.xls, and ch4-01c.xls.

2 Make the Asset 1001 sheet in file ch4-01b.xls active.

3 Click and highlight cells **B12** through **B16**.

4 Click the **Copy** tool on the Standard toolbar.

5 Make the Depreciation Comparison sheet in the file ch4-01a.xls active.

6 Click the chart once to select the Chart Area. This is best done by clicking in the upper left corner of the chart so as to not select any specific element of the chart, such as the legend, title, or plot area. The name box in the upper left corner of the chart should say Chart Area.

7 Click the **Paste** tool on the Standard toolbar.

8 Make the Asset 1001 sheet in file ch4-01c.xls active.

9 Click and highlight cells **B12** through **B16**.

10 Click the **Copy** tool on the Standard toolbar.

11 Make the Depreciation Comparison sheet in the file ch4-01a.xls active.

12 Click the chart once to select the Chart Area.

13 Click the **Paste** tool on the Standard toolbar.

14 Select the newly created line depicting double-declining balance depreciation.

15 Type **"Double-Declining Balance Depreciation"** as the first argument to the Series function as shown in Figure 4.10. Save.

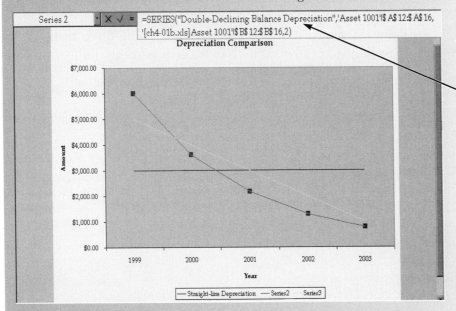

FIGURE 4.10

Changing the Name of a Chart Series

Type "Double-Declining Balance Depreciation" here to change the chart name

16 Press **Enter**.

17 Select the newly created line depicting sum-of-the-years digits depreciation.

18 Type **"Sum-of-the-years Digits Depreciation"** as the first argument to the Series function, then press **Enter**.

19 Adjust the size of the line name description box below the chart so that all names fit within the box. Your chart should now look like Figure 4.11.

FIGURE 4.11

Depreciation Comparison Chart

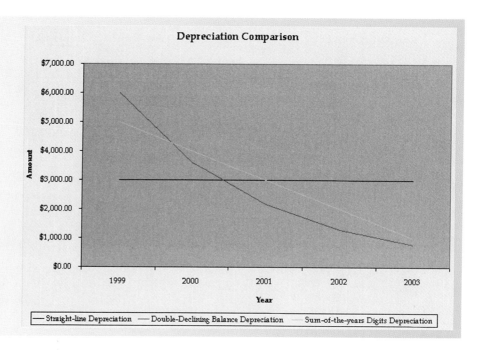

"That's just like I remember from my college classes," you comment. Kyle agrees and points out that straight-line depreciation will always produce a horizontal line reflecting a constant depreciation expense. Double-declining balance will always produce a curved line reflecting larger depreciation in the first years, declining thereafter. Sum-of-the-years digits will always produce a straight line going down from left to right reflecting larger depreciation in the first years, declining by a constant amount each year thereafter.

END NOTE

You've applied some of what you learned in the first three chapters to a specific accounting problem, the depreciation of fixed assets. In the next chapter you will learn how to use Excel to create loan amortization schedules.

practice

Chapter 4 Questions

1 What function is built-into Excel to help you calculate straight-line depreciation?

2 What arguments does the SLN function take?

3 Should the argument to the SLN function be values or references?

4 Which is preferred, values or references?

5 Should references used as arguments to the SLN function be absolute or relative?

6 What is the purpose of a depreciation summary?

7 What other depreciation functions are built into Excel?

8 What additional argument is added for these depreciation functions?

9 How do you add a new series of data to an existing chart?

10 Describe the three lines charted in a depreciation comparison chart depicting straight-line, double-declining balance, and sum-of-the-years digits depreciation.

Chapter 4 Assignments

1 *Add another depreciation schedule for Coast Jewelers*

Use the ch4-01a.xls worksheet you created in this chapter.

a Add a new depreciation worksheet labeled Asset 1003 using the Move or Copy Shortcut menu. Keep this sheet in the ch4-01a.xls workbook.

b The asset to be depreciated is Forge, purchased January 1, 2003 for $45,000. It has an estimated salvage value of $5,000 and is to be depreciated over four years using the straight-line method of depreciation.

c Update the summary worksheet to include information on this new asset. (Be careful to note the date this asset was acquired.)

d After placing your name, date, and filename in the footer of each worksheet, print a value view worksheet and a formula view worksheet for both the Summary and Asset 1003 worksheets.

e Save your file as **ch4-01a.xls**.

2 *Change depreciation methods for Coast Jewelers' new asset added above and modify data*

a Use the ch4-01a.xls worksheet you modified above.

(1) Use the Move or Copy Shortcut menu to copy the Asset 1003 sheet to a new workbook.
(2) Save the new workbook at **ch4-01d.xls**.
(3) Change the name of the sheet to **Asset 1003 DDB**.
(4) Change the depreciation method of Asset 1003 to DDB.
(5) Change the salvage value to $1,000.
(6) Change the cost to $40,000.
(7) After placing your name, date, and filename in the footer of each worksheet, print a value view worksheet and a formula view worksheet.
(8) Save the workbook.

b Use the ch4-01d.xls worksheet you modified above.

(1) Use the Move or Copy Shortcut menu to copy the Asset 1003 sheet the same workbook.
(2) Change the name of the sheet to **Asset 1003 SYD**.
(3) Change the depreciation method of Asset 1003 to SYD.
(4) After placing your name, date, and filename in the footer of each worksheet, print a value view worksheet and a formula view worksheet.
(5) Save the workbook.

c Use the ch4-01d.xls worksheet that you modified above.

(1) Create a chart comparing depreciation expense between the DDB and SYD methods.
(2) After placing your name, date, and filename in the footer of the worksheet, name the chart Depreciation Comparison for Asset 1003.
(3) Save the workbook.

Chapter 4 Case Problem: Kelly's Boutique

Kelly's Boutique owned the following equipment as of December 31, 2002:

- Asset #101— Shelving—Purchased: January 1, 2002—Cost: $3,500—Useful life: three years—Salvage value: $500.
- Asset #102—Computer—Purchased: January 1, 2002—Cost: $5,000—Useful life: five years—Salvage value: $1,000.
- Asset #103—Phone System—Purchased: January 1, 2002—Cost: $6,500—Useful life: five years—Salvage value: $500.

1 Create Kelly's Boutique's equipment depreciation summary and individual depreciation worksheets assuming straight-line depreciation given in the information above. Format Depreciation Summary to print without decimal places. Print a value view of each worksheet.

2 Create a worksheet for Asset #102 above assuming the company had decided to depreciate it using double-declining balance depreciation. Print a value view of the worksheet.

3 Create a worksheet for Asset #102 above assuming the company had decided to depreciate it using sum-of-the-years digits depreciation. Print a value view of the worksheet.

4 Create a line chart comparing the three deprecation methods for Asset #102. Print the chart.

5 Save the newly created file as **ch4-02.xls**.

Loan and Bond Amortization

In this chapter you will learn:

- How to use the payment function to calculate payments to retire a loan

- How to create a loan amortization schedule

- How to use what-if analysis with the payment function

- How to use names in a worksheet

- How to use the present value function to calculate the proceeds of a bond

- How to create a bond amortization schedule

- How to use Excel's what-if analysis and goal seeking abilities with the present value function

CASE: COAST JEWELERS, INC.
. . . .

Nathan and Meagan have been contemplating opening several new locations. They are somewhat strapped for cash and are interested in looking into their financing alternatives. On one hand they could borrow funds from their local banker. Alternatively, they could borrow money by issuing bonds to local investors. They are curious whether Excel could help them analyze the alternatives or at least help them determine the payments required to pay back a loan or bond.

"Can Excel perform these types of loan calculations?" Meagan asks.

"Yes," Kyle responds, "not only can Excel help you with the calculations but it can also help you with what-if sensitivity analysis to determine interest costs, loan payments, and balances."

LOAN CALCULATIONS
. . . .

Kyle explains that loans usually involve some constant periodic payment that pays both interest and principal over a specified period of time. Banks usually want to see a principal payment rather than interest-only payments that are often associated with bonds.

Excel has a built-in function that calculates the payment on a loan given three variables: interest rate, period, and loan amount. The PMT function takes three arguments and is written **=PMT** (rate, nper, pv) where *rate* is the periodic interest rate, *nper* is the number of periods, and *pv* is the present value (usually the loan amount). Kyle suggests that you create a worksheet to calculate the annual payment necessary on a three-year $100,000 loan with an interest rate of 10 percent.

To calculate a loan payment using Excel's built-in function:

1 Start Excel and open file ch5-01.xls. The worksheet should look like Figure 5.1.

FIGURE 5.1

Loan Worksheet

	A	B	C	D	E
1	Coast Jewelers, Inc.				
2	Loan Amortization Schedule				
3					
4	Amount				
5	Rate				
6	Term				
7	Payment				
8					
9					
10	Payment #	Payment	Interest	Principal	Balance
11					
12	1				
13	2				
14	3				

2 Type **100,000** in cell B4, **10%** in cell B5, and **3** in cell B6.

3 Type **=PMT(B5,B6,B4)** in cell B7, then press **Enter**. Note that the resulting amount is a negative number. This is Excel's way of indicating that cash must be paid out to repay the loan proceeds received.

4 Place a negative sign in front of the function PMT so that the formula reads as follows: **=–PMT(B5,B6,B4)**. This has the effect of making the payment a positive number.

5 Save your work to ch5-01a.xls.

Thus, a payment of $40,211.48, when made at the end of each year for three years will repay the loan, plus interest.

"How much of those payments is interest and how much principal?" Nathan asks. "Good question." Kyle responds. "That's why it is helpful to create a loan amortization schedule with each worksheet."

LOAN AMORTIZATION SCHEDULE

Kyle explains how a loan amortization schedule answers Nathan's question. In it each payment is broken down into the components of interest and principal. You remind Kyle that interest expense, based on the accrual accounting principal, is calculated as the balance owed multiplied by the periodic interest rate. The amount of payment that exceeds the interest owed is applied to the principal and reduces the loan amount.

"I can do that." you say.

To add a loan amortization schedule to your worksheet:

1 Type **=B4** in cell E11. This places the loan amount at the beginning of the schedule.

2 Type **=$B$7** in cell B12. This places the loan payment in the schedule. (This reference is absolute so that it can be replicated later.)

3 Type **=E11*$B$5** in cell C12. This formula calculates interest expense as the loan amount multiplied by the interest rate. (The reference to the interest rate is absolute so that it can be replicated later.)

4 Type **=B12–C12** in cell D12. This formula calculates the amount of the payment that reduces the loan amount, otherwise known as principal.

5 Type **=E11–D12** in cell E12. This formula calculates the new loan balance after the loan payment as the previous loan balance less principal reduction.

6 Replicate formulas located at cells B12 through E12 down through row 14.

7 The resulting worksheet should look like Figure 5.2.

FIGURE 5.2

*Loan Amortization
Worksheet*

	A	B	C	D	E
1	Coast Jewelers, Inc.				
2	Loan Amortization Schedule				
3					
4	Amount	$ 100,000.00			
5	Rate	10%			
6	Term	3			
7	Payment	$40,211.48			
8					
9					
10	Payment #	Payment	Interest	Principal	Balance
11					$ 100,000.00
12	1	$40,211.48	$ 10,000.00	$30,211.48	$ 69,788.52
13	2	$40,211.48	$ 6,978.85	$33,232.63	$ 36,555.89
14	3	$40,211.48	$ 3,655.59	$36,555.89	$ 0.00

8 Save your work to ch5-01a.xls.

Kyle points out that at the end of the loan period the balance should of course be zero, which it is in the worksheet.

"What is the payment if the interest rate is higher or lower?" Meagan asks. "Another good question," Kyle comments. "That leads us into the sensitivity features of Excel that we've worked on previously."

WHAT-IF ANALYSIS AND THE PAYMENT FUNCTION

Kyle explains that because you built the loan amortization worksheet with cell references, what-if analysis is easy. To investigate the effects of changing interest rates or different loan balances, Kyle suggests he determine the effect on the loan payment of interest rates of 11 percent and 9 percent, as well as loan balances of $150,000 or $75,000.

Using Excel, Kyle demonstrates how these variable changes affect the loan payment.

To perform a what-if analysis using the payment function:

1 Type **11%** in cell B5, then press **Enter**. Note the change in payment.

2 Type **9%** in cell B5, then press **Enter**. Again, note the change in payment. Your worksheet should look like Figure 5.3.

3 Type **10%** in cell B5, then press **Enter**.

4 Type **$150,000** in cell B4, the press **Enter**. Note the change in payment.

5 Type **$75,000** in cell B4, the press **Enter**. Note the change in payment. Your worksheet should look like Figure 5.4.

6 Type **$100,000** in cell B4.

FIGURE 5.3

Loan Amortization Schedule at 9%

	A	B	C	D	E
1	Coast Jewelers, Inc.				
2	Loan Amortization Schedule				
3					
4	Amount	$ 100,000.00			
5	Rate	9%			
6	Term	3			
7	Payment	$39,505.48			
8					
9					
10	Payment #	Payment	Interest	Principal	Balance
11					$ 100,000.00
12	1	$39,505.48	$ 9,000.00	$30,505.48	$ 69,494.52
13	2	$39,505.48	$ 6,254.51	$33,250.97	$ 36,243.56
14	3	$39,505.48	$ 3,261.92	$36,243.56	$ 0.00

FIGURE 5.4

Loan Amortization Schedule at $75,000

	A	B	C	D	E
1	Coast Jewelers, Inc.				
2	Loan Amortization Schedule				
3					
4	Amount	$ 75,000.00			
5	Rate	10%			
6	Term	3			
7	Payment	$30,158.61			
8					
9					
10	Payment #	Payment	Interest	Principal	Balance
11					$ 75,000.00
12	1	$30,158.61	$ 7,500.00	$22,658.61	$ 52,341.39
13	2	$30,158.61	$ 5,234.14	$24,924.47	$ 27,416.92
14	3	$30,158.61	$ 2,741.69	$27,416.92	$ 0.00

"Fascinating!" Meagan exclaims. "This is a great tool!"

"Yes, but these formulas get a bit confusing," Nathan comments. "I have trouble understanding what the payment function is doing with B5, B6, and B4. Isn't there a better way of describing the arguments to functions or what these cell references mean?"

Kyle decides to introduce the concept of named ranges to you, Nathan, and Meagan. He explains that cell references can also be named for clearer analysis.

NAMES IN A WORKSHEET

Excel provides a naming feature in every worksheet that allows you to define a cell or cells with a name that can then be used elsewhere in the worksheet. The are two steps involved in changing an existing worksheet from cell references to named references. Step 1 is defining cell names; Step 2 is applying those names throughout the worksheet.

Kyle suggests that you first name the variables Amount, Rate, Term, and Payment and then apply those names elsewhere in the loan amortization worksheet.

To use names in the loan amortization worksheet:

1 Select the cell range A4 through B7.

2 Select **Insert**, **Name**, **Create** from the menu as shown in Figure 5.5.

FIGURE 5.5
Selected Cells

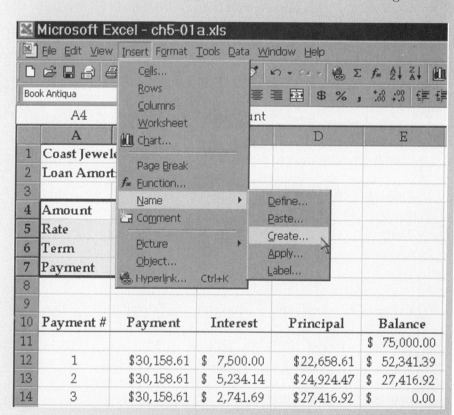

3 Click the **Create names in left column** checkbox in the Create Names window, then click **OK**. (Note that this action will define cells B4 to B7 based on the labels provided in the left column A4 to A7.)

4 Click in cell **E11**.

5 Now select **Insert**, **Name**, **Apply** from the menu.

6 Click **OK** in the Apply Names window. (Note that this action will apply the names created above to all references in the worksheet where cells B4 to B7 had been used.)

7 Click in cell **B7**. Note the new argument references to the payment function: =–PMT (Rate,Term,Amount).

8 Save your work to ch5-01a.xls.

Kyle explains that not all cell references will be replaced as you defined only four cells. However, all references to those cells will now refer to the names instead of specific cells such as B4, B5, etc.

"This looks much better," Nathan says. "Now I can clearly see that the payment function takes three arguments: Rate, Term, and Amount."

Kyle further explains that these named cells can be used in other ways as well. For example, Excel provides you with a Name Box that lists all the named cells and ranges on the worksheet. He suggests that you explore the use of names further.

To explore the use of named cells and ranges:

1 Click on the **drop-down arrow** of the Name box on the top left side under the printer to reveal the named cells on the worksheet. Then highlight Rate but don't click. See Figure 5.6.

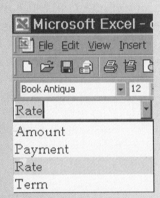

FIGURE 5.6

Name Box

2 Now click **Rate**. (Note how Excel now positions the active cell as B5, the location of the name Rate.)

3 Click on **Save** before closing Ch5-01a.xls.

Once names have been created, they can be used throughout the worksheet as you'll see in the next section. Kyle suggests that you now explore the use of worksheets as tools for bond calculations.

PRESENT VALUE IN BONDS

You recall having lots of trouble with present values and bonds while in school and are leery of using them in a worksheet. However, Kyle calms your fears by explaining how the use of a worksheet actually helped him better understand bonds and the concepts of present value.

"Whoa now!" Meagan comments. "Why should I learn about present values?"

"Present values are very helpful to an accountant and businessperson," Kyle explains. "In fact you just finished using present value concepts when you computed the loan payment above!"

Kyle reminds you that bonds are financial instruments that usually require a constant interest payment to the bondholder based on a stated interest rate and then a lump sum payment equal to the bond's face value at the end of a specified term. The proceeds from a bond's sale, however, are dependent on the market rate of interest at the time of sale.

He explains that Excel's present value function can compute those proceeds based upon the following variables: market interest rate, term, periodic interest payment, and the lump sum face value payment. The present value function is written: PV (rate, nper, pmt, fv) where *rate* is the market rate of interest, *nper* is the number of periods, *pmt* is the periodic interest payment, and *fv* is the future value that is paid at the end of the bond term.

You remember that if the stated rate of interest on a bond is different from the market rate of interest, the result will be bond proceeds different from the bond face value. If the stated rate is lower than the market rate, buyers will pay less than the face value resulting in a discount and if the stated rate is higher than the market rate, buyers will pay more than the face value resulting in a premium.

Kyle suggests you use Excel to calculate proceeds of a $100,000 bond paying 10 percent per year for five years given an 11 percent market rate of interest at the time of issuance.

To calculate bond proceeds:

1 Open file ch5-02.xls. The worksheet should look like Figure 5.7.

FIGURE 5.7
Bond Worksheet

	A	B	C	D	E	F
1	Coast Jewelers, Inc.					
2	Bond Amortization Schedule					
3						
4	Amount					
5	Stated Rate					
6	Market Rate					
7	Term					
8	Interest Payment					
9	Proceeds					
10	(Discount) / Premium					
11						
12	Payment #	Interest Payment	Interest Expense	Amortization	(Discount) Premium	Carrying Value
13						
14	1					
15	2					
16	3					
17	4					
18	5					

2 Type **100000** in cell B4 to identify the bond face value.

3 Type **10%** in cell B5 to identify the bond's stated interest rate.

4 Type **11%** in cell B6 to identify the market rate of interest.

5 Type **5** in cell B7 to identify the bond term.

6 Type **=B4*B5** in cell B8 to calculate annual interest payment.

7 Type **=–PV(B6,B7,B8,B4)** in cell B9 to calculate bond proceeds. [Don't forget the minus sign (–) in front of PV to make the proceeds positive.]

8 Type **=B9–B4** in cell B10 to calculate the bond discount or premium. Your worksheet should look like Figure 5.8.

FIGURE 5.8
Bond Proceeds

	A	B
1	Coast Jewelers, Inc.	
2	Bond Amortization Schedule	
3		
4	Amount	$ 100,000.00
5	Stated Rate	10.00%
6	Market Rate	11.00%
7	Term	5
8	Interest Payment	$10,000.00
9	Proceeds	$96,304.10
10	(Discount) / Premium	($3,695.90)

9 Name the various cells you just defined by selecting cells A4 to B10 then click **Insert**, **Name**, then **Create**.

10 Click the **Create names in left column** checkbox, then click OK.

11 Now select **Insert, Name, Apply** from the menu.

12 Click **OK** in the Apply Names window. (Note that this action will apply the names created above to all references in the worksheet where cells B4 to B10 had been used.)

13 Click on cell **B9** where the new formula should read as follows:
=–PV(Market_Rate,Term,Interest_Payment,Amount)

14 Save the file as ch5-02a.xls

Next you need to create a bond amortization schedule to summarize interest payments, interest expense, bond amortization, and remaining carrying value.

BOND AMORTIZATION SCHEDULE

A bond amortization schedule is in essence a reconciliation of interest payments and bond accounting. Interest expense, usually recorded using the "effective interest" method, is based on the market rate of interest and the carrying value of the debt.

Kyle suggests that you complete the bond amortization table using the named cell ranges you created above. In addition to the effective interest formula described above, you'll need to compute the bond discount/premium amortization as the difference between the interest expense recorded and the interest payment. The ending carrying value for each period will then be the previous period carrying value plus or minus the remaining discount or premium amortization.

To create the bond amortization schedule:

1 Select cell **E13**.

2 Click **Insert**, **Name**, then **Paste** from the menu.

3 Click **Discount____Premium** in the Paste Name window, then click **OK**, and press **Enter**. (*Note:* Pasting a name from a list is one way to use previously defined names.)

4 Type **=Amount+E13** in cell F13. Then replicate this formula down to cell F18. This calculation represents the sum of the discount or premium left to be amortized plus the face value of the note. (*Note:* Typing a name is another way of using previously defined names.)

5 Type **=Interest_Payment** in cell B14. Replicate this formula down to cell B18.

6 Type **=F13*Market_Rate** in cell C14. Replicate this formula down to cell C18. These cells will calculate interest expense as the previous period carrying value multiplied by the market rate of interest.

7 Type **=B14–C14** in cell D14. Replicate this formula down to cell D18. These cells will calculate the amortization for the period as the amount by which interest expense differs from the interest payment.

8 Type **=E13–D14** in cell E14. Replicate this formula down to cell E18. These cells will calculate the remaining amount of bond discount or premium to be amortized in future periods.

9 Type **=SUM(B14:B18)** in cell B19 to sum interest payments.

10 Format the cell with a top and double bottom border.

11 Replicate the formula to cell D19 to sum interest expense and amortization.

12 The resulting amortization table should look like Figure 5.9 below.

13 Save the file as ch5-02a.xls.

FIGURE 5.9

Bond Amortization Schedule

Payment #	Interest Payment	Interest Expense	Amortization	(Discount) Premium	Carrying Value
				($3,695.90)	$96,304.10
1	$10,000.00	$10,593.45	($593.45)	($3,102.45)	$96,897.55
2	$10,000.00	$10,658.73	($658.73)	($2,443.71)	$97,556.29
3	$10,000.00	$10,731.19	($731.19)	($1,712.52)	$98,287.48
4	$10,000.00	$10,811.62	($811.62)	($900.90)	$99,099.10
5	$10,000.00	$10,900.90	($900.90)	$0.00	$100,000.00
	$50,000.00	$53,695.90	($3,695.90)		

"I'll bet we can use this schedule to do some what-if analysis like we did with the loan amortization schedule," you suggest. "Exactly!" Kyle responds. "Let's see the impact of changing the effective interest rate on bond proceeds and interest expense."

WHAT-IF ANALYSIS AND GOAL SEEKING

Nathan is curious about the impact different market interest rates will have on the proceeds from a bond issuance and the impact on the interest expense. He suggests you try interest rates of 9 percent and 12 percent.

To assess the impact of different market rates:

1 Type **9%** into cell B6. Note the impact on bond proceeds and total interest expenses as shown in Figure 5.10.

FIGURE 5.10

Bond Amortization at 9%

	A	B	C	D	E	F
1	Coast Jewelers, Inc.					
2	Bond Amortization Schedule					
3						
4	Amount	$ 100,000.00				
5	Stated Rate	10.00%				
6	Market Rate	9.00%				
7	Term	5				
8	Interest Payment	$10,000.00				
9	Proceeds	$103,889.65				
10	(Discount) / Premium	$3,889.65				
11						
12	Payment #	Interest Payment	Interest Expense	Amortization	(Discount) Premium	Carrying Value
13					$3,889.65	$103,889.65
14	1	$10,000.00	$9,350.07	$649.93	$3,239.72	$103,239.72
15	2	$10,000.00	$9,291.57	$708.43	$2,531.29	$102,531.29
16	3	$10,000.00	$9,227.82	$772.18	$1,759.11	$101,759.11
17	4	$10,000.00	$9,158.32	$841.68	$917.43	$100,917.43
18	5	$10,000.00	$9,082.57	$917.43	$0.00	$100,000.00
19		$50,000.00	$46,110.35	$3,889.65		

2 Type **12%** into cell B6. Note the impact on bond proceeds and total interest expenses.

"Wow, that sure is useful." Nathan says. "We can use this information for our accounting record-keeping as well as for financial planning."

"Quite true," Kyle responds. "Excel also has a goal seek feature to help determine a stated rate given needed bond proceeds. Let's assume the company wants to issue a 5-year, $100,000 bond when the market rate of interest is 8 percent. If the company needs at least $95,000 from the proceeds, what stated rate of interest must be present in the bond?"

"I'll use the existing worksheet and try different stated rates to see how close I can get to $95,000," you comment. "Not necessary," Kyle explains. "We can use the existing worksheet formulas and simply use Excel's goal seek feature. First you change the variable information such as the market rate of interest. Then you invoke the goal seek command, set the location of the desired value (B9), specifying the desired value (95,000), and identify the location of the variable to be changed to achieve the desired value (B5). In this case that location is the cell containing the stated interest rate."

"I'll try that," Meagan says.

To use the goal seek feature:

1 Type **8%** into cell B6. Note the impact on bond proceeds as the old stated rate of 10% provides for a bond premium to be paid.

2 Now click **Tools**, then **Goal Seek** from the menu.

3 Type **$B$9** in the Set cell: edit box. (Alternatively, you could click in the Set cell: edit box and then click cell B9.)

4 Type **95000** in the To value: edit box.

5 Type **$B$5** in the By changing cell: edit box as shown in Figure 5.11.

FIGURE 5.11

Goal Seek Window

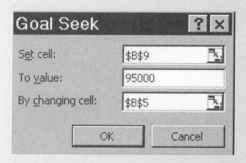

6 Click **OK**. The Goal Seek Status window should appear as shown in Figure 5.12 indicating that a solution has been found.

FIGURE 5.12

Goal Seek Status Window

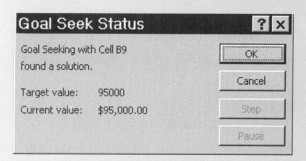

7 Click **OK** to view the solution as shown in Figure 5.13.

FIGURE 5.13

Goal Seek Solution

	A	B	C	D	E	F
1	Coast Jewelers, Inc.					
2	Bond Amortization Schedule					
3						
4	Amount	$ 100,000.00				
5	Stated Rate	6.75%				
6	Market Rate	8.00%				
7	Term	5				
8	Interest Payment	$6,747.72				
9	Proceeds	$95,000.00				
10	(Discount) / Premium	($5,000.00)				
11						
12	Payment #	Interest Payment	Interest Expense	Amortization	(Discount) Premium	Carrying Value
13					($5,000.00)	$95,000.00
14	1	$6,747.72	$7,600.00	($852.28)	($4,147.72)	$95,852.28
15	2	$6,747.72	$7,668.18	($920.46)	($3,227.25)	$96,772.75
16	3	$6,747.72	$7,741.82	($994.10)	($2,233.15)	$97,766.85
17	4	$6,747.72	$7,821.35	($1,073.63)	($1,159.52)	$98,840.48
18	5	$6,747.72	$7,907.24	($1,159.52)	$0.00	$100,000.00
19		$33,738.59	$38,738.59	($5,000.00)		

8 Click on **Save** before closing Ch5-02a.xls.

Kyle points out that the goal seek solution indicates that a stated rate of 6.75 percent yields the $95,000 proceeds needed given an 8 percent market rate for a 5-year $100,000 bond. In reality, the stated rate necessary to produce exactly $95,000 in proceeds is slightly smaller than 6.75. The B5 cell is formatted to show only two decimal places. If you formatted the cell to read additional decimal places it would have shown 6.74771772716582%. Kyle however contends that 6.75 percent is close enough!

END NOTE

You've applied some of what you learned in the first four chapters to better understand how Excel can be used to analyze loans and bonds. In addition you've learned some new functions: payment (PMT) and present value (PV) and a new feature: Goal Seeking. In the next chapter you'll explore cash flow budgets.

practice

chapter

5

Chapter 5 Questions

1 Explain the difference between a loan and a bond.

2 What function is used to calculate a loan payment?

3 What arguments does the loan payment function take?

4 Why does the payment function result in a negative number?

5 What does a loan amortization schedule do?

6 Describe the formula to compute interest expense each period for a loan.

7 What are the two steps necessary to incorporate names in a worksheet?

8 What function is used to calculate bond proceeds and what arguments does that function take?

9 Describe the formula to compute interest expense each period for a bond.

10 Describe the goal seek process.

Chapter 5 Assignments

1 *Loan Amortization Schedule for Coast Jewelers*

Create a worksheet similar to that created and saved as ch5-01a.xls in this chapter that calculates the required annual payment for a $350,000, 10-year, 8 percent interest loan and includes a loan amortization schedule. (Be sure to use names in a worksheet as illustrated in the chapter.)

   a Save your file as **ch5-03.xls**.
   b Print the value and formula view worksheets you create.
   c Print the value view worksheet created if the interest rate had been 9 percent.
   d Print the value view worksheet created if the interest rate had been 7 percent.

2 *Bond Schedule for Coast Jewelers*

Create a worksheet similar to that created and saved as ch5-02a.xls in this chapter that calculates the bond proceeds for a $700,000, 15-year, 6 percent stated interest bond issued when the market rate of interest is 6.5 percent and includes a bond amortization schedule. (Be sure to use names in a worksheet as illustrated in the chapter.)

   a Save your file as **ch5-04.xls**.
   b Print the value and formula view worksheets you create.

 c Print the value view worksheet created if the stated interest
rate had been 9 percent.

 d Print the value view worksheet created if the stated interest
rate had been 7 percent.

 e Print the value view worksheet created if the stated interest
rate had been 5 percent and the market rate of interest had
been 5.5 percent.

3 *Bond Schedule with Goal Seek for Coast Jewelers*

Use the worksheet created in Problem 2 with the original values
(stated rate 6 percent, market rate 6.5 percent)

 a What stated interest rate is necessary for bond proceeds of
$690,000?

 b Reset the stated interest rate to 6 percent. What market interest rate is necessary for bond proceeds of $710,000?

Chapter 5 Case Problem: Kelly's Boutique

Kelly's Boutique is contemplating several alternative means of financing
an expansion. One alternative is to borrow $500,000 from a local bank.
Another alternative is to borrow the same $500,000 from investors by
issued bonds. Both alternatives involve a five-year debt period.

1 Create a worksheet to compute a loan payment and loan amortization if the interest rate was 6 percent, 7 percent, 8 percent, or
9 percent.

 a Label this sheet **Loan**.

 b Save the newly created file as **ch5-05.xls**.

 c Print a copy of each value view worksheet.

2 Create another worksheet (in the same workbook) to compute
the bond proceeds and amortization if the stated rate is 6 percent,
7 percent, 8 percent, or 9 percent given a market rate of interest
of 7.5 percent.

 a Label this sheet **Bond**.

 b Save the modified file as **ch5-05.xls**.

 c Print a copy of each value view worksheet.

6

Cash Flow Budget

In this chapter you will learn:

- How to prepare a sales budget

- How to use the AutoFormat tool

- How to prepare a purchases budget

- How to prepare a sales and administrative expenses budget

- How to prepare a cash receipts budget

- How to prepare a cash disbursements budget

- How to prepare a summary cash budget

CASE: COAST JEWELERS, INC.

Nathan and Meagan have been contemplating an expansion of their business to include jewelry repair, which will require some new equipment. Nathan is certain they don't have the cash resources necessary to pull it off. Meagan believes that with the right financing, they'll be okay. At Kyle's suggestion, they have contacted their bankers who recommended that they prepare a cash budget for the next year that specifically addresses their cash needs.

"You'll need a complete cash budget that includes forecasts of sales, purchases, expenses, cash receipts, and cash disbursements for the year," Kyle informs them.

"I'll bet we could use Excel to help us!" Meagan responds. "However, since I'm not much of an accountant I'll need help."

"I did some cash budgeting in my accounting classes," you comment. "If Kyle can help me get started I'm sure this can be done on Excel."

"The first place to start is with the sales budget," Kyle says.

SALES BUDGET

Kyle explains that most budgets are broken into periods smaller than a year. He suggests that you prepare a quarterly budget with an annual summary column. He reminds you that you'll need to plan for both product and repair revenue and that no cost of goods sold or expenses will appear on this part of the budget.

Nathan estimates product sales to be $425,000, $400,000, $375,000, and $450,000 for the first through the fourth quarters, respectively. He thinks he'll bill 1,500, 1,600, 1,700, and 1,800 hours of jewelry repair for the first through the fourth quarters, respectively, at $50 per hour.

To prepare a sales budget:

1 Start Excel and open file ch6-01.xls. The worksheet should look like Figure 6.1.

FIGURE 6.1

Sales Budget Worksheet

	A	B	C	D	E	F
1	Coast Jewelers, Inc.					
2	Sales Budget					
3						
4						
5				Quarter		
6		1st	2nd	3rd	4th	Year
7	Professional services:					
8	Repair hours					
9	Hourly rate					
10	Professional services revenue					
11						
12	Product sales:					
13						
14	Total revenue					

2 Type **1500** into cell B8, **1600** into cell C8, **1700** into cell D8, and **1800** into cell E8.

3 Format those cells with commas and no decimals. (*Hint:* Use the comma style and decimal tools.)

4 Type **50** into cells B9 through E9 and format those cells using the currency style tool.

5 Type the formula **=B8*B9** into cell B10 to compute professional services revenue. (Note how the formatting from B9 is transferred to cell B10.) Fill the formula across to cells C10 through E10.

6 Type the product sales estimates from the information provided above into cells B12 through E12, respectively. Format these cells with the currency tool.

7 Type the formula **=B10+B12** into cell B14 to calculate total revenue. Fill the formula across to cells C14 through F14.

8 Type the formula **=SUM(B8:E8)** into cell F8 to calculate annual repair hours.

9 Copy the formula you placed in cell F8 to cells F10 and F12. Format all three cells (F8, F10, and F12) with the currency tool.

10 The completed worksheet should look like Figure 6.2.

	A	B	C	D	E	F
1	Coast Jewelers, Inc.					
2	Sales Budget					
3						
4						
5				Quarter		
6		1st	2nd	3rd	4th	Year
7	Professional services:					
8	Repair hours	1,500	1,600	1,700	1,800	6,600
9	Hourly rate	$ 50.00	$ 50.00	$ 50.00	$ 50.00	
10	Professional services revenue	$ 75,000.00	$ 80,000.00	$ 85,000.00	$ 90,000.00	$ 330,000.00
11						
12	Product sales:	$ 425,000.00	$ 400,000.00	$ 375,000.00	$ 450,000.00	$ 1,650,000.00
13						
14	Total revenue	$ 500,000.00	$ 480,000.00	$ 460,000.00	$ 540,000.00	$ 1,980,000.00

FIGURE 6.2
Completed Sales Budget

11 Save your work to ch6-01a.xls.

This now completed worksheet provides some important information for calculated cash receipts and disbursements. It is not, however, complete. Kyle explains that Excel's AutoFormat tool can turn a boring-looking schedule into a professional-looking analysis.

"What's the difference?" Nathan asks. "The numbers will still be the same!"

"Yes, but the professional appearance will affect the bankers' perceptions. If nothing else, they will be impressed with your style," Kyle responds.

AUTOFORMATTING A SCHEDULE

Excel's AutoFormat tool will reformat a worksheet by letting you choose from a variety of pre-designed templates. These templates provide number, border, font, patterns, alignment, and width/height formats.

"I can do that!" you say.

To autoformat the sales budget:

1 Select the range of cells A5 to F14.

2 Click **Format**, then **AutoFormat** from the menu.

3 Click the **Options...** button.

4 The AutoFormat window shown in Figure 6.3 will appear.

FIGURE 6.3

The AutoFormat Window

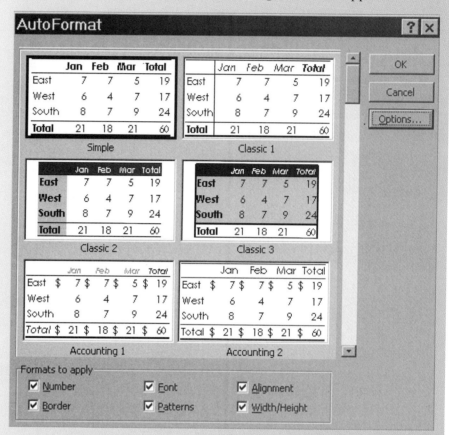

5 Scroll down the AutoFormat window and view all the possible formats available, then return to the top of the window and select format **Classic 3**.

6 Uncheck the **Number**, **Alignment**, and **Width/Height** check boxes in the Formats to apply section. This is because you have already established number formats in the worksheet and the Alignment and Width/Height characteristics are acceptable as is.

7 Click **OK** in the AutoFormat window.

8 Note the various changes that have taken place with only a few clicks.

9 Select the range of cells A1 to A3. Make them bold and change the font color of these cells to dark blue by selecting the large **A** with the drop-down arrow to the right (or click the More Buttons drop-down arrow to display the button) and select the color.

10 The results of your autoformatting are shown in Figure 6.4.

FIGURE 6.4

Formatted Sales Budget

	A	B	C	D	E	F
1	Coast Jewelers, Inc.					
2	Sales Budget					
3						
4						
5				Quarter		
6		1st	2nd	3rd	4th	Year
7	*Professional services:*					
8	Repair hours	1,500	1,600	1,700	1,800	6,600
9	Hourly rate	$ 50.00	$ 50.00	$ 50.00	$ 50.00	
10	Professional services revenue	$ 75,000.00	$ 80,000.00	$ 85,000.00	$ 90,000.00	$ 330,000.00
11						
12	Product Sales:	$ 425,000.00	$ 400,000.00	$ 375,000.00	$ 450,000.00	$ 1,650,000.00
13						
14	*Total revenue*	$ 500,000.00	$ 480,000.00	$ 460,000.00	$ 540,000.00	$ 1,980,000.00

11 Save your work to ch6-01a.xls.

"Now that is much more professional looking than our first attempt," Nathan admits. "And it was so easy!"

"Yes, but we have much more to do," Kyle explains. "Next we have to estimate purchases, which of course will be based on sales and inventory requirements."

PURCHASE BUDGET

Kyle explains that quarterly purchases are dependent on beginning inventory, the cost of expected sales, and the desired amount of ending inventory. For example, assume a beginning inventory of $500, and that Coast expects to sell $1,500 of merchandise (that cost them $900). Further, assume they would like to keep an inventory of $400 on hand for next month's sales. They will need to purchase $800 of inventory during the quarter. This is computed using the following formula: cost of expected sales (900) + desired ending inventory (400) − beginning inventory (500) = required purchases (800).

Nathan estimates that the cost of most of his inventory is 60 percent of sales value. For example, a necklace Coast sells for $100 cost them $60. Further, he would like to maintain an inventory on hand each month of 80 percent of expected sales in the following month.

Kyle recommends that you take a shot at producing the desired purchases budget and to explain the process to Meagan and Nathan.

To create a purchases budget:

1 Click the **Purchases** sheet of the ch6-01a.xls file you worked with while creating the sales budget.

2 Type **60%** in cell B7 to indicate the cost of sales estimated percentage.

3 Type the formula **=$B$7*Sales!B12** in cell C7. The absolute reference to B7 will allow you to fill the formula across cells later.

(Remember, instead of typing the reference to B12 on the Sales sheet you can point to the cell on that worksheet after typing =$B$7*.)

4 Fill that formula across to cells D7, E7, and F7.

5 Type **80%** in cell B8 to indicate the percentage of next quarter's sales you desire as ending inventory.

6 Type the formula **=$B$8*$B$7*Sales!C12** into cell C8. This formula multiplies the sales for the second quarter by the cost percentage to calculate the cost of next period's sales. That value is then multiplied by the desired inventory percentage entered in the last step.

7 Fill that formula across to cells D8, E8, and F8. Note, however, that the formula in F8 refers to the amount of sales located at Sales!F12, which is annual sales, not the next quarter sales which would be the first quarter of next year.

8 Replace Sales!F12 with **500000** (an estimate of sales in the first quarter of next year).

9 Type **125000** in cell C9 (an estimate of beginning inventory).

10 Type **=C8** in cell D9 (because last quarter's ending inventory is this quarter's beginning inventory).

11 Fill that formula across to cells E9 and F9.

12 Type **=C7+C8–C9** in cell C11 to calculate required purchases.

13 Fill that formula across to cell D11, E11, and F11.

14 Type **=SUM(C7:F7)** in cell G7 to calculate total cost of sales for the year.

15 Type **=F8** in cell G8 to reference ending inventory for the year.

16 Type **=C9** in cell G9 to reference beginning inventory for the year.

17 Type **=SUM(C11:F11)** in cell G11 to calculate total required purchases for the year.

18 Select the range of cells A5 to G11.

19 Click **Format**, then **AutoFormat** from the menu.

20 Click the **Options . . .** button.

21 Scroll down the AutoFormat window and view all the possible formats available, then return to the top of the window and select format **Classic 3**.

22 Uncheck the **Number**, **Alignment**, and **Width/Height** check boxes in the Formats to apply section. This is because you have already established number formats in the worksheet and the Alignment and Width/Height characteristics are acceptable as is.

23 Click **OK** in the AutoFormat window.

24 Format cells C7 to G7, and cells C11 to G11 in a currency format.

25 Format cells C8 to G8, and cells C9 to G9 in a comma format.

26 Select the range of cells A1 to A3. Change the font color of these cells to dark blue and make them bold.

27 The results of your autoformatting are shown in Figure 6.5.

	A	B	C	D	E	F	G
1	Coast Jewelers, Inc.						
2	Purchases Budget						
3							
4							
5					Quarter		
6			1st	2nd	3rd	4th	Year
7	Cost of expected sales	60%	$ 255,000.00	$ 240,000.00	$ 225,000.00	$ 270,000.00	$ 990,000.00
8	Plus: required ending inventory	00%	192,000.00	180,000.00	216,000.00	240,000.00	240,000.00
9	Less: beginning inventory		125,000.00	192,000.00	180,000.00	216,000.00	125,000.00
10							
11	Required purchases		$ 322,000.00	$ 228,000.00	$ 261,000.00	$ 294,000.00	$ 1,105,000.00

FIGURE 6.5

Formatted Purchases Budget

28 Save your work to ch6-01a.xls.

"As you can see, the purchases budget is based on the sales budget we had previously created and some additional facts and assumptions, such as the relationship between sales and costs of goods sold," Kyle notes.

"How does all this relate to cash flow?" you ask.

"Cash flow encompasses cash inflow from sales as well as cash outflow for purchases and expenses," Kyle answers. "Next up is budget for sales and administrative expenses."

SALES AND ADMINISTRATIVE EXPENSE BUDGET

Kyle explains to you, Nathan, and Meagan that the sales and administrative expense budget won't be linked to either sales or purchases. Instead the budget will be based on expected costs to be incurred for advertising, depreciation, payroll, and utilities. Advertising is expected to increase $5,000 per quarter over the year and depreciation will increase $1,000 per quarter, based on new equipment purchases. Payroll will vary based on the expected expansion of business and seasonal sales. Utilities will be based on prior year's actual results. The resulting analysis provides the following budget estimates:

	first	second	third	fourth
Advertising	$ 25,000.00	$ 30,000.00	$ 35,000.00	$ 40,000.00
Depreciation	8,000.00	9,000.00	10,000.00	11,000.00
Payroll	125,000.00	150,000.00	150,000.00	185,000.00
Utilities	15,000.00	18,000.00	17,500.00	19,000.00

Kyle suggests that you prepare the sales and administrative expense budget based on this data.

To create a sales and administrative expense budget:

1 Click the **Selling and Administrative Exp** sheet of the ch6-01a.xls file you worked with while creating the purchases budget.

2 Enter the information provided above.

3 Use the Sum function to provide totals in cells B12 through F12 and in cells F7 through F10.

4 Format the cells A5 through F12 as you have done in previous budget sheets using the AutoFormat function and the Classic 3 style.

5 Your completed sales and administrative expense budget should look like Figure 6.6, including the currency and comma formats and title font formatting.

FIGURE 6.6

Completed and Formatted Sales and Expense Budget

	A	B	C	D	E	F
1	Coast Jewelers, Inc.					
2	Selling and Administrative Expense Budget					
3						
4						
5				*Quarter*		
6		*1st*	*2nd*	*3rd*	*4th*	*Year*
7	Advertising	$ 25,000.00	$ 30,000.00	$ 35,000.00	$ 40,000.00	$ 130,000.00
8	Depreciation	8,000.00	9,000.00	10,000.00	11,000.00	38,000.00
9	Payroll	125,000.00	150,000.00	150,000.00	185,000.00	610,000.00
10	Utilities	15,000.00	18,000.00	17,500.00	19,000.00	69,500.00
11						
12	*Total*	$ 173,000.00	$ 207,000.00	$ 212,500.00	$ 255,000.00	$ 847,500.00

6 Save your work to ch6-01a.xls.

"Now that revenues, cost of sales, and expenses have been identified, it is time to translate them into cash flow," Kyle states.

"How are they different?" Meagan asks.

"Timing," Kyle responds. "Not all revenues will be collected in the same quarter as they are earned because you offer your customers 30-day terms to pay their invoices."

CASH RECEIPTS BUDGET

Kyle further explains that the cash receipts budget must not only account for the timing of revenue collection but also recognize that not all revenues will be collected. Giving customers credit necessitates that businesses realize that some customers will default on their accounts and not pay. An estimate of uncollected accounts and the timing of account collection make up the cash receipts budget.

" I have experienced about a 2 percent default rate on sales over the last several years," Nathan says. "Also, based on the last two years, our customers usually pay 80 percent of what we've invoiced them in the quarter when sales were earned, and 18 percent in the next quarter."

Kyle suggests that you use that information, along with the data provided in the sales budget, to calculate a cash receipts budget.

"How will I know how much cash is collected in the first quarter from prior quarter sales?" you ask.

"I would estimate cash collections in the first quarter from prior quarter sales of $81,000," Meagan answers.

To create a cash receipts budget:

1 Click the **Cash Receipts** sheet of the ch6-01a.xls file you worked with while creating the sales and administrative budget.

2 Type **=Sales!B14** in cell C7. You will use this information to estimate your cash collected each period.

3 Fill this formula across to cells D7, E7, and F7.

4 Type **80%** in cell B8. You'll use this to calculate cash collected each quarter from the current quarter's sales.

5 Type **18%** in cell B9. You'll use this to calculate cash collected each quarter from the previous quarter's sales.

6 Type **=C7*$B$8** in cell C8. Use absolute referencing at B8 so that the formula can be replicated across several cells.

7 Fill this formula across to cells D8, E8, and F8.

8 Type **$81,000.00** in cell C9 as your estimate of cash collected from the previous quarter from last year's sales.

9 Type **=C7*$B$9** in cell D9. Use absolute referencing at B9 so that the formula can be replicated across several cells.

10 Fill this formula across to cells E9 and F9.

11 Type **=SUM(C8:C9)** in cell C10 to add cash receipts from the current and previous quarters.

12 Fill this formula across to cells D10, E10, and F10.

13 Type **2%** in cell B12. You'll use this to calculate cash *not* collected each quarter from the current quarter's sales.

14 Type **=C7*$B$12** in cell C12.

15 Fill this formula across to cells D12, E12, and F12.

16 Enter a formula into cells G7, G8, G9, G10, and G12 to add each row.

17 Format the cells A5 through G12 as you have done in previous budget sheets using the AutoFormat function and the Classic 3 style.

18 Your completed cash receipts budget should look like Figure 6.7, including the currency and comma formats and title font formatting.

19 Save your work to ch6-01a.xls.

Kyle explains that the next logical step is to create a cash disbursements budget that will be coupled later with the just completed cash receipts budget to summarize cash flow for the year.

FIGURE 6.7

*Completed and Formatted
Cash Receipts Budget*

	A	B	C	D	E	F	G
1	Coast Jewelers, Inc.						
2	Cash Receipts Budget						
3							
4							
5					Quarter		
6			1st	2nd	3rd	4th	Year
7	Total revenue		$ 500,000.00	$ 480,000.00	$ 460,000.00	$ 540,000.00	$ 1,980,000.00
8	Collections in quarter of service or sale	80%	$ 400,000.00	$ 384,000.00	$ 368,000.00	$ 432,000.00	$ 1,584,000.00
9	Collections in quarter following service or sale	18%	81,000.00	90,000.00	86,400.00	82,800.00	340,200.00
10	*Total cash receipts*		$ 481,000.00	$ 474,000.00	$ 454,400.00	$ 514,800.00	$ 1,924,200.00
11							
12	*Uncollectible billings*	2%	$ 10,000.00	$ 9,600.00	$ 9,200.00	$ 10,800.00	$ 39,600.00

CASH DISBURSEMENTS BUDGET

The cash disbursements budget, like the cash receipts budget you just completed, is also a timing-based analysis. In this case, the timing issue is when payments are made. Nathan's analysis indicates that approximately 75 percent of purchases made in a quarter are paid in that same quarter and 25 percent are paid the following quarter.

"Can we budget some percentage of nonpayment like we did in the cash receipts budget?" Meagan asks.

"Wouldn't that be great?" Kyle responds. "However, it's not appropriate to budget your nonpayment of bills!"

Nathan further estimates that all of the company's sales and administrative expenses are paid in the same quarter as incurred except, of course, depreciation. Depreciation, being an expense that does not affect cash, is excluded from this analysis. Lastly, he anticipates $16,000 of purchases will be payable in the first quarter from the last year's purchases.

To create the cash disbursement budget:

1 Click the **Cash Disbursement** sheet of the ch6-01a.xls file you worked with while creating the cash receipts budget.

2 Type **=Purchases!C11** in cell C7. You will use this information to estimate your cash payments for purchases each period.

3 Fill this formula across to cells D7, E7, and F7.

4 Type **75%** in cell B8. You'll use this to calculate cash paid each quarter from the current quarter's purchases.

5 Type **25%** in cell B9. You'll use this to calculate cash paid each quarter from the previous quarter's purchases.

6 Type **=C7*$B$8** in cell C8. Use absolute referencing at B8 so that the formula can be replicated across several cells.

7 Fill this formula across to cells D8, E8, and F8.

8 Type **16000** in cell C9 as your estimate of cash paid from the previous quarter from last year's purchases.

9 Type =C7*$B$9 in cell D9. Use absolute referencing at B9 so that the formula can be replicated across several cells.

10 Fill this formula across to cells E9, and F9.

11 Type =SUM(C8:C9) in cell C10 to add cash payments made in the current quarter.

12 Fill this formula across to cells D10, E10, and F10.

13 Type ='Selling and Administrative Exp'!B12-'Selling and Administrative Exp'!B8 in cell C11. You'll use this to calculate cash paid for total selling and administrative expenses. The formula subtracts depreciation expense from total selling and administrative expenses each quarter.

14 Fill this formula across to cells D11, E11, and F11.

15 Type =C10+C11 in cell C12 to add payments for purchases to payments for expenses.

16 Fill this formula across to cells D12, E12, and F12.

17 Enter a formula into cells G7, G8, G9, G10, G11 and G12 to add each row.

18 Format the cells A5 through G12 as you have done in previous budget sheets using the AutoFormat function and the Classic 3 style.

19 Your completed cash disbursements budget should look like Figure 6.8 including the currency and comma formats and title font formatting.

FIGURE 6.8

Completed and Formatted Cash Disbursements Budget

	A	B	C	D	E	F	G
1	Coast Jewelers, Inc.						
2	Cash Disbursements Budget						
3							
4							
5					*Quarter*		
6			*1st*	*2nd*	*3rd*	*4th*	*Year*
7	Total purchases		$ 322,000.00	$ 228,000.00	$ 261,000.00	$ 294,000.00	$ 1,105,000.00
8	Payments in quarter of acquisition	75%	$ 241,500.00	$ 171,000.00	$ 195,750.00	$ 220,500.00	$ 828,750.00
9	Payments in quarter following acquisition	25%	16,000.00	80,500.00	57,000.00	65,250.00	218,750.00
10	Total payments for purchases		$ 257,500.00	$ 251,500.00	$ 252,750.00	$ 285,750.00	$ 1,047,500.00
11	Other cash payments		165,000.00	198,000.00	202,500.00	244,000.00	809,500.00
12	Total		$ 422,500.00	$ 449,500.00	$ 455,250.00	$ 529,750.00	$ 1,857,000.00

20 Save your work to ch6-01a.xls.

"Are we ready to pull this information all together?" you ask.

"I'm ready," Meagan says. "I'm anxious to see how this all helps us understand the total cash picture."

"I'm interested in seeing where financing and equipment purchasing fits into this budget," Nathan says. "I've seen revenues and expenses, but what about cash outlays for debt repayment, equipment purchases, or better yet additional borrowings!"

Kyle explains that we'll deal with all three next.

SUMMARY CASH BUDGET
. . . .

Kyle explains to you, Nathan, and Meagan that the summary cash budget does just that. It pulls information from the cash receipts and disbursements budgets and incorporates plans for debt repayment, equipment acquisitions, and additional financing.

"What are your plans for the coming year?" Kyle asks.

"Well, I'd like to purchase some new equipment in the second quarter for about $300,000," Nathan says. "The bank is willing to lend me $250,000, provided these budgets support the stories I've been telling them about the business. The quarterly payment on the loan, which includes interest, is about $20,000."

"How much cash will you have at the beginning of the budgeted period?" Kyle asks.

"Right now my best estimate is about $25,000," Nathan responds.

"That's all the information we need to create the summary cash budget," Kyle says. "Let's have our student here finalize the budget."

To create the summary cash budget:

1 Click the **Summary Cash Budget** sheet of the ch6-01a.xls file you worked with while creating the cash disbursements budget.

2 Type =**'Cash Receipts'!C10** in cell B7 to transfer the results of your cash receipts analysis to the summary budget.

3 Fill this formula across to cells C7 through F7.

4 Type =**'Cash Disbursements'!C12** in cell B8 to transfer the results of your cash disbursements analysis to the summary budget.

5 Fill this formula across to cells C8 through F8.

6 Type =**B7–B8** in cell B9 to calculate change in cash for that quarter.

7 Fill this formula across to cells C9 through F9.

8 Type **250,000.00** in cell C11 to represent the borrowings to be made in the second quarter.

9 Type **300,000.00** in cell C12 to represent the equipment purchases to be made in the second quarter.

10 Type **20,000.00** in cells D13 and E13 to represent the payments to be made on the loan in those quarters.

11 Type =**B9+B11–B12–B13** in cell B15 to calculate the change in cash balance for the first quarter based on the change in cash from cash receipts less disbursements, plus loan proceeds, less equipment purchases, less loan payments.

12 Fill this formula across to cells C15 through E15.

13 Type **25,000.00** in cell B16 representing beginning cash for the first quarter.

14 Type =**B15+B16** in cell B17 to calculate the ending cash balance for the first quarter.

15 Fill this formula across to cells C17 through F17.

16 Type **=B17** in cell C16 to reference the previous quarter's ending cash balance as the current quarter's beginning cash balance.

17 Fill this formula across to cells D16 through E16.

18 Type **=SUM(B11:E11)** in cell F11 to calculate the annual loan proceeds.

19 Fill this formula down to cells F12 and F13.

20 Type **=SUM(B15:E15)** in cell F15 to calculate the annual change in cash.

21 Type **=B16** in cell F16 to identify beginning cash balance for the year.

22 Format the cells A5 through F17 as you have done in previous budget sheets using the AutoFormat function and the Classic 3 style.

23 Make your completed summary cash budget look like Figure 6.9, including the currency and comma formats and title font formatting.

	A	B	C	D	E	F
1	Coast Jewelers, Inc.					
2	Summary Cash Budget					
3						
4						
5				Quarter		
6		1st	2nd	3rd	4th	Year
7	Cash receipts	$ 481,000.00	$ 474,000.00	$ 454,400.00	$ 514,800.00	$ 1,924,200.00
8	Cash disbursements	422,500.00	449,500.00	455,250.00	529,750.00	1,857,000.00
9	Change in cash	$ 58,500.00	$ 24,500.00	$ (850.00)	$ (14,950.00)	$ 67,200.00
10						
11	Proceeds from loan		250,000.00			250,000.00
12	Equipment purchase		300,000.00			300,000.00
13	Payment of loan			20,000.00	20,000.00	40,000.00
14						
15	Change in cash balance	$ 58,500.00	$ (25,500.00)	$ (20,850.00)	$ (34,950.00)	$ (22,800.00)
16	Cash balance, beg	25,000.00	83,500.00	58,000.00	37,150.00	25,000.00
17	Cash balance, end	$ 83,500.00	$ 58,000.00	$ 37,150.00	$ 2,200.00	$ 2,200.00

FIGURE 6.9

Completed and Formatted Summary Cash Budget

24 Save your work to ch6-01a.xls.

The resulting cash budget leaves the company with only $2,200 at the end of the fourth quarter, which as Nathan explains, is not acceptable. "We must have done something wrong, as I'm sure the bank will reject my application if I present them this budget," he says.

"Perhaps we can use Excel's What-If feature to manipulate the budget to give us a better-ending balance?" Meagan suggests. "I propose we increase the hourly rate we charge for repairs from $50 to $75 per hour."

"We can also use the goal seek feature we used before to determine what changes need to be made to achieve a certain target value for ending cash," you say. "For instance if we want an ending cash balance of $25,000, what cost of expected sales percentage could you use?"

Kyle suggests you experiment with your newly-created cash budget by using what-if analysis and goal seeking for the two scenarios described.

To use what-if analysis and goal seeking with the cash budget:

1 Change the hourly rate charged for repairs to **$75** in cells B9 through E9 on the Sales sheet.

2 The result should be ending cash of $155,800, assuming the change in hourly rate had no effect on the projected repair hours or uncollectible billings.

3 Change the hourly rate charged for repairs back to **$50** in cells B9 through E9.

4 Use goal seek by setting cell F17 on the summary cash budget to **$25,000** by changing cell B7 (the % cost of expected sales) on the purchases budget sheet.

5 The result should be a percent cost of sales of 59% (actually 58.8171206225681% before rounding).

6 Close the workbook ch6-01a.xls, but don't save the changes made.

"Now, that is a powerful tool." Nathan says. "I think I can shave off a little on the percentage of cost of sales by increasing my markup slightly."

END NOTE
. . . .

You've applied some of what you learned in the first five chapters to better understand how Excel can be used to analyze cash. In addition, you've learned a new feature of Excel (autoformatting) and experimented with what-if and goal seeking as analytical tools.

practice

Chapter 6 Questions

1 What information is provided by the sales budget?

2 What information is provided by the purchases budget?

3 What information is provided by the sales and administrative expense budget?

4 What information is provided by the cash receipts budget?

5 What information is provided by the cash disbursements budget?

6 What information is provided by the summary cash budget?

7 What does the AutoFormat feature in Excel accomplish?

8 What optional formats can you apply when using the AutoFormat feature?

9 How are revenues different from cash receipts?

10 How was the goal seek feature used in this chapter?

Chapter 6 Assignments

1 *AutoFormat*

Open the workbook created in this chapter (ch6-01a.xls).

a Save the workbook as **ch6-02.xls**

b Use AutoFormat and change the sales sheet by using a Classic 1 format, then print the value view worksheet.

c Use AutoFormat and change the purchases sheet by using a Classic 2 format, then print the value view worksheet.

d Use AutoFormat and change the summary cash budget sheet by selecting None from the AutoFormat options, then print the value view worksheet.

2 *What-if Analysis Using Cash Budgeting*

Open the workbook created in this chapter (ch6-01a.xls). Determine the ending cash balance in the fourth quarter if:

a Required ending inventory percent is 75 percent instead of 80 percent.

b Cash collections in the quarter of service or sale are 78 percent instead of 80 percent and cash collections in the quarter following service or sale are 20 percent instead of 18 percent.

c Cash payments in the quarter of acquisition are 70 percent instead of 75 percent and cash payments in the quarter following acquisition are 30 percent instead of 25 percent.

(Remember to reset each cell changed before recalculating ending cash. In other words, the preceding scenarios are independent of each other.)

Chapter 6 Case Problem: Kelly's Boutique

Kelly's Boutique is contemplating several alternative means of financing their acquisition of $100,000 in special equipment. One alternative is to borrow $100,000 from a local bank for 10 years at 12 percent per annum. The bank has asked them to produce a one-year cash budget broken down by months (January through December).

1 Create a sales budget based on sales of $30,000 in the first month, with each month after increasing 2 percent.

2 Create a purchases budget based on an expected cost of sales of 50 percent and a required ending inventory of 70 percent of next month's sales. Beginning inventory is estimated at $5,000. Sales for January next year are expected to be $26,000.

3 Create a selling and administrative budget based on advertising of $900, depreciation of $800, interest of $1,000, payroll of $8,000, supplies of $500, and utilities of $600 per month, respectively. *Note:* The company expects income taxes of 10 percent. To calculate income tax, subtract the cost of expected sales and subtotal of expenses from the product sales for each month. Then multiply this value by 10%. All expenses except depreciation are paid in the month in which they are incurred, including income taxes.

4 Create a cash receipts budget based on collections in the month of sale to be 50 percent, collections in the month following a sale to be 40 percent, collections in the following month to be 10 percent. Collections in January are expected to include $8,000 from December and $2,000 from November of the prior year. Collections in February are expected to include $2,000 from December.

5 Create a cash disbursements budget based on payments in the month of acquisition to be 60 percent and payments in the month following acquisition to be 40 percent. Payments in January are expected to include $6,000 from acquisitions in December.

6 Create a summary cash budget based upon receiving the $100,000 in June, purchasing the equipment for $100,000 in June, and in July starting to make monthly payments of $1,400. Beginning cash balance in January was $10,000.

7 Autoformat each sheet in Accounting 1 style.

8 Save the newly created workbook as **ch6-03.xls**.

9 Print a copy of each budget sheet in value view, landscape orientation, and formatted to fit on one page with footers including your name, the sheet name, and the filename.

part

2

Access for Accounting

Access Tour

In this chapter you will learn:

- **Access basics**

- **Access's help system**

- **An introduction to tables**

- **An introduction to queries**

- **An introduction to forms**

- **An introduction to reports**

CASE: COAST JEWELERS, INC.

Nathan and Meagan have expressed an interest in other software that might be able to help them in their jewelry business. Kyle asks them what kinds of records they keep for customer orders and inventory control.

"We keep records by hand now and it is very tedious and problematic," Meagan responds. "I have a file for customers, suppliers, products, etc. but often they get misplaced and are frequently out of date. It's difficult to keep track of it all!"

"Well, perhaps a database management system might help you out," suggests Kyle.

"What's a database management system?" asks Nathan.

Kyle explains that as their business grows the information available to them will increase as well and a database management system (DBMS) can help. "Essentially, a DBMS is a tool for storing, retrieving, and interpreting information in an effective and useful way. These days, Microsoft's Access program, a relational database management system, has proven to be a very successful tool in combating information overload."

"Hold on," warns Nathan. "What is a relational database?"

"Ok, let's go slowly," responds Kyle. "Let me walk you and our student assistant through the basics and I'll define relational database then."

"Great," you respond. "I know businesses use databases every day and this way I can get a better insight on how they are created and used."

ACCESS BASICS

In this section you will become familiar with the Access window, its toolbars, layout, and functions.

What Is Access?

Access is a DBMS, which organizes a collection of related information used for a specific purpose. For example, information about Coast's customers, its suppliers, and its products could be three different databases in and of themselves. A relational database is one in which information is divided into separate stacks of logically related information, each of which is stored in a separate table in the file. Thus, tables are a critical part of a DBMS and the relations among the tables are key to its success.

Tables can be related in three different ways: one-to-many, one-to-one, and many-to-many. For instance, the supervisor of an accounting department may have many employees who work under her, however, all the employees who work for her have only one supervisor. This would be a one-to-many relationship: one supervisor to many employees. Another example is the chief financial officer (CFO) who reports to the chief executive officer (CEO). This is a one-to-one relationship since there is only one CEO and one CFO. Still another example is the construction worker who works on many different jobs and each job has many different workers. This is an example of a many-to-many relationship. The most common of these, and the ones you'll experience here, are the one-to-many relationships.

The DBMS includes more than just tables, of course. Queries, forms, and reports based on the data stored in tables are what make up the management component of DBMS. Before you get too far, Kyle suggests you learn how to start Access.

Starting Access

To begin, Kyle explains that starting Access is similar to starting Excel.

To start Access:

1 Click the **Start** button.

2 Select the **Office 2000** menu and look down the list for Access. An example of what you might see is shown in Figure 7.1.

3 Once you've located the Access program, click and release the **Access icon** or name.

trouble? Your Start menu may be completely different from that shown below. See your instructor or lab manual to identify the location of the Access shortcut needed to start the program.

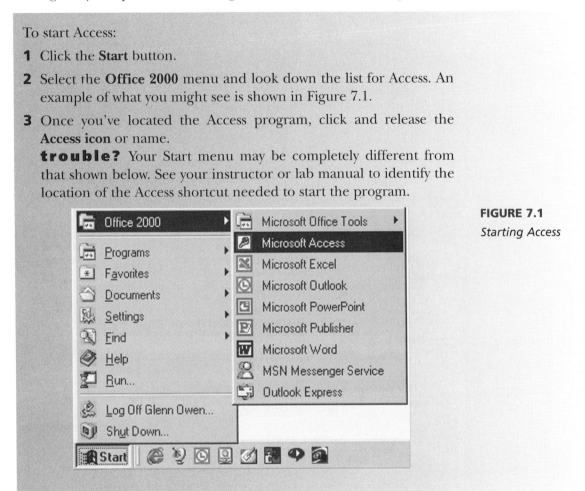

FIGURE 7.1
Starting Access

Now that you've started Access, you can begin to learn how to use it.

The Access Window

Access always opens a Microsoft Access window when first started as shown in Figure 7.2. Kyle explains that this window gives you the opportunity to start either a new blank Access database, a new pre-set Access database, or an existing Access database file. Kyle asks you to start a new blank Access database.

"Let's take some basic information on Coast Jewelers, Inc.'s inventory and set it up as a database."

FIGURE 7.2
Access Startup Screen

To create a new blank Access database:

1 Click in the option button next to the words **Blank Access database**, then click **OK**.

2 Type **Inventory.mdb** in the filename: edit box, then click **Create**.

3 The Access window shown in Figure 7.3 should appear.

FIGURE 7.3
Access Window

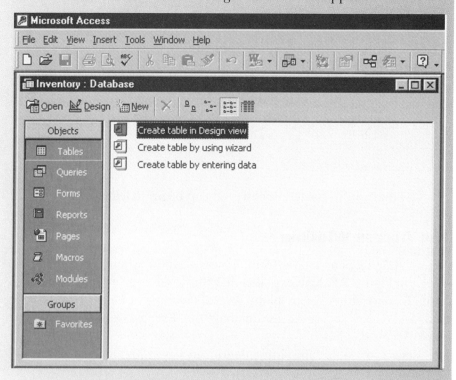

The Access window shown in Figure 7.3 lists a group of objects that will be a part of every database: tables, queries, forms, reports etc. Your focus will be to create a basic inventory system for Coast Jewelers, Inc. by creating several tables, queries, forms, and reports. But first it is important to understand Microsoft Access's help system.

The Help System

Access has a built-in help system to assist you in your learning experience. For example, new users to Access, like you, can use the help system to better understand how to create and design tables.

To enter and use the help system to learn more about tables:

1 Click **Help** on the menu bar, then click **Microsoft Access Help**. (Alternatively, you could simply press the F1 key.)

2 Move both the vertical and horizontal scroll boxes of the Microsoft Access Help window to the top and left respectively.

3 Click once on the **+** sign next to the Getting Help topic if it is open. Now click once on the topic **Getting Started with Microsoft Access**. Now your screen should look like Figure 7.4.

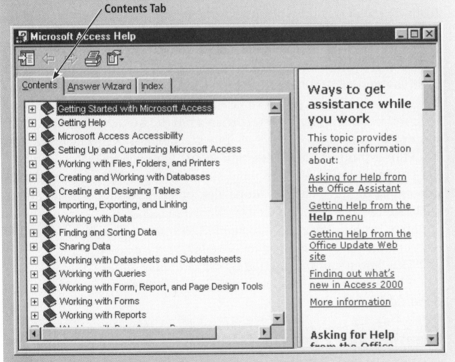

FIGURE 7.4
The Help Window

4 Click the **+** sign next to Creating and Designing Tables.

5 Click **Tables: What they are and how they work**, then click the graphic displayed.

6 View each of the five pages provided, moving between pages by clicking on the page numbers shown at the bottom of the window.

7 Close the Microsoft Access Help windows by clicking in the close window **X** in the upper right corner of each Help window.

You can use the help system any time Access is open to learn new techniques or remember how to do something you thought you already knew! Now you are ready to create your first database file.

TABLES
. . . .

Step 1 in the creation of any database is developing and understanding of the business and its information needs. Initially, that will take the form of table creation and separation. Rather than placing all information in one table, it's important to separate information into manageable chunks or tables. In our inventory example, Coast has information about its products, product suppliers, and product categories, which could be combined, but since every product has one supplier but some suppliers provide more than one product, a one-to-many relation exists between suppliers and products. Likewise, every product falls under one category, but most categories help define many products. Thus, we should separate product, supplier, and category information into three separate tables with the common relationship being the supplier identification number (ID) and category identification number (ID).

Step 2 is deciding what information we need for each table, what form (or data type) that information takes, and what properties exist for each field. This means that for each table (product, supplier, and category) we need to identify fields where information is to be stored. A common technique in database creation is to establish a unique identification number (ID) field for each record. This field will also be identified as our Primary Key. A primary key field, by definition, holds data that uniquely identifies each record in a table. Thus, our first field, common to all information entered into the table, is a product ID. Next would be a product name, description etc. For each field a corresponding data type (number, text, currency etc.) must be established and, depending on the data type, properties for each field must be identified (field size, format, caption etc.).

Step 3 is inputting the information into the tables. Now we gather information about each product, supplier, and category.

"How about running all that by me one more time?" you ask.

"I'll do you one better," responds Kyle. "I'll let you watch me create the product table."

Creating the Product Table

Kyle explains that in addition to creating fields for a product ID, name, and description, he will create fields which link the product to a specific inventory category, supplier, and identify the product's serial number, unit price, reorder level, and required lead time.

To create the product table:

1 Select the **Tables** object then double-click **Create table in Design view**. See Figure 7.3.

FIGURE 7.5
Product Table

Primary Key

Click here after entering field names, data types, and captions.

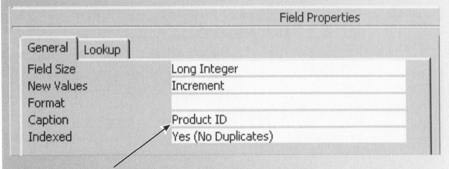

Field Name	Data Type
ProductID	AutoNumber
ProductName	Text
ProductDescription	Memo
SupplierID	Number
CategoryID	Number
ProductNumber	Text
UnitPrice	Currency
ReorderLevel	Number
LeadTime	Text

2 Enter the information shown in Figure 7.5 <u>exactly as typed</u> (ProductID). *Note:* Each data type has different field property characteristics. All allow you to specify a caption. Be sure to separate the field name for clarification and enter it as each field's caption. See Figure 7.6 for an example (Product ID). Continue with the rest of the fields, changing ProductName to Product Name, ProductDescription to Product Description, etc.

trouble? Do not change AutoNumber in the Data Type column. AutoNumber is a data type, not a field name.

FIGURE 7.6

Field Properties (for the ProductID Field)

Field Properties

General	Lookup
Field Size	Long Integer
New Values	Increment
Format	
Caption	Product ID
Indexed	Yes (No Duplicates)

Caption has been changed from ProductID to Product ID. The caption has changed, not the field name.

3 Once you have entered all the field names, data types, and correct captions, right-click in the box to the left of ProductID, the Primary Key button (shown in Figure 7.5), then select **Primary Key**.

4 Close the table window and save the table as **Product Table**.

You have created a placeholder for product information, now its time to create a placeholder for supplier information.

Creating the Supplier Table

Once again, similar to the product table creation, several fields will be required to capture information about each supplier. A supplier ID, supplier name, and contact name are just a few of the critical pieces of information necessary. In addition, Kyle suggests you should also gather information about the contact's title, address, and phone and fax numbers.

To create the supplier table:

1 Select the **Tables** object then double-click **Create table in Design view**. See Figure 7.3.

2 Enter the information shown in Figure 7.7 <u>exactly as typed</u>. *Note:* Each data type has different field property characteristics. All allow you to specify a caption. Be sure to separate the field name for clarification and enter it as each field's caption. See Figure 7.8 for an example. Continue with the rest of the fields, changing SupplierName to Supplier Name, ContactName to Contact Name, etc.

trouble? Note that changing the field's <u>caption</u> does not change the field's <u>name</u>.

FIGURE 7.7

Supplier Table

Primary Key

Click here after entering field names, data types, and captions.

Field Name	Data Type
SupplierID	AutoNumber
SupplierName	Text
ContactName	Text
ContactTitle	Text
Address	Text
City	Text
PostalCode	Text
StateOrProvince	Text
Country	Text
PhoneNumber	Text
FaxNumber	Text

FIGURE 7.8

Field Properties (for the SupplierID Field)

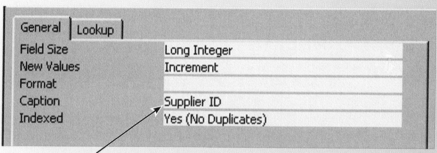

General	Lookup
Field Size	Long Integer
New Values	Increment
Format	
Caption	Supplier ID
Indexed	Yes (No Duplicates)

Caption has been changed from SupplierID to Supplier ID. The caption has changed, not the field name.

3 Once you have entered all the field names, data types, and correct captions, right-click the Primary Key box to the left of SupplierID, then select **Primary Key**.

4 Close the table window and save the table as Supplier Table.

You have now created a placeholder for supplier information. All that is left is to create a table with category information so that you can separate products into identifiable categories.

Creating a Category Table

The final table necessary to complete the inventory database is a category table that will consist of only two fields: a category ID and a category name.

"Why not just add the category to each product in the product table?" you ask.

"Remember, in a relational database we try to conserve space and eliminate redundancy," Kyle responds. "In this case every product has one category but every category may have multiple products. This is a one-to-many relationship."

To create a category table:

1 Select the **Tables** object then double-click **Create table in Design view**.

2 Create two fields: CategoryID as an AutoNumber data type and CategoryName as a Text data type.

3 Change the caption names as in previous tables.

4 Set the CategoryID field as the primary field, as in previous tables.

5 Close the table window and save the table as Category Table.

Your table structure is complete. All you need now is information.

Entering Data into Tables

With the table structure complete, you volunteer to enter information about the company's products, suppliers and categories. Nathan provides the information in Figures 7.9, 7.10, and 7.11.

To enter data into the three tables:

1 Select the **Tables** object then double-click the **Category Table**.

2 Enter the information as specified in Figure 7.9. Note the Category ID field will be automatically assigned as you tab to the Category Name field and enter information. After you type each record, press the **Enter** key to begin a new category.

3 Close the Category Table window after you have typed all the information.

4 Select the **Tables** object then double-click the **Supplier Table**.

5 Enter the information as specified in Figure 7.10. Note the Supplier ID field will be automatically assigned as you tab to the Supplier Name field and enter information. After you type each record, press the **Enter** key to begin a new supplier.

6 Close the Supplier Table window after you have typed all the information.

7 Select the **Tables** object then double-click the **Product Table**.

8 Enter the information as specified in Figure 7.11. Note the Product ID field will be automatically assigned as you tab to the Product

CategoryID	1	2	3	4
CategoryName	Watches	Rings	Necklaces	Earrings

FIGURE 7.9

Category Table Information

FIGURE 7.10 *Supplier Table Information*

SupplierID	1	2	3	4	5
SupplierName	Johnson Wholesale Jewelry Supply	Jewelry Inc.	Seiko USA	Robert Rose	Casio USA
ContactName	Ben Nimitz	Sara Munoz	Nancy Bearfoot	Paul Moo	Kelly O'Leary
ContactTitle	VP Sales	Sales	Western Sales	Salesman	Regional Sales
Address	100 8th Ave.	909 S. Washington	111 Macarthur Blvd.	385 5th Ave.	571 Mount Pleasant
City	New York	Pilot Pt.	Mahwah	New York	Dover
PostalCode	10035	76258	07430	10001	07801
StateOrProvince	NY	TX	NJ	NY	NJ
Country	USA	USA	USA	USA	USA
PhoneNumber	212-555-1354	940-555-0817	201-555-5730	212-555-4166	201-555-3215
FaxNumber	212-555-6874	940-555-1187	201-555-3872	212-555-9718	201-555-8741

FIGURE 7.11 *Product Table Information*

ProductID	1	2	3	4	5	6	7
ProductName	Flower Drop Earrings	Kinetic Auto Relay	LeGrand Sport	G-Shock	Engagement Ring	Diamond Earrings	Diamond Heart Slide
ProductDescription	These elegant earrings have a classy, refined look. The crystal stone top is attention-getting marcasite look, followed by a dainty drop that is a faceted black bead.	Energy storage for up to four years of time memory.	Step-motion second hand will move at 2-second intervals.	Shock resistant, daily and schedule alarm.	This engagement ring is set in 14K white and yellow gold.	A dazzling pair of dangle diamond earrings.	A gorgeous diamond heart slide is designed in 14K white and yellow gold.
SupplierID	4	3	3	5	1	2	1
CategoryID	4	1	1	1	2	4	3
Product#	136305	SMA113	SKA040	DW004B-4V	LGR29	ER-764	PD-241
UnitPrice	$6.00	$425.00	$275.00	$49.00	$400.00	$510.00	$525.00
ReorderLevel	5	2	2	2	1	1	2
LeadTime	10	11	14	10	15	30	30

Name field and enter information. After you type each record, press the **Enter** key to begin a new product.

9 Close the Product Table window after you have typed all the information.

Next up, establishing relationships among the three tables.

Establishing Table Relationships

One final step is necessary when you create multiple tables: to create relationships between the tables. Recall the earlier discussion about one-to-one, one-to-many, and many-to-many relationships. In the Coast Jewelers' database, you created three tables. Now you must define each relationship. For example, every product belongs in a particular category and has a supplier. Thus, there is a one-to-many relationship between the supplier table and the product table and a one-to-many relationship between the category table and the product table.

Kyle suggests you establish those relationships using Access's relationship tool.

To establish relationships between tables:

1 Select the **Relationships** tool from the standard toolbar.

2 Click each table in the **Show Table** window and click the **Add** button.

3 Move the Show Table window by clicking and dragging on the title bar of the window to view the three tables. If all three are showing in the Relationships window, click **Close** in the Show Table window.

4 Resize the Product table and the Supplier Table so that all fields are visible and the vertical scroll bars disappear as shown in Figure 7.12.

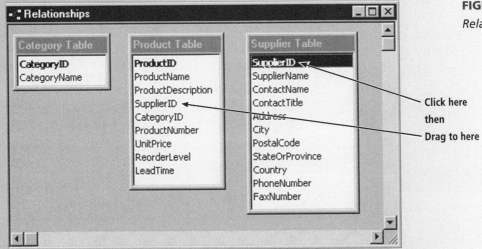

FIGURE 7.12
Relationships Window

5 Click on the **CategoryID** field in the Category Table. Hold the mouse button down and drag to the CategoryID field in the Product Table, and then release the mouse button.

6 When the Edit Relationships window appears click **Create**.

7 Click on the **SupplierID** field in the Supplier Table. Hold the mouse button down and drag to the SupplierID field in the Product Table, then release the mouse button.

8 When the Edit Relationships window appears click **Create**. The Relationships window should now show lines connecting the common fields between each table.

9 Close the Relationships window and click **Yes** to save the changes.

Now that relations have been established you can create queries, reports, and forms which use information from one or more tables. However, it is always important to have a physical copy of your tables for backup and reference.

Printing Tables

Occasionally you may want to print the tables to make sure information has been entered correctly. Later you will use the report feature of Access to print specific information available in the tables in a format that more effectively provides information needed.

To print all three tables:

1 Select the **Tables** object then double-click the **Category Table**.

2 Click the **Print Preview** button to view a reduced-size version of the table to be printed.

3 Click the **Print** button to print a copy of the table, then close the Table window.

4 Select the **Tables** object then double-click the **Supplier Table**.

5 Click the **Print Preview** button to view a reduced-size version of the table to be printed.

6 Click the **Print** button to print a copy of the table, then close the table window.

7 Select the **Tables** object then double-click the **Product Table**.

8 Click the **Print Preview** button to view a reduced-size version of the table to be printed.

9 Click the **Print** button to print a copy of the table.

10 Close the Table window.

QUERIES

Queries are essentially questions of the information provided in the database, such as: What products do we sell? From whom do we buy products? etc. In each query it is important to identify where the information can be found, what information is required, what criteria has been established, and how the information is reported.

Creating a Query

Kyle explains that for each query, tables are identified which contain the information to be requested. He suggests you create a query to list all products. Specifically, he wants you to provide the category name, product name, unit price, supplier name, and supplier phone number.

To create a query:

1 Select the **Queries** object then double-click the **Create query by using wizard**.

2 Select **Table: Category Table** from the Table/Queries drop-down list.

3 Click the field **CategoryName** from the list of available fields, then click the **>** button. This action will place the field CategoryName into the list of selected fields. See Figure 7.13.

trouble? If you select the wrong field, or click the wrong buttons, you can use the > or < buttons to move fields back and forth between the list of available fields and the list of selected fields.

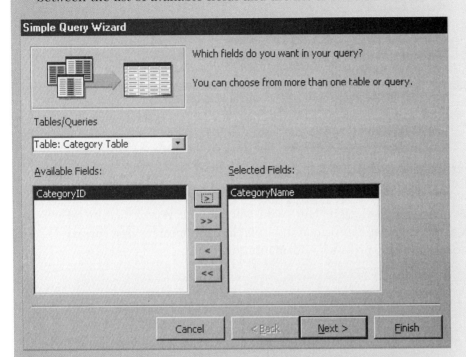

FIGURE 7.13

Simple Query Wizard Window

4 Select **Table: Product Table** from the Table/Queries drop-down list.

5 Click the field **ProductName** from the list of available fields, then click the **>** button. This action will place the field ProductName into the list of selected fields.

6 Click the field **UnitPrice** from the list of available fields, then click the **>** button. This action will place the field UnitPrice into the list of selected fields.

7 Select **Table: Supplier Table** from the Table/Queries drop-down list.

8 Click the field **SupplierName** from the list of available fields, then click the **>** button. This action will place the field SupplierName into the list of selected fields.

9 Click **Next** in the Simple Query Wizard window.

10 Make sure the Detail button is selected in the window presented, then click **Next**.

11 Change the title of the query to **Query1**, then click the **Open the query to view information** button, then click **Finish**.

12 The resulting query lists all seven products as shown in Figure 7.14.

FIGURE 7.14 *Query 1*

Category Name	Product Name	Unit Price	Supplier Name
Earrings	Flower Drop Earrings	$6.00	Robert Rose
Watches	Kinetic Auto Relay	$425.00	Seiko USA
Watches	Le Grand Sport	$275.00	Seiko USA
Watches	G-Shock	$49.00	Casio USA
Rings	Engagement Ring	$400.00	Johnson Wholesale Jewelry Supply
Earrings	Diamond Earrings	$510.00	Jewelry Inc.
Necklaces	Diamond Heart Slide	$525.00	Johnson Wholesale Jewelry Supply

Printing a Query

Occasionally you may want to print the query to make sure information has been properly selected. Later you will use the report feature of Access to print specific information available from a query in a format that more effectively provides information needed.

To print the query:

1 Select the **Query** object then double-click **Query1**.

2 Click the **Print Preview** button to view a reduced-size version of the query to be printed.

3 Click the **Print** button to print a copy of the query.

4 Close the Query window.

Access has another helpful feature, called forms, for capturing or viewing information in a database.

FORMS

Forms have a variety of purposes. One purpose is to provide a dialog box for access to pre-designed queries, other forms, or reports. Another purpose is to provide a dialog box to capture information from a user and use it to carry out an action.

Creating a Form

Kyle suggests that you use a form to capture information about additional Coast Jewelers' products. He reminds you that entering information into a form updates the table containing that information automatically. The form itself is just a means to update the table either by editing existing information or adding new information, like a new record.

To create a form to capture additional products:

1 Select the **Forms** object then double-click the **Create form by using wizard**.

2 Select **Table: Product Table** from the Table/Queries drop-down list.

3 Click the **>>** button to select all the fields available then click **Next**.

4 Select the **Columnar** layout, then click **Next**.

5 Select the **Sumi Painting** style, then click **Next**.

6 Name the new form title **Products**, then click **Finish**.

7 The resulting form should look like Figure 7.15.

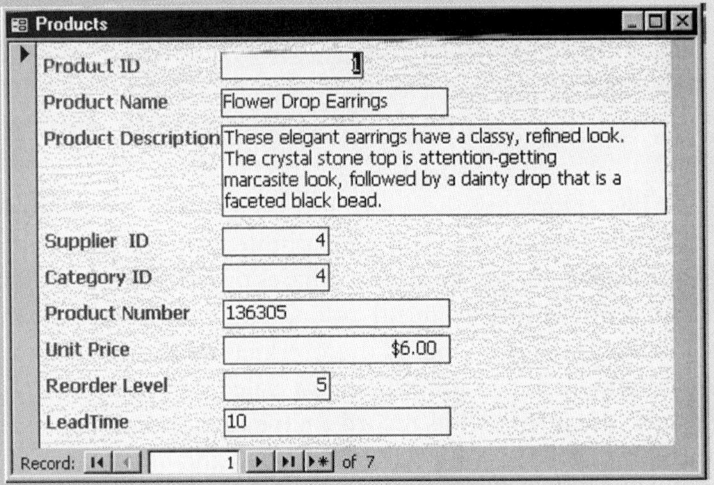

FIGURE 7.15

Products Form

Using a Form to View, Edit, or Add Information

This newly created form can be used to enter new information, edit existing information, and view existing information for each product. Nathan offers to try out the new form viewing each record. He also volunteers to enter a new product and edit a reorder level for one product.

To use a form to view and edit existing products and add an additional product:

1 Select the **Forms** object then double-click the **Products** form.

2 Click the **Next** button (the right arrow) at the bottom of the Products form and view each product. Continue to view each record until you reach record 5, Engagement Ring.

3 Click in the **Reorder Level** edit box and change the reorder level from 1 to 2.

4 Click the **New Record** button (the right arrow with the asterisk).

5 Press the **Tab** key to move the cursor to the Product Name field.

6 Type **Diamond Wedding Ring** as the new product name. Note that once you start typing the new product name the Product ID field changes to 8, as the AutoNumber process executes.

7 Complete the form as shown in Figure 7.16.

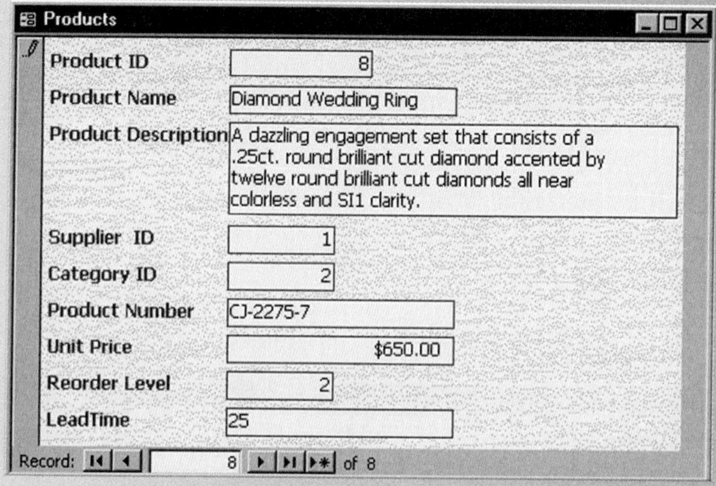

FIGURE 7.16

New Product Form

8 Close the Products Form window.

Nathan has completed the form and, as a result, edited an existing record and added a new one. This new product is now a part of the product table and will be present for future queries or reports. Most of the information in a form comes from an underlying record source. In Coast Jewelers, Inc. this includes some of the product information derived from the product table. Using graphical objects called controls Nathan created a link between the form and its record source, the product table. He used the most common type of control used to display and enter data: a text box.

Other information in the form is stored in the form's design. In the Coast Jewelers, Inc. form just created, this would include the descriptive text such as headers and footers and graphic elements such as the horizontal rule. In other forms this might include a calculation that comes from an expression stored in the form's design.

Printing a Form

Occasionally you may want to print a single form.

To print a single form:

1 Select the **Forms** object then double-click **Products**.

2 Select **Print** from the File menu. This is done to view the Print window so that you can specify which record to print.

3 Click **Selected Record(s)** to print the form of record 1 (Flower Drop Earrings). Note that record 1 will be printed since you were in record 1 when you activated the Print window.

4 Click **OK** to print the selected record.

5 Close the Products form.

"How do I get a report of the information in my new database?" asks Nathan.

"Good question," Kyle answers. "Let's generate a report for you now."

REPORTS
. . . .

Reports are a way for a user to get information out of a database in a format that helps the analytical process. To be useful, reported information needs to be properly formatted, sorted, and/or grouped. Reports are more than listings of information. For instance, a user may want to create mailing labels, which would require a different level of formatting than a report of items grouped in particular categories. Your report may need a chart, a logo, subtotals, or grand totals. It may need a date, a special title, headers, or footers by item or category, etc. Lastly, your report requirements may necessitate only certain items in your database that meet specific criteria, such as those items which cost more than a certain dollar amount or only those items from a particular category.

Creating a Report

Kyle suggests that your first report utilize Access's report wizard and simply list all the products, their product ID, product name, and unit price, listed by product number. There are five steps necessary to create a report:

1 Identify which fields you want in your report and in what tables those fields are present.
2 Specify grouping levels, if any.
3 Specify sort order, if any.
4 Specify a report layout.
5 Specify a report style.

To create a report of all products listed by product number:

1 Select the **Reports** object then double-click **Create report by using wizard**.

2 Select **Table: Product Table** from the list of Tables/Queries.

3 Click **ProductID** from the list of Available Fields, then click the **>** button to move ProductID from the list of Available Fields to the list of Selected Fields.

4 Click **ProductName** from the list of Available Fields, then click the **>** button to move ProductName from the list of Available Fields to the list of Selected Fields.

5 Click **UnitPrice** from the list of Available Fields, then click the **>** button to move UnitPrice from the list of Available Fields to the list of Selected Fields.

6 Click the **Next** button.

7 Click the **Next** button again since no grouping is required for this report.

8 Select **ProductID** in the first sort order list box. Make sure the sort order is from A to Z and not Z to A, and then click **Next**.

9 Click **Tabular Layout**, **Portrait Orientation**, and make sure the Adjust the field width so that all fields fit on a page check box is checked, then click **Next**.

10 Click **Corporate** from this list of available report styles, and then click **Next**.

11 Type **Products by ProductID** as the name of the report. Select the **Preview the Report** option button, then click **Finish**. Your report should look like the one shown in Figure 7.17.

12 Leave the Report window open.

FIGURE 7.17

Product by ProductID Report

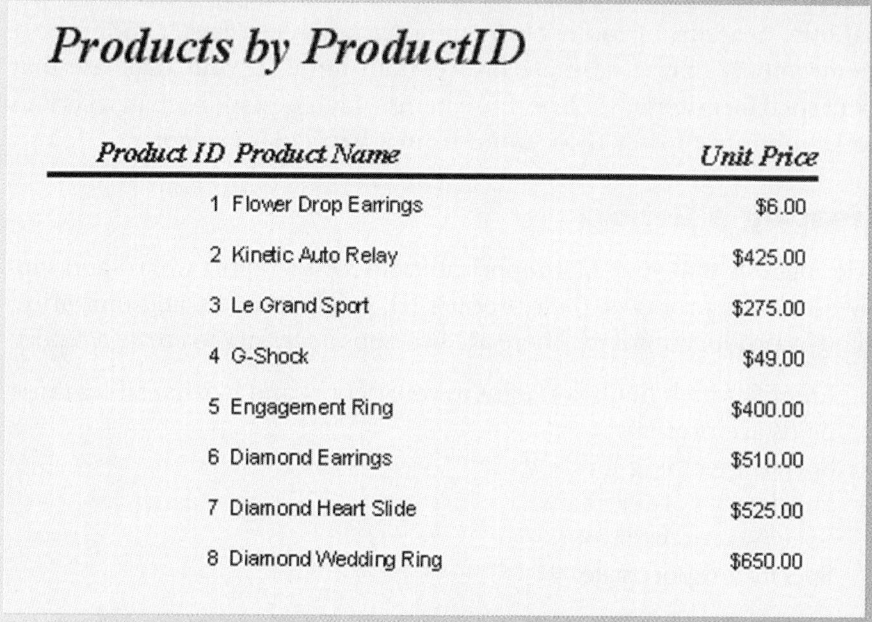

Products by ProductID

Product ID	Product Name	Unit Price
1	Flower Drop Earrings	$6.00
2	Kinetic Auto Relay	$425.00
3	Le Grand Sport	$275.00
4	G-Shock	$49.00
5	Engagement Ring	$400.00
6	Diamond Earrings	$510.00
7	Diamond Heart Slide	$525.00
8	Diamond Wedding Ring	$650.00

Editing a Report

You can edit this report at any point and change its characteristics. When you closed the Report window a Design View window appeared. The resulting design view is shown in Figure 7.18. You can now switch between the Design view and the Layout view by clicking on the View tool. Once in the Layout view you can customize the report as necessary.

Meagan suggests that centering the product ID title and data, narrowing the width of the unit price field, and narrowing the horizontal rule could improve the report just generated. You offer to make the changes she has suggested.

To edit the Product by Product ID report:

1 Change to the Design view by clicking the **View** button tool to the left of the Printer button tool.

2 Click **Product ID** located in the Page Header section, then click the **Center** tool on the Format toolbar.

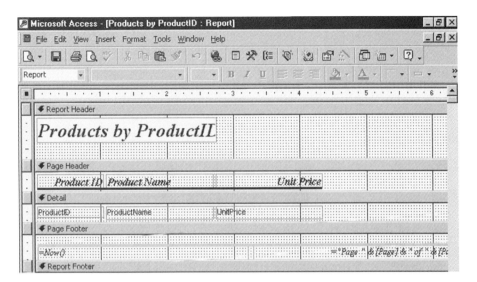

FIGURE 7.18

Product by ProductID Report Design View

3   Click **ProductID** located in the Detail section, and click the **Center** tool on the Format toolbar.

4   Click **Unit Price** located in the Page Header section. Hold the **Shift** key down and click **UnitPrice** in the Detail section as well. (Holding the Shift key down allows you to select both the header and the detail field at the same time.)

5   Click the right handle on the UnitPrice field and drag to the left until the right-most edge of both the UnitPrice field and the Unit Price header are lined up with the 3½-inch marker on the ruler. See Figure 7.19.

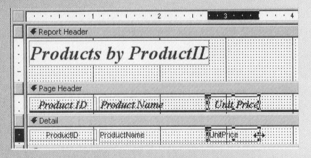

FIGURE 7.19

Resizing Fields in a Report

6   Click anywhere in the **Report window** to unselect the Unit Price fields, then click the **horizontal rule** to select it.

7   Hold the **Shift** key down then click the right-most part of the rule and drag it to the left until it falls just under the Unit Price header. (Holding the Shift key down in this case forces the line to maintain its level.)

8   Click the **View** tool to see the effects of these changes on the final report. Your report should now look like Figure 7.20.

9   Close both the Design and Report views of the Products by ProductID report.

10   When prompted, click **Yes** to save the changes in the Products by ProductID report.

FIGURE 7.20

Resized Report

Products by ProductID

Product ID	Product Name	Unit Price
1	Flower Drop Earrings	$6.00
2	Kinetic Auto Relay	$425.00
3	Le Grand Sport	$275.00
4	G-Shock	$49.00
5	Engagement Ring	$400.00
6	Diamond Earrings	$510.00
7	Diamond Heart Slide	$525.00
8	Diamond Wedding Ring	$650.00

Printing a Report

Often you will want to print the reports created.

To print the Products by ProductID report:

1 Select the **Reports** object then double-click the **Products by ProductID** report.

2 Click the **Print Preview** button to view a reduced-size version of the report to be printed.

3 Click the **Print** button to print the report.

4 Close the Products by ProductID report window.

Nathan and Meagan are both pleased with your changes and impressed with your skills. They recognize that they have just scratched the surface of what Access can do for their business and are anxious to learn more.

END NOTE

In this chapter, you have learned some basics of the Access program, some features of the help system, and how to work with tables, queries, forms, and reports. There is much more to the Access program and much more to know about tables, queries, forms, and reports. The following four chapters will elaborate on each of these, bringing you a keener understanding of how Access is used in accounting.

practice

Chapter 7 Questions

1 What is a database management system?

2 What is Access?

3 What is a relational database?

4 How are tables related in a relational database?

5 Why isn't all information entered into a single table?

6 Identify and describe the first three steps followed in the creation of a database.

7 Which tool is used to establish relationships between tables?

8 What are queries?

9 What facts must be identified for each query?

10 What questions are asked by the simple query wizard?

11 What are the purposes of forms?

12 From where does most of the information in a form come?

13 How are controls used to create forms?

14 Are headers and footers also a part of the record source?

15 What questions does the simple form wizard ask?

16 What are reports?

17 To be useful, how should reports be organized?

18 What questions does the report wizard ask?

19 What are the five steps necessary to create a report?

20 How do you switch between the design view and the layout view when creating reports?

Chapter 7 Assignments

1 *Create new queries for Coast Jewelers*

   a Create and print a query for Coast Jewelers that lists the supplier name, contact name, and phone number of every supplier. (*Note:* Be sure to use the supplier table to locate field names.) Save the query as **Query2**.

   b Create and print another query for Coast Jewelers that lists the supplier name, address, city, and state of every supplier. (*Note:* Be sure to use the supplier table to locate field names.) Save the query as **Query3**.

2 *Create new forms for Coast Jewelers*

   a Create and print a form for Coast Jewelers that lists all fields from the supplier table in a columnar format, Sumi Painting style, using Suppliers as a title. (*Note:* Once again use the supplier table to locate field names.) Print just the first record. Save the form as **Suppliers**.

   b Create and print a form for Coast Jewelers that lists all fields from the category table in a columnar format, Sumi Painting style, using Categories as a title. (*Note:* Use the category table to locate field names.) Print just the first record. Save the form as **Categories**.

3 *Create new reports for Coast Jewelers*

   a Create and print a report for Coast Jewelers that lists the supplier ID, supplier name, and city from the supplier table. (*Note:* Once again use the supplier table to locate field names.) The report should have no grouping, be sorted by supplier ID, in a tabular layout, portrait orientation, in a formal style, and be labeled Suppliers by Supplier ID.

   b Create and print a report for Coast Jewelers that lists the supplier name, contact name, contact title, and phone number from the supplier table. (*Note:* Once again, use the supplier table to locate field names.) The report should have no grouping, be sorted by supplier name, in a tabular layout, portrait orientation, in a corporate style, and be labeled Suppliers by Supplier Name. Make sure all fields are wide enough to present all data by widening the supplier name field and narrowing the contact name field in the report.

4 *Create a new table for Coast Jewelers*

   a Create and print a new table for Coast Jewelers that includes fields labeled BuyerID, BuyerName, and BuyerPhone. The first field (BuyerID) is an AutoNumber data type; the rest are text data types. All should have captions that separate each word (like Buyer ID). Set the BuyerID field as the primary key and save the new table as **Buyers Table**.

   b Enter the following buyer information into the Buyers table:

BuyerID	BuyerName	BuyerPhone
1	Lopez	555-7894
2	Ng	555-1324
3	Fortier	555-9137

   c Add a field to the Product table called BuyerID, a number data type.

   d Add the specific BuyerID information to the following products in the Products table:

ProductID	BuyerID
1	3
2	3
3	2
4	1
5	2
6	3
7	1
8	2

e Establish a one-to-many relationship between the Buyers table and the Product table.

f Create and print a query for Coast Jewelers that lists the product name, buyer name, and buyer phone number for every product. (*Note:* Be sure to use both the product and buyer tables to locate field names.) Save the query as **Query4**.

Chapter 7 Case Problem: Kelly's Boutique

Kelly's Boutique, located in Pewaukee, Wisconsin, sells a unique combination of books and women's shoes. Customers love to peruse her book inventory while trying on the latest in shoe fashions, often buying both books and shoes even though they came in to buy only one. Casey, Kelly's youngest son, a college student studying accounting, is home for the holidays and can't wait to help his mom come in from the dark ages and use computers in her business. In this chapter, and those that follow, Casey will make every attempt to bring his mom up to speed by teaching her the use of Access as it applies to her accounting and business needs.

To begin, Casey suggests that Kelly use a database to keep a record of her book inventory. She does not maintain a large inventory, but she does carry books that she thinks moms in the community might be interested in reading or buying as gifts for their children or friends.

Kelly has a partial list of books she purchases that she thinks should be part of the database. This list includes each book's ISBN, department name, related supervisor, and phone number of the supervisor, the book title, publisher, publisher contact, publisher phone number, author, and list price.

Casey thinks it best to split this information into three tables shown on the following page.

1   Use the information below to create a book table, department table, and publisher table:

Book Table:

ISBN	Dept	Book Title	PubNum	Author	ListPrice
684872153	Adult	*Angela's Ashes*	7	McCourt	$ 7.99
60244151	Children	*Betsy–Tacy*	2	Lovelace	$12.95
670175919	Children	*Blueberries for Sal*	5	McCloskey	$16.99
27136701	Children	*Caddie Woodlawn*	4	Brink	$17.00
140286276	Adult	*Deep End of the Ocean*	3	Mitchard	$12.95
60173289	Adult	*Divine Secrets of the YaYa Sisterhood*	2	Wells	$24.00
394800168	Children	*Green Eggs and Ham*	6	Seuss	$ 7.99
439064864	Children	*Harry Potter and the Chamber of Secrets*	9	Rowling	$17.95
439136350	Children	*Harry Potter and the Prisoner of Azkaban*	9	Rowling	$17.95
590353403	Children	*Harry Potter and the Sorcerer's Stone*	9	Rowling	$17.95

Dept Table:

Dept	Supervisor	Phone
Adult	Nancy Wine	555-9754
Children	Barbara Manchester	555-1974

Publisher Table:

PubNum	Publisher	Contact	Phone
1	Mass Market Paperback	Smith	555-9745
2	Harper Collins	Potter	555-7481
3	Penguin	Frued	555-8974
4	Simon & Schuster	Gonzalez	555-9874
5	Viking Press	Hu	555-1654
6	Random House	Ouimet	555-9144
7	Scholastic Press	Salazar	555-9888
8	Touchstone Books	Chi	555-1112
9	Arthur A. Levine Books	Robinson	555-5118

2   Establish the appropriate relationship between each table.

3   Print each table.

4   Create and print a query that lists deptartment, book title, author, supervisor, publisher, and contact.

5 Create a form and print the first record of that form which shows all fields from the book table, in a columnar format, in a blends style, and label it Book Form.

6 Create and print a report that contains the ISBN, book title, publisher, and phone with no grouping, sorted by book title, and in a tabular portrait layout, and in a bold style with the title Book Report.

Tables

In this chapter you will learn to:

- **Add, change, and delete records**

- **Add a picture with an OLE field**

- **Change the structure of a database**
  - **Change field data types, row heights, and column widths**
  - **Create field validation rules**
  - **Create field default values**
  - **Create field formats**

- **Specify referential integrity**

CASE: COAST JEWELERS, INC.

Nathan and Meagan are impressed with the features of Access as a database program. Kyle cautions them that there is a lot more to Access than what they have seen so far. He explains that the tables they have created can be structured in different ways and that each field can be set up with specific formats, default values, validation rules, etc.

"Wait just a minute," exclaims Nathan. "This sounds more complicated than what we might need!"

"On the contrary," responds Kyle. "These table features, and ones I'll explain later for queries, forms, and reports, are important to the validity of the data included in your database and helpful in making your database useful."

"Let's just take it one step at a time," says Meagan.

Kyle then enlightens them both on the importance of data validity and integrity. He explains that information in your database is of little use if it is incorrect, incomplete, or in an inconsistent format. Over the next few days he plans on explaining tables in more detail.

Let's begin by reviewing the basic procedures for adding, changing, or deleting records from a table.

ADD, CHANGE, AND DELETE RECORDS

In this section, you will learn how to add, change, and delete records from tables. This process can also be done via forms, which will be discussed in a future chapter.

Add Records

You have already added records to the inventory database in Chapter 7 but decided to try it again one more time. Kyle observes your input of adding one more record to the product table.

To add a new record to a table:

1 Using Windows Explorer, copy Chapter 8 Access files from your student disk to your hard drive. Start Access and open the file titled Ch 8 - Coast.mdb from your hard drive. (This is the completed Coast Jewelers Inventory file from Chapter 7.)

2 Select the **Tables** object then double-click the **Product Table**.

3 Click in the Product Name field of a new record next to the (AutoNumber) reference in the Product ID field. Type **Diamond Pendant** in the Product Name field.

4 Press the **Tab** key and type **A one caret top of the line diamond in a gold leaf setting** in the Product Description field.

5 Press the **Tab** key and type **3** as the Supplier ID.

6 Press the **Tab** key and type **3** as the Category ID.

7 Press the **Tab** key and type **1235** as the Product Number.

8 Press the **Tab** key and type **375** as the Unit Price.

9 Press the **Tab** key and type **2** as the Reorder Level.

10 Press the **Tab** key and type **10** as the Lead Time.

11 Press the **Tab** key and type **1** as the Buyer ID.

12 Press the **Tab** key again and note that a new record (product) has been added to the table.

Change Records

Changing records in the table is equally as easy. Kyle suggests you change the supplier for the diamond pendant you just entered from **3** to **2** and change the buyer from **1** to **3**.

To change a record in a table:

1 Double-click the **Supplier ID** field for the Diamond Pendant you just entered. Type **2** to replace the *3* currently listed in this field.

2 Double-click the **Buyer ID** field for the Diamond Pendant you just entered. Type **3** to replace the *1* currently listed in this field. You may have to use the horizontal scroll bars at the bottom of the table to view this field.

3 Press the **Tab** key to move to a new record.

Changing fields for a particular record in a table is easy. So is the procedure for deleting a record.

Delete Records

Kyle warns you that deleting records in a table is a permanent act. It is important to be sure you want to delete a record before proceeding. Access will warn you of this and give you an opportunity to undo your deletion.

To delete a record from a table:

1 Click on the far left side of the table next to the row containing information on Product ID 7. See Figure 8.1.

2 With the Product ID 7 record selected, right-click anywhere in that record to bring up a shortcut menu.

3 Click **Delete Record**. (Alternatively, you could have clicked the Delete Record tool on the Standard toolbar or selected the Delete Record menu item from the Edit menu to delete the record once it was selected.)

FIGURE 8.1 *Deleting a Record from a Table*

Product ID	Product Name	Product Description	Supplier ID	Category ID	Product Numbe
1	Flower Drop Earrings	These elegant earrings h	4	4	136305
2	Kinetic Auto Relay	Energy storage for up to	3	1	SMA113
3	Le Grand Sport	Step-motion second ha	3	1	SKA040
4	G-Shock	Shock resistant, daily ar	5	1	DW004B-4V
5	Engagement Ring	This is a very uniquely de	1	2	LGR29
6	Diamond Earrings	A dazzling pair of dang	2	4	ER-764
7	Diamond Heart Slide	A gorgeous diamond h	1	3	PD-241
8	Diamond Wedding Ri	A dazzling engagemen	1	2	CJ-2275-7
9	Swiss Army Watch	A timely tour of duty...C	5	1	24277
10	Diamond Pendant	A one caret top of the	2	3	1235

Record: ◄◄ ◄ 7 ► ►◄ ►* of 10

4 An Access dialog-warning box appears asking if you are sure you want to delete this record. Click **Yes**, and the record is deleted. See Figure 8.2. Close if you do not continue at this time.

FIGURE 8.2

Delete Warning

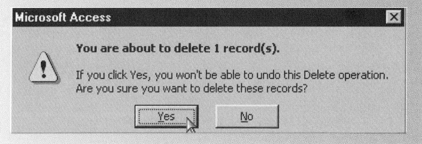

"That was easy," you comment. "Let's continue."

ADD A PICTURE WITH AN OLE FIELD

In this section, you will add a special field to the table and insert pictures to enhance the database. The process requires two steps. Step one is adding a new field to the table, step two is adding a picture to each record.

Add an OLE Field to a Table

Kyle decides to add a picture field to the Product table. The picture, in this case pictures of the jewelry Coast Jewelers sells, is created by either taking a digital picture of each product, or scanning a picture of each product. Nathan has taken digital pictures of each product and saved them as bitmaps (.bmp) files. Since these are not objects Access created, but instead objects created with another application, they need to be inserted as objects into the database. OLE (Object Linking/Embedding) is the integration of objects from other applications.

To add an OLE field to the Product table:

1 Change your view of the table to Design from Datasheet by clicking the **View** tool on the Standard toolbar. (This is presuming you still have the Product table open. If not, open it now.)

2 Scroll down the Design view and click in the **blank field name** under BuyerID.

3 Type **Picture** as the new field name.

4 Press **Tab** to move the cursor to the Data Type column.

5 Select **OLE Object** from the drop-down list of data types.

6 Save the modified table by clicking the **Save** tool on the Standard toolbar. (*Note:* There is no Save command for the database itself. Access automatically saves all data record entries. There is, however, a Save command for changes to table design, query design, form design, etc.)

The table is now ready for additional data. You will need to switch from the design view of the table back to the datasheet view to add pictures of each product.

Add Pictures to the Table

To add pictures to the table you will need your student disk, which has all the bitmap files you'll need to insert into the Product table.

To add a picture to the product table:

1 Change your view of the table to Datasheet from Design by clicking the **View** tool on the Standard toolbar.

2 Scroll to the right of the table to view the Picture field.

3 Right-click the **Picture** field on the first record to reveal the Shortcut menu, then click **Insert Object**.

4 Select **Create** from File. See Figure 8.3 below.

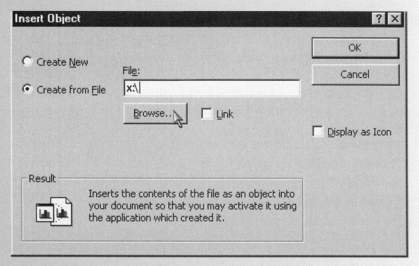

FIGURE 8.3
Insert OLE Object

5 Insert your student disk into your CD-ROM drive.

6 Change the File: edit box to your CD-ROM drive.

7 Click **Browse**.

8 Open the Access folder, then the Chapter 8 folder, then open the Images folder.

9 Several bitmap (.bmp) images should be available. Double-click on **prodid1.bmp** to insert that picture into the Product ID 1 record.

10 Click **OK** in the Insert Object window. This window should then close and the table should now contain the words Bitmap Image in the Picture field of the Product ID 1 record. (*Note:* The name of the .bmp image corresponds to the product number for each product.)

11 Add pictures to the *three* next products following the same procedures.

12 Close the Product table.

You have now added both a placeholder and some data for the picture field. You will enter more pictures later.

"Why don't I see the pictures in the table?" Meagan asks.

"The pictures are there, they are just not shown." Kyle responds. "You'll need to add the picture field to your previously created Product Form to view each picture. We can do that next week when we spend time modifying and creating new forms."

CHANGE THE STRUCTURE OF A DATABASE

When you initially created the Inventory database, you defined its structure by specifying the names, data type, and sizes of all the fields in each table. Often, as was the case in the preceding effort to add a picture field, you will need to change the structure of the database. In addition to adding fields, you may also need to change the field size, resize the field rows or columns, or change the data type.

Additional changes that impact the validity of the data entered include the creation or modification of field validation rules, default values, and field formats.

"That is a very important issue for us," says Nathan. "We can't use this database if the information isn't accurate and reliable. We also need to make it easier for our employees to enter data into the database."

"Exactly the reason for validation rules, default value, and field formats!" Kyle replies.

Change a Field Size, Row Height, Column Width, and Data Type

If you recall, when you first created the Inventory tables, every field you created with a Data Type = Text set the initial field size to 50. That means that a maximum of 50 characters could be entered into that field. In some instances limiting the field size helps prevent errors. For instance, the supplier table has a field for State or Province. If you wanted only a two-character designation for each State or Province, you could set the field size to 2.

To change a field size:

1 Select the **Tables** object then double-click the **Supplier Table**.

2 Change the view to from Datasheet to Design.

3 Click the **StateOrProvince** field name.

4 Under Field Properties, change the Field Size from 50 to **2**. See Figure 8.4.

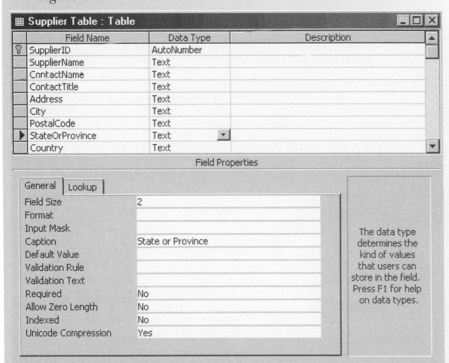

FIGURE 8.4
Changing Field Size

5 Click the **Save** tool on the Standard toolbar.

6 A Some data may be lost warning should appear. Click **Yes** to continue.

7 Change the view from Design to Datasheet.

8 Scroll across to the last suppliers record under the State or Province field. Try to replace NJ with **New Jersey**. Note that you are restricted to two characters.

9 Change the field back to **NJ**.

10 Close the Supplier table.

Viewing data in table format is a quick way to look at all the information available in the table without generating a query or report. Sometimes, however, the information available in a table is not very readable. Take, for instance, the Product table and the related product description. Only part of the description is viewable. That is easily fixed by modifying the row height of each record.

"There is also a lot of wasted space in those tables where the columns are too wide as well," remarks Meagan.

"Let's fix them both," says Kyle.

To modify the Product table's row height and column width:

1 Open the Product table.

2 Place the cursor between product 1 and 2.

3 Click and drag down until the entire product description is revealed as shown in Figure 8.5. Notice how the cursor changed its composition once it was over the line separating each record.

FIGURE 8.5

*Resizing a Record's
Row Height*

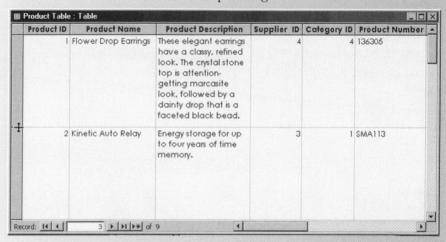

4 Place the cursor between the Product Name and Product Description fields at the top of the table. Note how the cursor has once again changed its composition.

5 Click and drag to the left to resize the column size of the Product Name field as shown in Figure 8.6. Note that because the row was resized you can still see the product name.

FIGURE 8.6

*Resizing a Field's
Column Width*

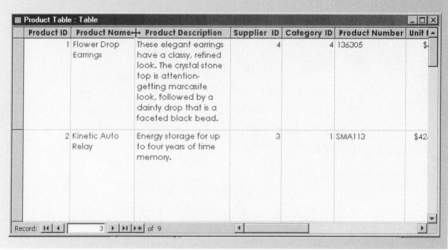

"I have a question," says Meagan. "When I was watching you create the Product table, I noticed you set up the LeadTime field as a data-type text. Why isn't it considered a number?"

"Good question," Kyle responds. "If we plan to use the lead time information as just information for each product, then it doesn't matter whether we set it up as a data type text or number. However, if we later on want to use this field in a calculation, the text data type wouldn't work. I'll show you how easy it is to change a field's data type."

To change a field's data type:

1 Change the view of the Product table from Datasheet to Design.

2 Scroll down the fields listed and click in the Data Type column next to the field name LeadTime.

3 Select **Number** from the drop-down arrow as the new data type for this field as shown in Figure 8.7.

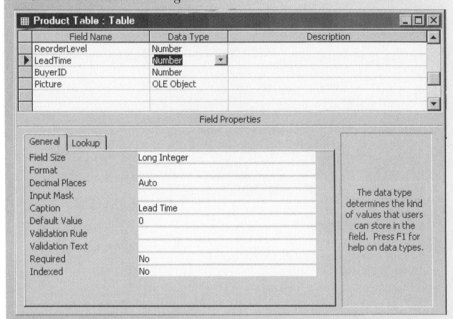

FIGURE 8.7

Changing a Field's Data Type

4 Close and save the changed Product table.

By changing a table's row height and column width, and editing a field's data type and field size, you have been successful in changing the basic structure of a database. Additional changes to a table are possible, including establishing validation rules, default values, and formats, which will be addressed next.

Create Validation Rules

Kyle explains that validation rules improve data integrity and validity. A validation rule checks information entered into the database, a field, for example, and tests the entry to see if it meets certain criteria. If the information entered passes the test the entry is allowed. If the entry fails the test, a warning is provided and the entry is rejected.

"For example, in the Product table, every product should have a unit price entered and every price should be reasonable. You wouldn't want to have a unit price of $0.00 or something greater than $1,000.00," says Kyle.

"This would then prevent someone from entering an unreasonable price but it wouldn't prevent him from entering an incorrect price, right?" asks Nathan.

"Right," Kyle responds. "Validation rules can test for limits like greater than 0 and less than 1,000, or just greater than 100."

Kyle explains that in addition to validating a user's entry into a database, the validation rule can also provide specific feedback to a user as to why the validation test failed. He suggests that you help Meagan and Nathan establish the unit price restriction for the Product table and insure that a price is entered.

To create a validation rule:

1 Open the **Product** table in Design view.

2 Select the **UnitPrice** field.

3 With the UnitPrice field selected, click in the Validation Rule text box and type **>0 And <1000**.

4 With the UnitPrice field still selected, click in the Validation Text text box and type **Unit Price must be > $0 and < $1,000**, as shown in Figure 8.8

FIGURE 8.8

Validation Rules and Text

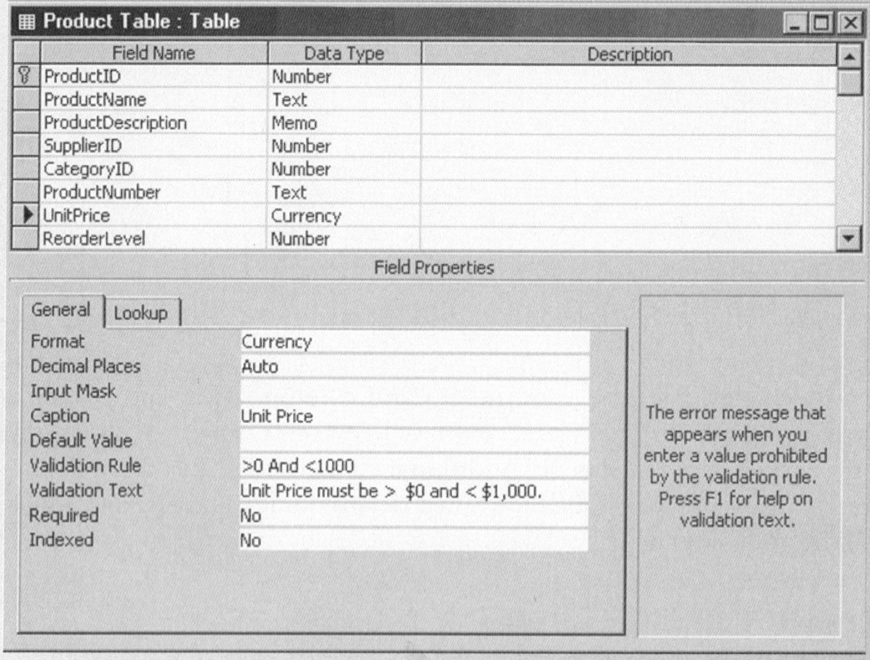

5 Save your changes to the table by clicking on the **Save** tool on the toolbar.

6 Before Access will allow you to save the changes in validation rules it will first ask if you want to test the existing data in the table (specifically the UnitPrice field) to see if it meets with the new rule. See Figure 8.9. Click **Yes** to check the validity of existing information.

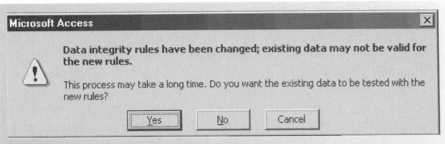

FIGURE 8.9
Warning Message for Changing Validation Rules

7 With the UnitPrice field still selected, change the Required text box from **No** to **Yes**. (This will require that all new records in the Product table have a unit price entered.)

8 Change the view in the Product table to Datasheet.

9 Click **Yes** in the dialog box provided to save the revised table design.

10 Also click **Yes** in the next dialog box provided to once again test to see that existing data meets the new rules.

11 Change the unit price of product ID 1 from **6** to **1500**, then press **Tab**.

12 The dialog box shown in Figure 8.10 should appear.

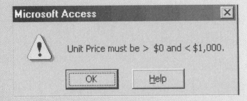

FIGURE 8.10
Validation Text Dialog Box

13 Click **OK**.

14 Change the unit price of Product ID 1 back to **6**, then press **Tab**.

15 Now delete the unit price of Product ID 2, then press **Tab**. The dialog box shown in Figure 8.11 should appear stating that an entry is required in this field.

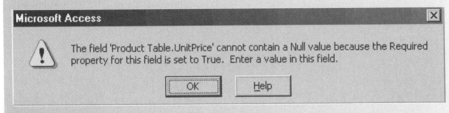

FIGURE 8.11
Required Value Warning

16 Click **OK**.

17 Change the unit price of Product ID 2 back to **425**, then press **Tab**.

18 Close the Product table.

You've now established validation rules, text, and field requirement rules, which will help you maintain data integrity. Another way to insure that valid information is entered into the database is to create default values.

Create Default Values

Default values, as the name implies, provides the person entering data into a database with pre-existing information for certain fields. This can both insure that valid data is entered as well as speed up the process for entering information into a database.

"Repetitive information or information that is present in many or most records is ideal for Access' Default Value option," Kyle explains. "For example, if most of your suppliers are located in New York, then you could set the default value for the state field of the supplier table to **NY**."

"What if a supplier's home state is something other than New York?" you ask.

"Then you simply type over the default value," Kyle answers. "But since most of your suppliers are in the state of New York that won't happen very often."

"Could we also set the default value for country given that most of our suppliers are also located in the United States"?

"Now you're catching on!" Kyle responds.

Kyle instructs you to add a new supplier after you establish NY as the default value for the state field and USA as the default value for the country field of the supplier table.

To create default values:

1 Open the Supplier table in Design view.

2 Select the **StateOrProvince** field.

3 With the StateOrProvince field selected, click in the **Default Value** text box and type **NY** as shown in Figure 8.12.

FIGURE 8.12

Entering Default Values

Field Name	Data Type	Description
City	Text	
PostalCode	Text	
StateOrProvince	Text	
Country	Text	
PhoneNumber	Text	
FaxNumber	Text	

Field Properties

General | Lookup

Field Size	2
Format	
Input Mask	
Caption	State or Province
Default Value	NY
Validation Rule	
Validation Text	
Required	No
Allow Zero Length	No
Indexed	No
Unicode Compression	Yes

A value that is automatically entered in this field for new records

4 Select the **Country** field.

5 With the Country field selected, click the **Default Value** text box and type **USA**.

6 Close the Supplier table and click **Yes** to save your changes.

"Now that should save time as we enter more suppliers," you comment.

Kyle explains that formats and input masks also help insure valid data entry as well as make information meaningful.

Create Formats and Input Masks

Kyle explains that format properties in tables vary depending on the data type assigned each field. For example, a number data type can be pre-formatted as currency ($1,234.56), fixed decimal (1234.56), standard decimal (1,234.56), percent (123%), or other formats. A date/time data type can be pre-formatted as a short date (1/23/03), a long date (Sunday, January 23, 2003), etc. On the other hand, a text data type is not usually subject to a particular format.

"I'd like to add a date to our supplier table so that I know how long I've been doing business with each supplier," Nathan comments. "Can that date be formatted like you mentioned?"

"Certainly," Kyle responds.

"How about formatting phone numbers?" Meagan asks. "Can we format phone numbers so the area code, prefix, and number are always displayed the same?"

"The best way to solve that issues is by using another Access feature called input masks." Kyle answers.

He explains that input masks are used to control how data is entered. This is quite different from the format property referred to previously, which affects only how a value is displayed, not how it is stored in the table. A display format is not applied until the data entered is saved—nothing is displayed in the field to suggest or control the format in which data is entered. If you need to control how data is entered, Kyle suggests you use an input mask in addition to, or instead of, a data display format in those cases.

An input mask ensures that the data will fit in the format you define, and only the kind of values specified can be entered in each blank. In Meagan's example, an input mask would require that all entries contain exactly enough digits to make up a U.S. area code and telephone number, and that only digits, not alpha characters, be entered in each blank.

Kyle instructs you to work with Nathan and Meagan by adding a first purchase date field to the Supplier table and have it displayed in a short date format. In addition, he suggests you modify the Supplier table: phone number field using a phone number mask.

To utilize the format and input mask capabilities of Access:

1   Open the Supplier table in Design view.

2   Create a new field by clicking in the field name text box located under the last field titled FaxNumber.

3   Type **Firstpurchasedate** as the new field name.

4   Select **Date/Time** as the data type for the new field.

5   Select **Short Date** as the format for the new field.

6   Type **First Purchase** as the caption for the new field. Your screen should look like Figure 8.13.

FIGURE 8.13
Setting a Format for a Field

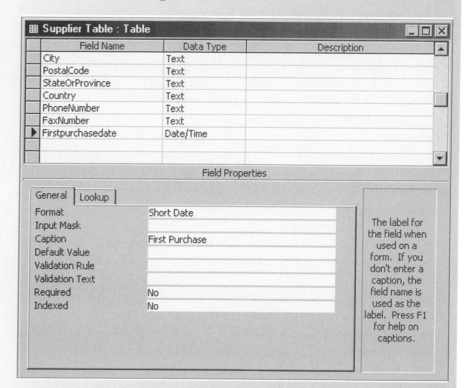

7   Select the **PhoneNumber** field.

8   With the PhoneNumber field selected, click in the Input Mask text box and select the **down arrow** on the far right.
    trouble? The input mask feature may not be installed on your version of Access. If not installed, a message may pop up asking if you want to install it now. If you are in a lab environment please check with your lab administrator before proceeding. If you are at your own computer, have your installation disk handy and follow the instructions to install this feature.

9   Select the **Phone Number** input mask as shown in Figure 8.14, then click **Next**.

10 Click **Next** again to accept the underscore as a placekeeper.

11 Click the option button next to **With the symbols in the mask, like this** to store the symbols with the data.

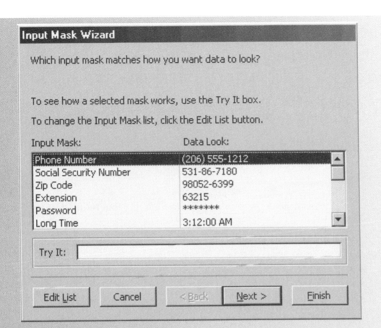

12 Click **Next**, then click **Finish**. Your Supplier table should look like Figure 8.15.

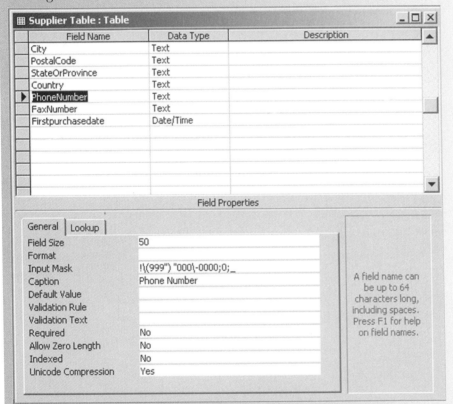

13 Save the changes made to the design of the Supplier table.

14 Change to the **Datasheet view** of the Supplier table.

15 Type **1/01/03** in the First Purchase field of Supplier ID 1.

16 Click in the **First Purchase** field of Supplier ID 2. Note that the date displayed for Supplier ID 1 has changed to 1/1/2003.

17 Type **February 12, 2003** in the First Purchase field of Supplier ID 2.

18 Click in the **First Purchase** field of Supplier ID 3. Note that the date displayed for Supplier ID 2 has changed to 2/12/2003.

19 Type **Mar 20, 2003** in the First Purchase field of Supplier ID 3.

20 Click in the **First Purchase** field of Supplier ID 4. Note that the date displayed for Supplier ID 3 has changed to 3/20/2003.

21 Type **4/30/03** in the First Purchase field of Supplier ID 4 and 5. Part of your screen should look like Figure 8.16.

FIGURE 8.16

Supplier Table after First Purchase Dates Are Entered

		Postal	State	Country	Phone Number	Fax Number	First Purchase
	+	10035	NY	USA	212-555-1354	212-555-6874	1/1/2003
▶	+	76258	TX	USA	940-555-0817	940-555-1187	2/12/2003
	+	07430	NJ	USA	201-555-5730	201-555-3872	3/20/2003
	+	10001	NY	USA	212-555-4166	212-555-9718	4/30/2003
	+	07801	NJ	USA	201-555-3215	201-555-8741	4/30/2003
	+		NY	USA			

Supplier Table : Table

22 Add a new supplier to the Supplier table by typing **Rolex** as the Supplier Name, then press **Tab**.

23 Type **Paula Lyon** as the Contact Name, then press **Tab**.

24 Type **Sales associate** as the Contact Title, then press **Tab**.

25 Type **10332 5th Avenue** as the Address, then press **Tab**.

26 Type **New York** as the City, then press **Tab**.

27 Type **10003** as the Postal Code, then press **Tab**.

28 Press **Tab** twice to accept the default State and Country values of NY and USA.

29 Type **2125551345** as the Phone Number, then press **Tab**. Note the input mask will place the parentheses and dashes accordingly. (Applying the input mask will have an effect on future entries into this field. However, existing entries will not have the area code in parentheses.)

30 Type **2125551346** as the Fax Number, then press **Tab**. Note here that since there is no input mask the data is accepted as is.

31 Go back to the Fax Number field and re-enter the fax number as **212-555-1346** to be consistent with previous entries, then press **Tab**.

32 Type **6/1/03** as the First Purchase field.

33 Close the Supplier table and save any changes you made.

You have now seen the affects and benefits of default values, formatting, and input masks. Perhaps now is a good time to see how Access can enforce additional constraints on data entry to insure that only valid data, available in database tables, is entered as a part of a record.

REFERENTIAL INTEGRITY

In the previous chapter you established relationships between the product, supplier, category, and buyer tables. This action identified the common fields between each table. You can further define that relationship through the use of referential integrity.

Kyle explains that referential integrity is a system of rules that Microsoft Access uses to ensure that relationships between records in related tables are valid, and that you don't accidentally delete or change related data. When referential integrity is enforced, you must observe the following rules.

1 You cannot enter a value in the foreign key field of the related table that does not exist in the primary key of the primary table. A foreign key is a field that refers to the primary key field in another table and indicates how the tables are related—the data in the foreign key and primary key fields must match, though the field names do not have to be the same.

2 You cannot delete a record from a primary table if matching records exist in a related table.

3 You cannot change a primary key value in the primary table if that record has related records.

If you want Microsoft Access to enforce these rules for a relationship, you would select the Enforce Referential Integrity check box when you create or edit the relationship. If referential integrity is enforced and you break one of the rules with related tables, Microsoft Access displays a message and does not allow the change.

"Wait just a minute!" Nathan exclaims. "Primary key, foreign key, referential integrity, I'm confused!"

"I know," responds Kyle. "Let me give you an example and show you how this impacts our product, supplier, category, and buyer tables and I think you will have a better understanding."

Kyle explains that one of the foreign keys he was referring to included the SupplierID field located in the Product table. It is considered a foreign key field since it refers to a primary key field in another table. In this case, the primary key it is referring to is the SupplierID field located in the Supplier table. Kyle also notes that this field, SupplierID, is the primary key field in the Supplier table.

Further, Kyle explains, to insure validity in the Product table we should enforce referential integrity. In doing so, every entry in the SupplierID field of the Product table will have to match one of the records in the SupplierID field of the Supplier table.

"This is still a bit baffling," says Meagan.

"Just watch as I establish referential integrity for the SupplierID field and test it by adding another record," responds Kyle.

To establish referential integrity:

1 Open the Relationships window by either clicking on the **Relationships** tool on the toolbar or selecting Relationships from the Tools menu.

2 Move the tables around the screen so they match Figure 8.17 by clicking in the title bar of each window.

FIGURE 8.17

Relationships Window

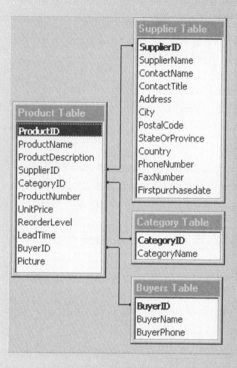

3 Double-click the line which connects the SupplierID field of the Product table with the SupplierID field of the Supplier table.

4 Check in the **Enforce Referential Integrity** check box in the Edit Relationships window as shown in Figure 8.18, then click **OK**.

FIGURE 8.18

*Edit Relationships
Window*

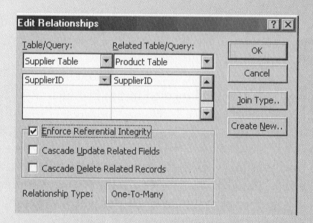

5 Note the changed line connecting the two tables. In particular, note the one-to-many reference shown by the dark line, the 1, and the infinity symbol. Then close the Relationships window. Click **Yes** to save changes.

6 Now open the Product table.

7 Create a new product by typing **11** in the Product ID field, then press **Tab**. Note how the Auto Number feature places item #11 for you.

8 Type **Diamond Studs** in the Product Name field, then press **Tab**.

9 Type **A brilliant pair of .5 ct round cut diamonds**. in the Product Description field, then press **Tab**.

10 Type **10** in the Supplier ID field, then press **Tab**.

11 Type **4** in the Category ID field, then press **Tab**.

12 Type **ER 800** in the Product Number field, then press **Tab**.

13 Type **750** in the Unit Price field, then press **Tab**.

14 Type **1** in the Reorder Level field, then press **Tab**.

15 Type **14** in the Lead Time field, then press **Tab**.

16 Type **1** in the Buyer ID field, then press **Tab**.

17 Press **Tab** again since we do not yet have a picture for this product.

18 Note that the last Tab completes the entry for this new product. However, since you established referential integrity, an error message (see Figure 8.19) appears. This occurred because there is no Supplier ID 10 in the Supplier table, thus Access rejected your entry. Click **OK** in the error message to return to the Product table.

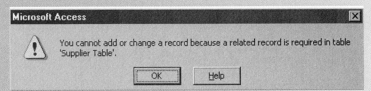

FIGURE 8.19
Access Error Message

19 Type **2** in the Supplier ID field, then close the Product table. This time Access accepts the entry in the Supplier ID field because it matches a record found in the Supplier ID field of the Supplier table.

"That makes more sense now," Meagan and Nathan agree.

END NOTE

In this chapter, you have learned more about the use of tables in the Access program. You have learned how to add, change, and delete records, how to add a picture with an OLE field, and change the structure of a database, including changing field data types and column widths, and changing record row heights. You have also learned how to create field validation rules, default values, and formats. Lastly, you have learned the advantages and functionality of specifying referential integrity. Next you will experience more of the query process.

practice

chapter

8

Chapter 8 Questions

1   Describe the process for deleting a record from a table.

2   Define OLE.

3   What can you do in Access to change the structure of a database?

4   Why would you want to change the column width and/or row height of a table?

5   What do validation rules do?

6   What is the process for adding a validation rule to a field?

7   Why would you establish default values for a field?

8   What are input masks?

9   What is referential integrity?

10   What rules must be followed if referential integrity is enforced?

Chapter 8 Assignments

Make the following changes for Coast Jewelers using the Ch 8 - Coast.mdb file found on your student disk *after* you have completed all the changes specified in the chapter.

1   *Add, change, and delete records to the Coast Jewelers database*

    a Add the following record to the Buyers table: ID 4, Farley, 555-7187.

    b Add Bracelets as a category to the Category table.

    c Delete the following record from the Buyers table: ID 2, Ng.

    d Change the buyer for the following Product IDs from buyer 2 to buyer 4: Product ID 3, 5, 8, and 9.

    e Print the first page of the product, buyers, and category tables as modified.

2   *Add pictures with an OLE field to the Coast Jewelers database*

    a Add pictures for the remaining products in the Product table utilizing picture files found in the images folder for this chapter on your student disk. Each product has a picture associated with it and labeled with the product ID number.

    b Print page 4 of the Product table as modified.

3   *Change the structure of the Coast Jewelers database*

    a Resize the column width of each field and the record's row height of the Product table so that they fit on one page when printed. (Don't worry if not all the information is shown or if the field name isn't fully visible when the table is printed.)

b Add the following product to the Product table: 12, Pearl Necklace, "A 14K gold 18 inch cable chain holds a genuine 6mm round cultured pearl.", 1, 3, PRLN652, 95, 3, 7, 1, prodid12.bmp.

c Change the column widths of the Supplier table so that each heading is fully visible.

d Create a validation rule for the Reorder Level field of the Product table to make the field a required field and to make sure the reorder level is greater than 0 but less than 100 units. Create your own feedback statement and insert it as the validation text.

e Establish the default value for the Lead Time field of the Product table to 7.

f Establish a phone number input mask for the BuyerPhone field of the Buyers table.

g Enforce referential integrity between the Product table and the Buyer and Category tables.

h Print the Product and Supplier tables.

i Print the relationships window. (Choose Print Relationships from the File menu while the Relationships window is open.)

Chapter 8 Case Problem: Kelly's Boutique

In the last chapter you created a database for Kelly's Boutique, which consisted of a book table, department table, and a publisher table. You created an initial form, query, and report. Kelly would now like you to make some adjustments to the tables you created by adding and deleting some records, adding some OLE fields and pictures, and changing the structure of the database. Make the following changes for Kelly using the Ch 8 - Kelly.mdb file found on your student disk:

1 Add Warner as the tenth publisher to the Publisher table with a contact Yee and phone 555-7894.

2 Add the following records to the Book table:

ISBN	Dept	Book Title	Pub Num	Author	List Price
039480029	Children	*Hop on Pop*	6	Seuss	7.99
039480001	Children	*The Cat in the Hat*	6	Seuss	7.99
446676098	Adult	*The Notebook*	10	Sparks	16.95

3 Add a Picture field for OLE objects to the Book table.

4 Add pictures to the Book table for *Green Eggs and Ham*, *Hop on Pop*, *Prisoner of Azkaban*, *Divine Secrets*, and *Deep End of the Ocean*. Picture files are labeled by book name and are located on your student disk.

5 Resize the column width of each field and the record's row height of each table so that they fit on one page when printed.

6 Establish a phone number input mask for the Phone field of the Publisher and Department tables.

7 Enforce referential integrity between the Book table and the Department and Publisher tables.

8 Create a validation rule for the Listprice field of the Book table to make the field a required field and to make sure the price is greater than or equal to $1 but less than or equal to $100. Create your own feedback statement and insert it as the validation text.

9 Establish the default value for the Department field of the Book table to Children.

10 Print the Book, Department, and Publisher tables.

11 Print the Relationships window. (Choose Print Relationships from the File menu while the Relationships window is open.)

9

Queries

In this chapter you will learn to:

- Use a query to display selected records
- Use character data in criteria in a query
- Use wildcards in criteria
- Edit a query
- Use comparison operators and sorting
- Use compound criteria and limit output
- Perform calculations
- Use computed fields
- Compute statistics
- Use an action query to update records
- Use a parameter query
- Use an action query to delete records

CASE: COAST JEWELERS, INC.

Kyle decides to take Meagan and Nathan to the next level of database use by explaining the query process.

"What good is all this information if you can't use it?" he explains. "Access provides you tables as a holder of information, but queries are used to ask questions of the data and retrieve a subset of the total information available."

"Do we have to learn a special language in order to ask questions of the database?" asks Meagan.

"No, but you do need to know some characteristics of the data so that you can use Access's Query By Example (QBE) method of inquiry," he responds.

Kyle decides that he'll begin by explaining how to go about querying the database for specific information such as what necklaces Coast has in inventory and then continue with more complicated queries like which necklaces Coast has in inventory that are above one price but below another.

QUERYING SELECTED RECORDS

Kyle explains that the querying you accomplished in your introduction to Access involved listing specific data from various tables. In these queries you didn't establish any criteria to select specific records, you just specified what specific information you wanted from all records. The next level of inquiry will require you to establish specific criteria for certain fields to narrow down your search for particular records. These are referred to as *select* queries.

"We'll begin with character data, wildcards, and numbers to specify what records we're looking for," Kyle explains.

Using Character Data in a Select Query

Queries can be generated either by using a query wizard as was done in the introduction to Access, or by using the Design view, which is more sophisticated and flexible in query design. Kyle suggests you use the Design view to create a simple query of your inventory file, which has been updated to include a total of 20 records. If a customer was looking for a specific item she may have seen elsewhere, she might ask you if you have a particular watch. You could look that item up in your database by generating a query asking for a specific match to a specific name.

"Why don't we ask the database if it has a specific Seiko watch with a product number of SMA113?" asks Meagan.

"Good idea," Nathan responds. "Let's create such a query which then displays the product number, name, and supplier."

To create a query using character data:

1 Start Access and open the file on your student disk titled Ch 9 - Coast.mdb.

2 Select the **Queries** object, then double-click **Create query in Design view** as shown in Figure 9.1.

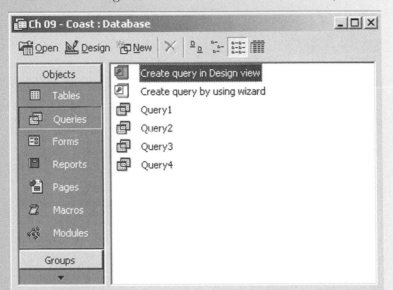

FIGURE 9.1
Creating a Query in Design View

3 Add the Product and Supplier tables to the query, then click the **Close** button on the Show Table window.

4 Double-click the **ProductNumber**, **ProductName**, and **SupplierName** fields from the appropriate tables shown in the query.

5 Type **SMA113** in the criteria section of the query in the Product-Number column of the design grid as shown in Figure 9.2 on the following page.

6 Click **Run** from the Query menu or click the **!** icon from the toolbar. The resulting Datasheet view of the query should look like the query solution in Figure 9.3.

7 Close the Query window and save it as Query5.

The character-based queries work well when you have a specific name or set of characters (like the product number) you are looking for. However, Access users are often in search of records which match some, but perhaps not all of a specific criteria. Wildcards provide that ability.

Using Wildcards in a Select Query

Queries using wildcards allow the user to find such things as field values, records, or filenames. The asterisk (*), which matches any number of characters, can be used as a wildcard as the first or last character in the character string. For example, if Nathan wanted to list all the products he had in inventory that contained the name Seiko, he would type Seiko* as the criteria under the ProductName column.

FIGURE 9.2

Establishing Criteria for Record Selection

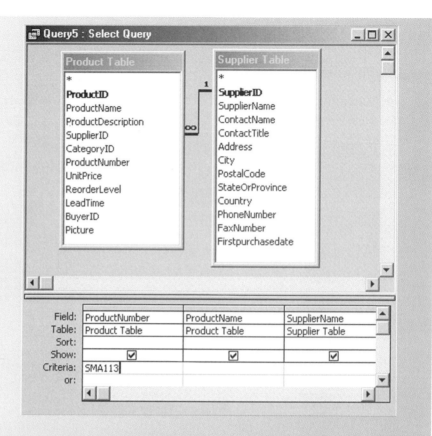

FIGURE 9.3

Query Solution

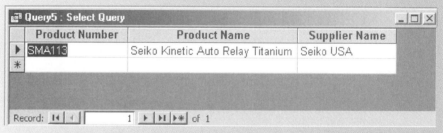

To search for a product using wildcards:

1 Double-click **Create query in Design view** once again.

2 Add the Product table to the query, then click the **Close** button on the Show Table window.

3 Double-click the **ProductName** and **UnitPrice** fields from the Product table shown in the query.

4 Type **Seiko*** in the criteria section of the query in the ProductName column of the design grid as shown in Figure 9.4.

5 Click **Run** from the Query menu or click the **!** icon from the toolbar. The resulting Datasheet view of the query should look like the query solution in Figure 9.5.

6 Close the Query window and save it as Query6.

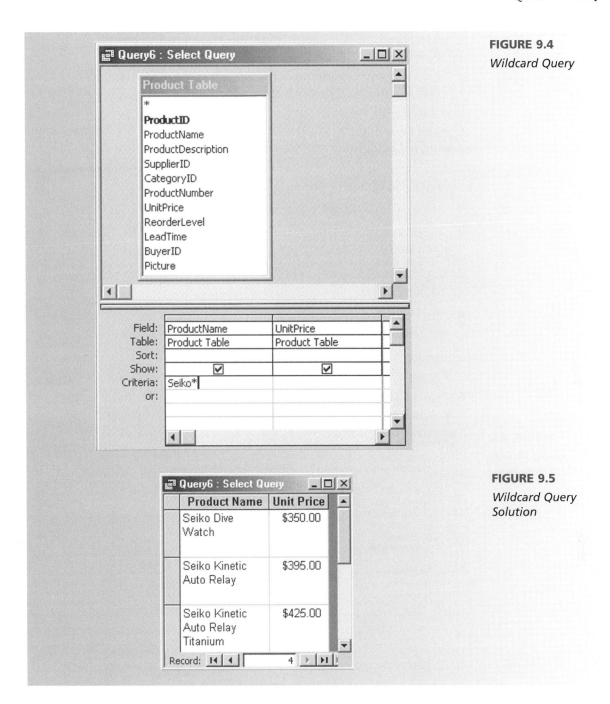

FIGURE 9.4
Wildcard Query

FIGURE 9.5
Wildcard Query Solution

"That's all well and good," Meagan says. "But what if I wanted to add more fields to my query solution?"

"Good question," Kyle responds. "It's easy to change your existing query but you'll notice that Access has saved your query in a slightly different form from how you created it.

Editing a Select Query

Once you've saved a query it can be re-run any number of times. Query5, for instance, which looked up a particular product number from the database could be run again for the same or a different product number.

Query6 could be run again using the same criteria but asking for the same or different fields of information.

Kyle suggests you demonstrate the query editing features of Access by modifying Query5 to look up a different product number (LGR29) and adding the buyer's name to the result. He also suggests you modify Query6 to look up all product names containing the word *diamond* and adding the category name to the result.

To edit Query5 and Query6:

1 Double-click **Query5** from the Query listing.

2 Select **Design View** from the View menu or click the View icon on the toolbar.

3 Select **Show Table** from the View menu or click the Show Table icon on the toolbar.

4 Add the Buyers table to the query, then click the **Close** button on the Show Table window.

5 Double-click the **BuyerName** field from the Buyers table shown in the query.

6 Type **LGR29** in the criteria section of the query in the ProductNumber column as shown in Figure 9.6 below.

FIGURE 9.6

Edited Query5 in Design View

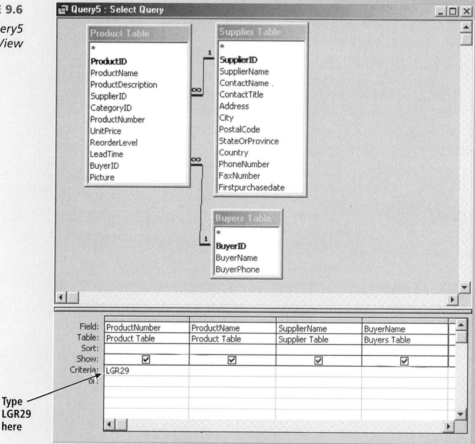

Type LGR29 here

trouble? Before typing the new criteria specified for this query, note that the previous product number has automatically been placed in quotes. You don't need to initially type the quotes in before making this query but Access knows that quotes are needed for future instances of this query.

7 Click **Run** from the Query menu or click the **!** icon from the toolbar. The resulting query now shows an engagement ring from Johnson Wholesaler Jewelry Supply and Coast Jewelers' buyer Farley.

8 Click **Save As** from the File menu and save this revised query as Query7. Close the Query window.

9 Double-click **Query6** from the Query listing.

10 Select **Design View** from the View menu or click View icon on the toolbar.

11 Sclect **Show Table** from the View menu or click the Show Table icon on the toolbar.

12 Add the Category table to the query, then click the **Close** button on the Show Table window.

13 Double-click the **Category Name** field from the Category table shown in the query.

14 Type **Diamond*** in the criteria section of the query in the ProductName column as shown in Figure 9.7 below.

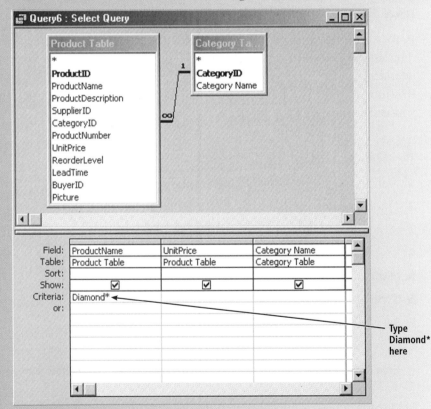

FIGURE 9.7

Edited Query6 in Design View

trouble? Before typing the new criteria specified for this query, note that the previous criteria had automatically been replaced. When you typed Seiko* after running the query, Access saved the query with the criteria Like "Seiko*". Once again you don't need to initially type the quotes in before making this query but Access knows that quotes are needed for future instances of this query and that the Like reference delineates the wildcard nature of the query.

15 Click **Run** from the Query menu or click the **!** icon from the toolbar. The resulting query now shows six different products which have Diamond in the ProductName field; one ring, two necklaces, and three earrings.

16 Click **Save As** from the File menu and save this revised query as Query8.

17 Close the Query window.

"I'm impressed!" exclaims Meagan. "This query stuff isn't so difficult; in fact it's rather intuitive."

Kyle continues with his explanation of queries by showing additional examples of the query process. So far he has used characters in his queries. Now it is time to demonstrate the use of numbers in queries and show how comparison operators can be used in a select query.

Using Comparison Operators and Sorting in a Select Query

Before continuing, Kyle thought you might like to add some additional data to your inventory database. Specifically, each item of inventory would normally have some balance on hand at a particular date. Once this information is a part of your database you'll be able to track items you're running short of or items you need to place on sale.

To enter quantity on hand:

1 Continue with the Ch 9 - Coast.mdb file.

2 Open the Product table to create a new field.

3 Switch to the Design view.

4 Right-click on the row header for the UnitPrice field.

5 Click **Insert Rows**.

6 Type **Quantity** as the field name and set the Data Type to **Number**.

7 Save the table, then switch to the Datasheet view.

8 Enter the following quantities for each Product ID:

Prod. ID	Quan.	Prod. ID	Quan.	Prod. ID	Quan.	Prod. ID	Quan.
1	10	6	2	11	3	16	5
2	4	7	4	12	15	17	8
3	5	8	5	13	3	18	1
4	10	9	3	14	9	19	0
5	12	10	7	15	7	20	2

9 Close the Product table and save any changes.

Now that your database contains quantity information Kyle suggests you create a select query to find all inventory items for which quantity balances are running low (less than or equal to two items, for instance). To do so, Kyle explains that you simply modify your criteria to include comparison operators like the < symbol, which signifies less than. He cautions you, however, that the less than symbol, just like the greater than symbol (>), is not inclusive of the number specified. Thus to generate a query that selects those records for which inventory quantities are less than or equal to a certain number, it will be important to include both the < and the = symbols.

To select records for which inventory quantities are less than or equal to 2:

1 Click **Create query in Design view** from the Query window.

2 Include the Product table only in this query.

3 Include only the ProductName and Quantity fields in this query.

4 Type **<=2** in the criteria row of the Quantity field of the design grid.

5 Run the query. Your results should look like Figure 9.8 below.

6 Save the query as Quantity <= 2.

Product Name	Quantity
Seiko Kinetic Auto Relay	1
Seiko Dive Watch	0
Rolex Oyster Submariner	2
Diamond Earrings	2

FIGURE 9.8

Quantity Query Results

"Wouldn't you get the same results if you set the criteria as <2?" Nathan asks.

"No, you wouldn't." responds Kyle. "Let me demonstrate."

To select records with criteria of <2:

1 Modify the query saved above.

2 Type **<2** in the criteria row of the Quantity field of the design grid, replacing the <=2.

3 Run the query. Your results should look like Figure 9.9 below.

4 Close the query but do not save changes.

Product Name	Quantity
Seiko Kinetic Auto Relay	1
Seiko Dive Watch	0

FIGURE 9.9

Modified Quantity Query Results

Kyle compares the two query results to demonstrate to Nathan the differences. He explains that the equal sign was important so that all records with a quantity of 2 or fewer were selected.

"What other comparison operators are available in Access?" asks Meagan.

Kyle responds that in addition to the < and = symbols, Access allows you to select records using any combination of <, =, or >. For instance you could ask for records in which the price was between $500 and $1,000 by using the < and > symbols together. Or you could not use the symbols and simply ask for the records in which the unit price was between 500 and 1000.

"Could we also sort the results from lowest to highest price?" asks Meagan.

"Yes," Kyle answers. "Access queries allow for sorting the results in either ascending or descending order.

To select records with a price between $500 and $1,000 and sort the results:

1 Click **Create query in Design view** from the Query window.

2 Include the Product table only in this query.

3 Include only the ProductName and UnitPrice fields in this query.

4 Type **>500 And <1000** in the criteria row of the UnitPrice field of the design grid.

5 Click **Ascending** from the drop-down menu in the Sort cell of the UnitPrice field as shown in Figure 9.10.

FIGURE 9.10

Design View for Comparison Query

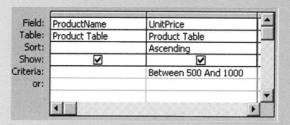

6 Run the query. Your results should look like Figure 9.11 below.

FIGURE 9.11

Unit Price Query Results

Product Name	Unit Price
Diamond Earrings	$510.00
Diamond Wedding Ring	$650.00
Diamond Studs	$750.00
Diamond Heart Slide	$875.00
Diamond Solitare Earrings	$995.00

7 Modify the criteria row of the UnitPrice field to read **Between 500 And 1000**.

8 Run the query. Your results should still look like Figure 9.11.

9 Save this query as Unit Price between 500 and 1000.

10 Close this query.

Kyle explains that so far you've specified criteria for only one field. Access allows you to specify criteria for more than one field using specific or comparison operators.

Using Compound Criteria and Limiting Output in a Select Query

Compound criteria allow you to select records from a database using more than one field. These criteria can be applied to require that all criteria be met or they can be applied such that only one criterion be met to select a record. The field upon which the criteria are applied must be included in the query but doesn't necessarily have to be included in the output.

"Let's create a query that includes product name and unit price for all products with a unit price greater than $500 and a buyer ID of 1 or 3 sorted by product name," suggests Kyle.

"Do we have to include the Buyers table in this query?" Meagan asks.

"No, since the buyer ID is a part of the Product table, it won't be necessary to include the Buyers table," answers Kyle.

To create a query which includes product name and unit price for all products with a unit price greater than $500 *and* a buyer ID of 1 or 3:

1 Click **Create query in Design view** from the Query window.

2 Include the Product table only in this query.

3 Include only the ProductName, UnitPrice, and BuyerID fields in this query.

4 Type **>500** in the criteria row of the UnitPrice field of the design grid. Make sure the Show check box in the UnitPrice field of the design grid is selected.

5 Type **1 Or 3** in the criteria row of the BuyerID field of the design grid.

6 Unselect the **Show** check box under the BuyerID field.

7 Click Ascending from the drop-down menu in the Sort cell of the ProductName field. Your screen should look like Figure 9.12.

Field:	ProductName	UnitPrice	BuyerID
Table:	Product Table	Product Table	Product Table
Sort:	Ascending		
Show:	☑	☑	☐
Criteria:		>500	1 Or 3
or:			

FIGURE 9.12

Design View for Compound Query

8 Run the query. Your results should look like Figure 9.13 below.

Product Name	Unit Price
Diamond Earrings	$510.00
Diamond Heart Slide	$875.00
Diamond Solitare Earrings	$995.00
Diamond Studs	$750.00

FIGURE 9.13

Results of Compound Query

9 Save this query as Unit Price > $500 AND Buyer 1 or 3, but do not close it.

As an alternative Kyle explains that the criteria specified on multiple fields can require that all records satisfy all criteria or that the criteria specified on multiple fields satisfy one or more criteria. For example, the previous query asked for all records in which the unit price was greater than $500 *and* for which the buyer was 1 or 3. Another query might ask for all records in which the unit price was greater than $500 *or* for which the buyer was 1 or 3. This, as you will see, will yield different results.

To create a query which includes product name, unit price, and buyer ID for all products with a unit price greater than $500 *or* a buyer ID of 1 or 3:

1 Move the **1 Or 3** in the criteria row of the BuyerID field down one row to the or: row of the design grid as shown in Figure 9.14.

FIGURE 9.14

Modified Design View for Compound Query

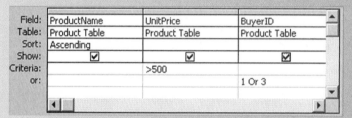

2 Select the **Show** check box under the BuyerID field.

3 Run the query. Your results should look like Figure 9.15 below.

FIGURE 9.15

Results of Modified Compound Query

Product Name	Unit Price	Buyer ID
Diamond Earrings	$510.00	3
Diamond Heart Slide	$875.00	1
Diamond Pendant	$375.00	3
Diamond Solitare Earrings	$995.00	3
Diamond Studs	$750.00	1
Diamond Wedding Ring	$650.00	4
Flower Drop Earrings	$6.00	3
G-Shock	$49.00	1
Pearl Necklace	$95.00	1
Rolex Oyster Submariner	$2,999.00	5
Seiko Kinetic Auto Relay Titanium	$425.00	3
Tanzanite Ring	$445.00	1
Topaz Necklace	$375.00	3

4 Close and save this query as Unit Price > $500 OR Buyer 1 or 3.

Kyle points out that in this modified query the G-Shock record is present even though its unit price is less than $500 since its buyer ID is 1 or 3. Likewise the Diamond Wedding Ring record is present even though its buyer ID is 4 since its unit price is greater than $500.

PERFORMING CALCULATIONS

Kyle explains that there are many types of calculations you can perform in a query. For example, you can calculate the sum or average of the values in one field, multiply the values in two fields, or calculate the date three months from the current date. When you display the results of a calculation in a field, the results aren't actually stored in the underlying table. Instead, Microsoft Access reruns the calculation each time you run the query so that the results are always based on the most current information in the database.

Displaying the Results of Calculations in a Field

To demonstrate the use of computations and the creation of a computed field Kyle suggests that you and Nathan create a query which calculates the cost of each item in inventory. He explains that to begin you'll first need to create a query which includes the field's product name, quantity, and unit price. Then you'll need to create a computed field to calculate the product of the quantity and the unit price fields. To create a computed field you'll need to type the name of the newly created field in a blank field row followed by the two fields used to compute total cost. Each field used must be surrounded by brackets like [Quantity]. After you've created the computed field you'll often need to format the field to a number or currency depending on how you want it displayed.

To create an inventory cost query:

1 Click **Create query in Design view** from the Query window.

2 Include the Product table only in this query.

3 Include only the ProductName, Quantity, and UnitPrice fields in this query.

4 In the fourth column on the Field row of the design grid type **Cost: [Quantity]*[UnitPrice]** as shown in Figure 9.16.

Field:	ProductName	Quantity	UnitPrice	Cost: [Quantity]*[UnitPrice]
Table:	Product Table	Product Table	Product Table	
Sort:				
Show:	☑	☑	☑	☑
Criteria:				
or:				

FIGURE 9.16

Creating a Calculated Field

5 Select **View** from the menu and **Properties** from the drop-down menu, which takes you to the Field Properties window.

6 Select **Currency** from the drop-down menu on the row labeled Format, then close the Field Properties window.

7 Run the query to yield the results shown in Figure 9.17 on the following page.

8 Save this query as Inventory Cost.

Once again the resulting value established in the Cost field is there only temporarily and can only be used in a later report or form if this query is run as well. In addition to creating a computed field, Access will allow you to perform statistics and summations from within a query.

FIGURE 9.17

Resulting Inventory Cost Query

Product Name	Quantity	Unit Price	Cost
Flower Drop Earrings	10	$6.00	$60.00
Seiko Kinetic Auto Relay Titanium	4	$425.00	$1,700.00
Le Grand Sport	5	$275.00	$1,375.00
G-Shock	10	$49.00	$490.00
Engagement Ring	12	$400.00	$4,800.00
Diamond Earrings	2	$510.00	$1,020.00
Diamond Heart Slide	4	$875.00	$3,500.00
Diamond Wedding Ring	5	$650.00	$3,250.00
Swiss Army Watch	3	$175.00	$525.00
Diamond Pendant	7	$375.00	$2,625.00
Diamond Studs	3	$750.00	$2,250.00
Pearl Necklace	15	$95.00	$1,425.00
Diamond Solitare Earrings	3	$995.00	$2,985.00
Tanzanite Ring	9	$445.00	$4,005.00
Blue Topaz Ring	7	$249.00	$1,743.00
Topaz Necklace	5	$375.00	$1,875.00
Amethyst Pendant	8	$195.00	$1,560.00
Seiko Kinetic Auto Relay	1	$395.00	$395.00
Seiko Dive Watch	0	$350.00	$0.00
Rolex Oyster Submariner	2	$2,999.00	$5,998.00

Computing Statistics

Access will allow you to calculate various statistical measures of your database including sum, average, maximum, and minimum for example.

"What if I needed to know my total inventory cost?" asks Nathan.

"No problem," Kyle responds. "Access has a sum function which will work on the cost variable we just created. All we need to do is turn on the sum function and then create a sum query using the cost field we defined. To do so it will be important to select the query we just created instead of an existing table."

To create a sum query:

1 Click **Create query in Design view** from the Query window.

2 Click the **Queries** tab in the Show Table window.

3 Double-click the **Inventory Cost** query, then close the Show Table window.

4 Double-click the **Cost** field.

5 Select **Totals** from the View menu or click the Totals button on the toolbar.

6 Select **Sum** from the drop-down menu on the Totals row as shown in Figure 9.18 on the following page.

7 Run the query to generate a summation of all inventory cost as shown in Figure 9.19.

8 Save the query as Inventory cost summary.

9 Close this query.

"Is there any way to find the total cost of inventory by category?" asks Nathan.

"Yes," Kyle answers. "Access uses the concept of grouping to provide statistical information on a database."

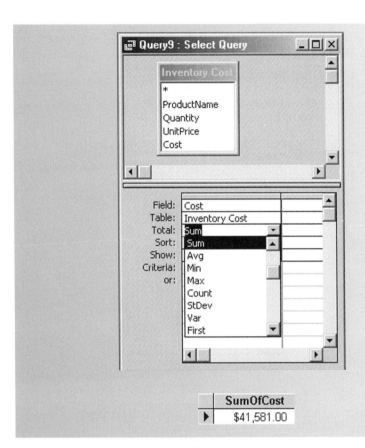

FIGURE 9.18
Using the Sum Function

SumOfCost
▶ $41,581.00

FIGURE 9.19
Resulting Sum Query

Kyle goes on to explain than since the field he summed previously was a calculated field, it is imperative that the category field be a part of that query before a sum query is run. He suggests that you edit the inventory cost query and include the category field in it before modifying the Inventory cost summary query you just created.

To create a sum query by category:

1 Open the Inventory Cost query, and click on **Design view**.

2 Click **Show Table** from the Query menu.

3 Add the **Category Table** to this query then close the Show Table window.

4 Double-click the **Category Name** field to add it to the query.

5 Close and save the revised query.

6 Re-open the Inventory cost summary query in the Design view.

7 Click and drag the **Category Name** field from the Inventory Cost table in the query to the existing Cost field as shown in Figure 9.20 on the following page.

8 The result should be the placement of the Category Name field to the left of the existing Cost field. (This is important since we want total cost of inventory by category.) See Figure 9.21.

9 Run the query to generate a summation of all inventory cost by category as shown in Figure 9.22.

FIGURE 9.20

*Click and Drag the
Category Name Field*

FIGURE 9.21

*Revised Design View
of the Inventory Cost
Summary Query*

FIGURE 9.22

*Resulting Sum Query
by Category*

Category Name	SumOfCost
Earrings	$6,315.00
Necklaces	$10,985.00
Rings	$13,798.00
Watches	$10,483.00

10 Save the query as Inventory Cost Summary by Category.

11 Close the query.

"That's great information," says Nathan. "Is there a way to find out how many watches, necklaces, etc. we have on hand or how many different products we have in each category?"

"Sure," responds Kyle. "We can use the sum feature again to sum up the quantity of each category and the count feature to count the number of products we have by category."

Kyle explains that the sum feature in this case can be used on the product and category tables since the information we want to display and sum is found in the tables and not any particular query. Likewise the count feature is used on the same two tables. He recommends that you and Meagan give it a try.

To create a sum query of quantities by category:

1 Click **Create query in Design view** from the Query window.

2 Add the Category and Product table to this query then close the Show Table window.

3 Double-click the **Category Name** and the **Quantity** fields to add them to the query.

4 Select **Totals** from the View menu or click the Totals button on the toolbar.

5 Select **Sum** from the drop-down menu on the Totals row in the Quantity field column.

6 Run the query. Your result should look like Figure 9.23.

7 Save the query as Sum of quantity by category. Close the query.

Category Name	SumOfQuantity
▶ Earrings	18
Necklaces	39
Rings	33
Watches	25

FIGURE 9.23

Sum of Quantity by Category

"That was fairly easy," Meagan says. "Let's let Nathan see if he can create the count query."

To create a sum query of quantities by category:

1 Click **Create query in Design view** from the Query window.

2 Add the Category and Product table to this query then close the Show Table window.

3 Double-click the **Category Name** and the **Product Name** fields to add them to the query.

4 Select **Totals** from the View menu or click the Totals button on the toolbar.

5 Select **Count** from the drop-down menu on the Total row in the ProductName field column of the design grid.

6 Run the query. Your result should look like Figure 9.24.

7 Save the query as Count of products by category. Close the query.

Category Name	CountOfProductName
▶ Earrings	4
Necklaces	5
Rings	4
Watches	7

FIGURE 9.24

Count of Products by Category

Next Kyle will explain the process of using action queries to affect many records at one time.

ACTION QUERIES (UPDATE, PARAMETER, AND DELETE)

. . . .

An action query is a query that makes changes to many records in just one operation. There are two types of action queries that Kyle would like to explain: update and delete. An update query makes global changes to a group of records in one or more tables. For example, you can raise costs or sales prices by 10 percent for all products, or you can raise salaries by 5 percent for the people within a certain job category. With an update query, you can change data in existing tables. A parameter query is a query that when run displays its own dialog box prompting you for information, such as criteria for retrieving records or a value you want to insert in a field. A delete query removes a group of records from one or more tables. With delete queries, you always delete entire records, not just selected fields within records.

Update Queries

Nathan would like to use an update query to increase the cost of all products by 5 percent. To do so he'll need to use an update query that includes the Product table and the field UnitPrice.

To create and update query to increase the cost of all products by 5 percent:

1 Click **Create query in Design view** from the Query window.

2 Add the Product table to this query then close the Show Table window.

3 Double-click the **UnitPrice** field to add it to the query.

   trouble? Unfortunately, there is no way to restore the information corrupted by selecting ProductName, for instance, instead of UnitPrice in an Update Query.

4 Select **Update Query** from the Query menu.

5 Type **[UnitPrice]*1.05** in the Update To: row of the design grid as shown in Figure 9.25.

FIGURE 9.25

Update Query

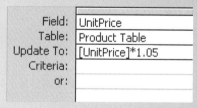

Field:	UnitPrice
Table:	Product Table
Update To:	[UnitPrice]*1.05
Criteria:	
or:	

6 Run the query.

7 Click **Yes** to continue the update process.

8 Save the query as Unit Price Update. Close the query.

9 Open the Product table and note that the unit prices have all been increased by 5 percent.

10 Close the Product table.

"Very slick and efficient!" says Meagan. "This software is going to be very helpful for us in maintaining our inventory. Do we always have to update all records or can we limit an update to just a few records?"

"You can limit your update by setting criteria for the update just like a select query," Kyle answers. "Let's have you update all records that have a reorder level of 1 to reflect a new reorder level of 2."

To create and update query to update reorder levels:

1 Click **Create query in Design view** from the Query window.

2 Add the Product table to this query then close the Show Table window.

3 Double-click the **ReorderLevel** field to add it to the query.

4 Select **Update Query** from the Query menu.

5 Type **2** in the Update To: row then type **=1** in the Criteria: row of the design grid as shown in Figure 9.26.

Field:	ReorderLevel
Table:	Product Table
Update To:	2
Criteria:	=1
or:	

FIGURE 9.26

Update Query

6 Run the query.

7 Click **Yes** to continue the update process.

8 Save the query as ReorderLevel Update. Close the query.

9 Open the Product table and note that there or no more products with a reorder level of 1. They have all been changed to a reorder level of 2.

10 Close the Product table.

Parameter Queries

Another type of action query is the parameter query, in which the query prompts the user with a dialog box asking for some criteria information to select records.

"When would I want to use this type of query?" Meagan asks.

These queries, Kyle explains, are used when you're not sure what criteria the user wants to specify for record selection. They provide flexibility in the query process and will be very handy in the future when forms and reports are generated for users who aren't that familiar with Access.

"Let's create a parameter query to provide information on who is responsible for buying each product," suggests Nathan. "Can this query just give us information on one buyer?"

"Yes," responds Kyle. "I suggest you and Meagan create this query now."

To create a parameter query for buyers:

1 Click **Create query in Design view** from the Query window.

2 Add the Product and Buyers tables to this query then close the Show Table window.

3 Add the BuyerName, ProductName, and Quantity fields to the query.

4 Type **[Enter Buyer's Name]** in the Criteria: row of the BuyerName field of the design grid as shown in Figure 9.27.

FIGURE 9.27

Parameter Query

Field:	BuyerName	ProductName	Quantity
Table:	Buyers Table	Product Table	Product Table
Sort:			
Show:	☑	☑	☑
Criteria:	[Enter Buyer's Name]		
or:			

5 Run the query.

6 Type **Lopez** in the Enter Parameter Value dialog box presented, then click **OK** to produce the results as shown in Figure 9.28.

7 Save the query as Buyer ?. Close the query.

FIGURE 9.28

Parameter Query Results

Buyer Name	Product Name	Quantity
Lopez	Diamond Studs	3
Lopez	Pearl Necklace	15
Lopez	Tanzanite Ring	9
Lopez	Diamond Heart Slide	4
Lopez	G-Shock	10

The last action query Kyle wants to demonstrate deletes specific records from your database.

Delete Queries

"Occasionally," Kyle explains, "you might want to delete some records from your database based on specific criteria. For example, you may want to delete all records in a table which have a quantity balance of zero."

"I'll bet you set the criteria to = 0, right?" asks Meagan.

"Well, almost," Kyle answers. "First you must create a specific delete query, include all the fields from the table, and then specify the criteria that must be met for the deletion of a record."

"Let's give it a try," says Nathan.

To use a delete query to delete specific records:

1 Click **Create query in Design view** from the Query window.

2 Add the Product table to this query then close the Show Table window.

3   Click the **arrow** next to the Query Type button on the toolbar and then click **Delete Query** or select Delete Query from the Query menu.

4   Add all fields to the query by double-clicking the ***** from the field list.

5   Double-click the **Quantity** field.

6   Note that the word From appears on the Delete: line of the design grid under Product Table.* and the word Where appears on the Delete: line under Quantity.

7   Type **0** in the Criteria: row of the design grid under the column Quantity as shown in Figure 9.29 below.

Field:	Product Table.*	Quantity
Table:	Product Table	Product Table
Delete:	From	Where
Criteria:		0
or:		

FIGURE 9.29

Parameter Query

8   Run the query.

9   Click **Yes** in the dialog box presented to delete one record from the Product table.

10 Save the query as **Delete zero quantity products**. Close the query.

11 Open the Product table and note that there are no more products with a quantity of 1. (Product ID 19 has been removed.)

12 Close the Product table.

END NOTE

· ·

In this chapter you have learned how to use select queries with characters, numbers, wildcards, comparison operators, and compound criteria. You've also performed calculations, computed statistics, created computed fields, and created parameter queries and action queries to update and delete records. In the next chapter you'll learn how to use forms.

practice

Chapter 9 Questions

1 Describe the difference between the query wizard and design view methods of creating a query.

2 Describe the process for using criteria in a query using the design view method.

3 How and why are wildcards used in a query?

4 Describe the process for adding a field to an existing query that exists in a table not currently included in the query.

5 What are the three key comparison operators used in a query?

6 What will compound criteria allow you to accomplish in Access?

7 Are the results of a calculation stored as a field in a table?

8 What is an action query? Give examples.

9 What is a parameter query?

10 When might you use a delete query?

Chapter 9 Assignments

1 *Create additional select queries for Coast Jewelers using specific criteria*

　　a Create and print a select query for Coast Jewelers that lists the buyer name, phone number, and product name of a product with a product number ER-800. Save this query as **Ch 9 Assignment 1a** before you print it.

　　b Create and print another select query for Coast Jewelers that lists whatever information you'd like from at least two tables. Specify the criteria from one field of your choice. (Be sure to write on your query the criteria you specified.) Save this query as **Ch 9 Assignment 1b** before you print it.

2 *Create additional select queries for Coast Jewelers using wildcards*

　　a Create and print a select query for Coast Jewelers that lists the product name, category name, and lead time for any product name that includes the words *Seiko Kinetic*. Save this query as **Ch 9 Assignment 2a** before you print it.

　　b Create and print another select query for Coast Jewelers that lists whatever information you'd like from at least two tables. Specify the criteria from one field of your choice. (Be sure to write on your query the wildcard criteria you specified.) Save this query as **Ch 9 Assignment 2b** before you print it.

3   *Edit select queries for Coast Jewelers*

   a Edit Query3 (created in the chapter) to include the fields product name and buyer name and to include only supplier *Casio USA*. Save this query as **Ch 9 Assignment 3a** before you print it.

   b Edit Query4 (created in the chapter) to include the field Category Name and to include only the category *Rings*. Save this query as **Ch 9 Assignment 3b** before you print it.

4   *Create additional select queries for Coast Jewelers using comparison operators*

   a Create and print a select query for Coast Jewelers that lists the product name, unit price, supplier name, and supplier contact name for any unit price between $300 and $600. Save this query as **Ch 9 Assignment 4a** before you print it.

   b Create and print a select query for Coast Jewelers that lists the product name, unit price, and category name for any unit price less than or equal to $200 sorted in ascending order by unit price. Save this query as **Ch 9 Assignment 4b** before you print it.

5   *Create additional select queries for Coast Jewelers using computed fields*

   a Create and print a select query for Coast Jewelers that lists the product name and sales price for all watches. *Hint:* You'll need to create a computed field titled Sales Price, the formula for which would be the product's unit price times 1 + the sales price markup. Be sure to format the computed field to Currency and to include the fields SalesMarkup and Category Name from the Category table and UnitPrice from the Product table even though they won't be shown in the resulting query. Save this query as **Ch 9 Assignment 5a** before you print it.

   b Open the query created above, then modify and print a select query for Coast Jewelers that lists the product name, sales price, quantity, and sales value for all rings. *Hint:* You'll need to create another computed field, *Sales Value*, the formula for which would be the previously computed sales price times quantity. You will also need to change the criteria from watches to rings. Be sure to format the computed field to Currency. Sort this query by sales price in descending order. Save this query as **Ch 9 Assignment 5b** before you print it.

6   *Create additional select queries for Coast Jewelers using statistics*

   a Create and print a select query for Coast Jewelers that calculates the sales value of all watches in inventory. *Hint:* You'll need to use your completed query from 5b above. Be sure to format this computed field to Currency with two decimal places. Save this query as **Ch 9 Assignment 6a** before you print it.

b Create and print a query for Coast Jewelers that includes all products by category name, product name, quantity, unit price, sales markup, and sales value (a computed field equal to the product of quantity times unit price times 1 plus the sales markup). Save this query as **Ch 9 Assignment 6b** before you print it.

c Next create and print a query which sums the sales value of each category using the query just created in (b) above as the source. Save this query as **Ch 9 Assignment 6c** before you print it.

7 *Create action queries for Coast Jewelers*

a Create and run an action query for Coast Jewelers that increases the sales markup 5 percent for all categories. *Hint:* You'll need to use an update query which adds .05 to the existing sales markup. Save this query as **Ch 9 Assignment 7a**. Print the resulting category table.

b Create a parameter query for Coast Jewelers that lists products purchased from a particular supplier. The query should ask "Enter supplier's name:" and list the supplier name, product name, quantity, and unit price. Save this query as **Ch 9 Assignment 7b**. Run and print the query entering *Casio USA* as the supplier.

c Create and run a delete query for Coast Jewelers that deletes all products identified with supplier's ID 1. Save this query as **Ch 9 Assignment 7c**.

d Create an additional query listing the product name and supplier ID of all the remaining products in the Product table sorted in ascending order by supplier ID. Save this query as **Ch 9 Assignment 7d**. Print the resulting query.

Chapter 9 Case Problem: Kelly's Boutique

In the last chapter you added and modified some tables for Kelly's Boutique. She would now like you to create, run, and print some select and action queries. Use the file labeled Ch 9 - Kelly.mdb on your student disk.

1 Create and print a select query that lists the author and book title for all books written by Seuss. Save this query as **Ch 9 Kelly Case 1** before you print it.

2 Create and print a select query that lists the book title and author for all books purchased and supervised by Barbara Manchester. Save this query as **Ch 9 Kelly Case 2** before you print it.

3 Create and print a select query that lists the book title and list price for all book titles that start with *Harry*. Save this query as **Ch 9 Kelly Case 3** before you print it.

4 Edit the query you just created. Add the field author and publisher and delete the field list price. Change the criteria from starting with

Harry to containing the word *Secrets*. (*Hint:* Place a wildcard character in front of and behind the word.) Save this query as **Ch 9 Kelly Case 4** before you print it.

5 Create and print a select query that lists the book title, contact, and phone number for all books with a list price greater than $20. Save this query as **Ch 9 Kelly Case 5** before you print it.

6 Create and print a select query that lists the ISBN, book title, and list price for all books with a list price greater than $30 or less than $10 sorted by list price. Save this query as **Ch 9 Kelly Case 6** before you print it.

7 Create and print a select query that lists the book title, list price, quantity, and retail value (a computed field, the product of list price times quantity) sorted in descending order by retail value. Be sure to format the field as Currency. Save this query as **Ch 9 Kelly Case 7** before you print it.

8 Create and print a select query that lists book title, list price, markup, unit cost, quantity, and cost. Unit cost is a computed field (list price divided by 1 + markup). Cost is another computed field (unit cost times quantity). Be sure to format both computed fields as Currency. Save this query as **Ch 9 Kelly Case 8** before you print it.

9 Create and print a select query that sums the total cost of the book inventory. *Hint:* Use the query created in (8) above as your source for this new query. Save this query as **Ch 9 Kelly Case 9** before you print it.

10 Modify the query you created in (8) above so that it includes the Department field. Save the query, then use that modified query as the source for a query that sums the cost of inventory by department. Save this query as **Ch 9 Kelly Case 10** before you print it.

11 Create and run an action query that increases all books' list price by 5 percent. Save this query as **Ch 9 Kelly Case 11**. Create and print another query which lists the book title and list price for all books. Do not save this query.

12 Create a parameter query that lists books from a particular publisher. The query should ask "Enter publisher's name:" and then list the publisher, book title, and quantity for that publisher. Save this query as **Ch 9 Kelly Case 12**. Run and print the query entering *Harper Collins* as the publisher.

13 Create and run a delete query that deletes all products with a quantity of *0*. Save this query as **Ch 9 Kelly Case 13**.

14 Create a query listing the book title and quantity for all the remaining books in inventory sorted by quantity in descending order. Save this query as **Ch 9 Kelly Case 14** before you print it.

chapter 10

Forms

In this chapter you will learn to:

- **Modify a form's labels and text box controls**

- **Use list and combo box controls**

- **Place a calculated control on a form**

- **Place a check box control on a form**

- **Use special combo box controls**

- **Place an option button control on a form**

- **Create a form with a subform**

CASE: COAST JEWELERS, INC.

Nathan and Meagan are now ready to expand the use of forms in their rapidly expanding database. They recall that forms have a variety of purposes. Previously they created a form to capture additional information about their products. Now Kyle suggests they create a form with more features.

Kyle tells them that they can add functionality to forms with such features as calculated fields, check boxes, option buttons, list boxes, combo boxes, and subforms.

"Once again this sounds like more than we need!" Nathan exclaims.

"Don't panic," says Meagan. "Kyle seems to know just how much of this stuff we can take. Give him a chance."

Kyle thanks Meagan for her confidence and convinces them that in the long run the use of forms in their database will allow them to more efficiently use their product database and improve the integrity of the data input.

LABELS AND TEXT BOX CONTROLS

In this section you will become familiar with the steps necessary to modify a form's labels and text box controls. Forms are often created using the Forms Wizard, but once created, they often need to be customized. Customization includes moving controls and labels and resizing the form itself.

Kyle suggests that you modify a form, previously created using a forms wizard, to be more in keeping with the form Nathan used to keep on each supplier.

"That would be helpful," Nathan comments. "I feel more comfortable using an electronic version of a form I've already worked with on paper."

Kyle explains that the purpose of this exercise is to get to know the process for moving controls and labels around a form.

To modify the Suppliers form:

1 Start Access and open the file on your student disk titled Ch 10 - Coast.mdb.

2 Select the **Forms** object, then double-click the **Supplier Form** button to view the Supplier form shown in Figure 10.1.

3 Change your view of the form to Design view from Form view by clicking the **View** tool on the Standard toolbar.

4 Click and hold in the lower right corner of the Supplier form to reveal the dragging tool and move the window down and to the right to reveal the Form Footer as shown in Figure 10.2. The process will expand the size of the Form Design view window so you can manipulate all the objects on the form.

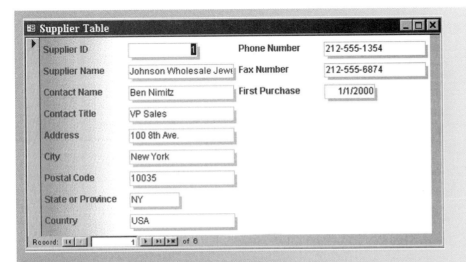

FIGURE 10.1

Supplier Form

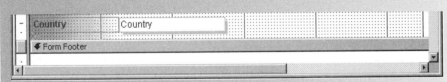

FIGURE 10.2

Expanding the Form Window

5 Click on the edge of the **Postal Code control** until the hand appears, then move the control approximately three inches to the right as shown in Figure 10.3. This process will move the control around the form.

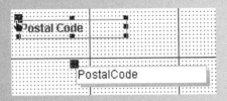

FIGURE 10.3

Moving a Control on a Form

6 Click on the upper left corner of the **Postal Code label** and then move it up and to the right as shown in Figure 10.4. This process is will separate the label from the control.

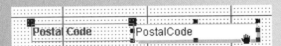

FIGURE 10.4

Separating a Label from a Control

7 Click on the upper left corner of the **Postal Code label** again, then press the **Delete** key. This process will delete the label from the window.

8 Remove the City, State or Province, and Country labels in the same way.

9 Click on the far right edge of the **City control**, then drag the control to the left to reduce its width as shown in Figure 10.5.

FIGURE 10.5

Resizing a Control

10 Resize controls and remove labels until your form looks like Figure 10.6.

FIGURE 10.6
Modified Supplier Form

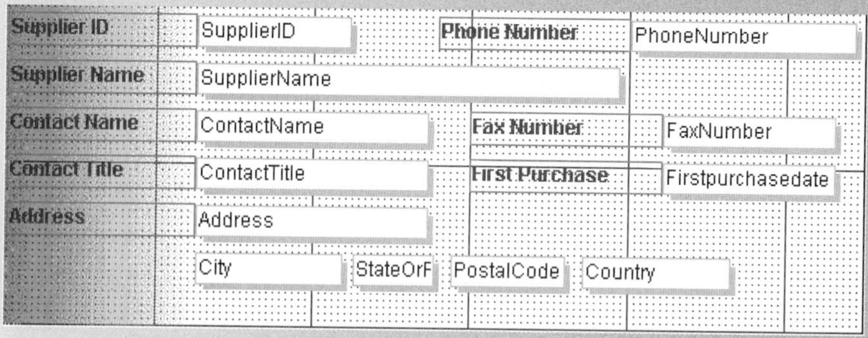

11 Save the new form as Supplier Form A.

"Modifying a form's labels and controls was fairly intuitive," Meagan comments.

Kyle agrees and now suggests that you and Nathan explore the use of form controls such as list and combo boxes to help simplify the data entry process and improve the integrity of information captured in your database.

LIST AND COMBO BOX CONTROLS

The form you just modified included a series of text box controls containing information such as a supplier's name, address, etc. These text boxes are referred to as a type of form control. You use text boxes on a form or report to display data from a record source. This type of text box is called a **bound** text box because it's bound to data in a field. In this case, for example, the text box control Supplier Name was bound to the field Supplier Name in the Supplier table. Text boxes can also be unbound. For example, you can create an unbound text box to display the results of a calculation or to accept input from a user. Data in an unbound text box isn't stored anywhere, but we will discuss unbound text boxes more later.

Kyle explains that in many cases, it's quicker and easier to select a value from a list than to remember a value when using a form to enter new information, such as a new supplier. A list of choices also helps to ensure that the value that's entered in a field is correct. If you have enough room on your form to display the list at all times, you might want to use a list box. When you want to create a control that displays a list but requires less room, you would use a combo box. Combo boxes are a control used on a form, which provide the combined functionality of a list box and a text box.

"Which should we use and when?" asks Meagan.

"Well, let's try something simple first, like modifying an existing text box control in our supplier form to a list box," answers Kyle.

List Box Control

Kyle explains that modifying a control on a form simply requires changing the form control (from text to list) and creating the list of choices.

"Let's modify the Country text box control on our previously created supplier form to a list box control," directs Kyle. "We will also add a new supplier from the United Kingdom."

To change the Country text box control to a list box control and add a new supplier:

1 Open Supplier Form A you saved previously, if it is not already open.

2 Change your view of the form to Design view from Form view by clicking the **View** tool on the Standard toolbar.

3 Right-click the **Country** text box control, then click **Change To**, then click **List Box** as shown in Figure 10.7.

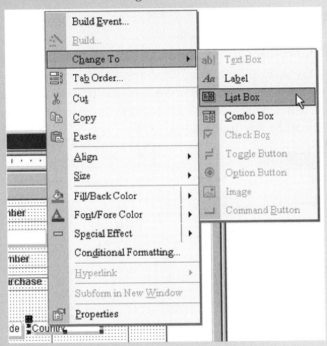

FIGURE 10.7

Changing Form Controls

4 Right-click the **Country** list box control, then click **Properties**.

5 In the Properties window for List Box: Country, click the **All** tab, change the Row Source Type to **Value List** and type **USA; CAN; UK** in the Row Source as shown in Figure 10.8.

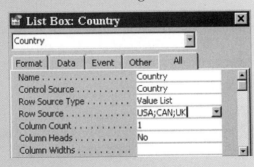

FIGURE 10.8

Changing the List Box Control Properties

6 Close the List Box: Country properties window.

7 The form should now look like Figure 10.9.

8 Change your view of the form to Form view.

9 Enter a new supplier by clicking on the **Add Record** button located at the bottom of the form and typing the information provided in Figure 10.10. Note that to specify the country for this new supplier all you had to do was click UK.

10 Save this new form as Supplier Form B, then close the form.

You have now modified an existing form to include a list box control. Now Kyle suggests you look at the combo box control as an alternative.

Combo Box Control

Once again, a combo box control is a control that provides the combined functionality of a list box and a text box and is used on a form. In this situation someone entering a new supplier using the Supplier form can either type new information into a combo box control (like a text box control) or select from an existing list of information (like a list box control) without taking up much space.

Kyle suggests you try out a combo box control by changing the State text box control to a combo box control listing four of the more common states in which your suppliers reside. Further he suggests you try this combo box control out by entering a new supplier.

To change the State text box control to a combo box control and add a new supplier:

1 Open Supplier Form B you saved previously, if it is not already open.

2 Change your view of the form to Design view from Form view by clicking the **View** tool on the Standard toolbar.

3 Right-click the **StateOrProvince** text box control, then click **Change To**, then click **Combo Box**.

4 Right-click the **StateOrProvince** combo box control, then click **Properties**.

5 In the Properties window for Combo Box: StateOrProvince, with the **All** tab selected, change the Row Source Type to Value List and type **CA;NY;MA;NJ** in the Row Source as shown in Figure 10.11.

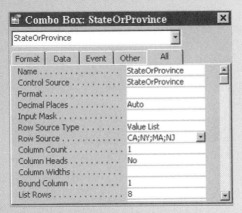

FIGURE 10.11

Changing the Combo Box Control Properties

6 Close the Properties window.

7 Change your view of the form to Form view.

8 Enter a new supplier by clicking on the **Add Record** button located at the bottom of the form and typing the information provided in Figure 10.12. Note that to specify the state for this new supplier all you had to do was click NJ.

9 Enter another new supplier who doesn't reside in one of the states listed in the combo box as follows: **Seawear, Dan Patrick, Consultant, 5405 Skalak Drive, Williamsburg, VA, 23188, USA, 757-555-1000, 757-555-5186.** Note that to specify the state for this new supplier all you had to do was type VA.

10 Save this new form as Supplier Form C, and then close the form.

FIGURE 10.12 *New Supplier Information*

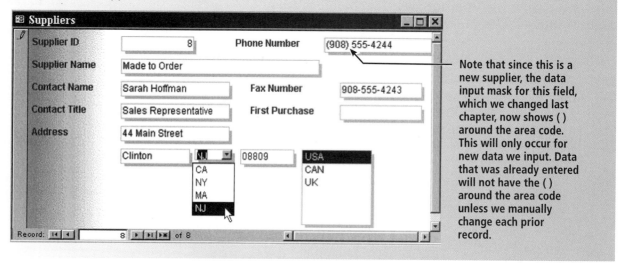

Note that since this is a new supplier, the data input mask for this field, which we changed last chapter, now shows ( ) around the area code. This will only occur for new data we input. Data that was already entered will not have the ( ) around the area code unless we manually change each prior record.

You have now created a combo box control on a form to ease the creation of new supplier records and found that it acts like both a text box and list box control. Now it is time to experiment with other features, such as calculated controls.

CALCULATED CONTROL

A calculated control uses an expression as its source of data. An expression is any combination of mathematical or logical operators, constants, functions, names of fields, controls, and properties that evaluate to a single value. For example, an expression can use data from a field in an underlying table or query of a form or report, or from another control on the form or report.

Bound controls get their data from fields in a table, while unbound controls don't have any particular data source other than an expression. Kyle explains that to calculate the total cost invested in any particular product, Nathan would have to multiply the units on hand times the unit cost. He demonstrates that both the units on hand and the unit cost are already on the product form as bound controls Quantity and UnitPrice. However, to create a control on the form which calculates the total cost he will have to create an unbound control (referred to in this case as a calculated control) to calculate the product of Quantity times Unit Price.

"Bound, unbound, I'm bound up just thinking about these," Meagan complains. "Do we really have to understand this to create a useful form?"

"Well," responds Kyle, "I think you'll find them useful in many forms you might create and they are really not that difficult. Here, let me show you."

To add a control to calculate the total cost in inventory of each item:

1 Open the Products form.

2 Change your view of the form to Design view.

3 Click the **Toolbox** button 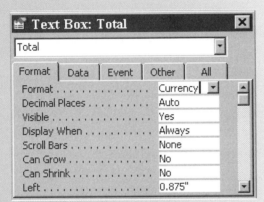 on the toolbar to reveal the toolbox floating toolbar.

4 Click the **Text box** button on the toolbox toolbar, then click in the Products design window.

5 Highlight the new text label and type **Total**.

6 Type =[**Quantity**]*[**UnitPrice**] to replace the word Unbound in the text box, then press the **Enter** key.

7 Right-click the newly created text box to reveal the Text Box Properties window. Note the expression you typed should be in the Control Source box.

8 Type **Total** as the name of this new control.

9 Click the **Format** tab of the Properties window, and then select **Currency** in the Format section of the Properties window as shown in Figure 10.13.

FIGURE 10.13
Formatting the New Text Box

10 Click the **All** tab in the Properties window to make sure you've typed the expression correctly. It should appear in the Control Source section of the Properties window as shown in Figure 10.14.

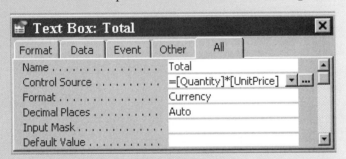

FIGURE 10.14
Properties Window of the New Text Box

11 Close the Properties window.

12 Change your view of the form to Form view. You should see the total cost of $63.00 if you're viewing the Flower Drop Earrings item.

> **trouble?** If you did not type the expression exactly as specified you may end up with the message *#Name?* in the text box where you expected to see the $63 cost. Reexamine the Control Source section of the Properties window for the total text box to verify you've typed the expression correctly.

13 Save this new form as Products A, and then close the form.

14 If still open, close the Toolbox Floating toolbar.

"Alternatively," Kyle explains, "you could have used the Access program's Expression Builder to create this calculated control."

"Would that help prevent typos?" Meagan asks.

"Definitely," Kyle responds. "Let's create the same total using the Expression Builder."

To add a control to calculate the total cost in inventory of each item using the expression builder:

1 Open the Products form, *not* the Products A form you just saved.

2 Change your view of the form to Design view.

3 Click the **Toolbox** button 🛠 on the toolbar to reveal the toolbox floating toolbar.

4 Click the **Text box** button ⌨ on the toolbox toolbar, then click in the **Products design** window.

5 Change the label to read **Total**.

6 Right-click the word **Unbound**. (Remember, unbound simply means this value is not linked or bound to any field in the database and thus is just a temporary placeholder and will not be saved once the form is closed.)

7 Click **Properties** from the Shortcut menu.

8 Type **Total** as the name of this new control.

9 Click on the **Expression builder** button ▭ located to the right of the term Control Source.

10 Double-click the **Forms** folder, then double-click on **Loaded Forms**.

11 Click the **Products** folder. This process reveals the various labels and controls available for the expression. See Figure 10.15.

FIGURE 10.15

Expression Builder

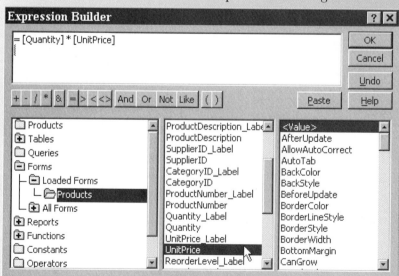

12 Click the **=** button at the top of the window.

13 Scroll down the list; then double-click **Quantity** from the list of labels and controls. Note the brackets [ ] that appear around the control in the Expression window.

14 Click the * button at the top of the window.

15 Scroll down the list; then double-click **UnitPrice** from the list of labels and controls. Again, note the brackets [ ] that appear around the control in the Expression window.

16 Click **OK** to close the Expression Builder window.

17 Click the **Format** tab of the Properties window, and then select **Currency** in the Format section of the Properties window.

18 Close the Properties window.

> **trouble?** Note that these are still the Properties window even though it says Text Box. Realize that when you open these Properties windows that you are changing *properties of controls*.

19 Change your view of the form to Form view. You should see the total cost of $63.00 if you're viewing the Flower Drop Earrings item.

20 Close the form without saving changes since you already created this form before naming it Products A.

You've now seen two different processes for creating a calculated control. Both Nathan and Meagan seem more comfortable with the terms and processes and are anxious to know if there are any other useful controls available in Access.

CHECK BOX CONTROL
. . . .

The check box control, implemented on a form, gives the user a choice from which all, none, or some of the check boxes can be activated or not. In each case, a check box control, if checked, returns a *Yes* value, while an unchecked check box control returns a *No* value. This control, like other controls, can be bound or unbound. To create a bound check box control, you must be working in a form or report that is bound to a record source.

Kyle asks Meagan if there are any situations in which she thinks a control like this might be helpful on a form. She suggests that in the Buyers table, it would be nice to know who specializes in what category of product. For instance, some buyers specialize in only one category, like rings, while others specialize in several categories.

"Would a check box control be appropriate here?" she asks.

"Yes," you respond. "But if you want to store this information for later use, doesn't it have to be a bound control? And if so, don't we have to create some new fields in the Buyers table?"

Kyle compliments you on your comprehension of this topic. He points out that this is a situation where a bound control is appropriate but first, the buyer table fields must be created and set up in a data type called Yes/No.

To create additional fields in the Buyers table:

1 Open the Buyers Table.

2 Change your view of the table to Design view.

3 Add five new fields to the table and specify each as a Yes/No data type as shown in Figure 10.16.

FIGURE 10.16

Modifying the Buyers Table

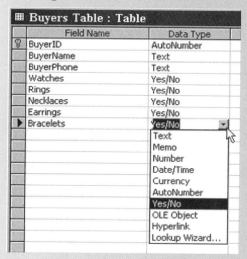

4 Close the Buyers Table. Choose **Yes** to save changes.

Now that the Buyers table includes the field for data storage you offer to modify the Buyers form to include check boxes for quick data entry.

"How do I create check boxes on the form?" you ask. "Do I need to use the toolbox toolbar again?"

"Actually, no," Kyle responds. "All you'll need to do is add the fields you just created in the Buyers table to the Buyers form. Since they are of the data type Yes/No, they will automatically be added to the form as a check box control."

To create a check box control bound to a field:

1 Open the Buyers form.

2 Change your view of the form to Design view.

3 Click the **Field List** button on the Form Design toolbar to reveal the Buyers Table field list shown in Figure 10.17.

FIGURE 10.17

Buyers Table Field List

4 Enlarge the Buyers form so you have room to place the new fields.

5 Click and drag all five category fields you just created, one at a time, to the Buyers form as shown in Figure 10.18. Be sure to line them up as close to Figure 10.18 as possible.

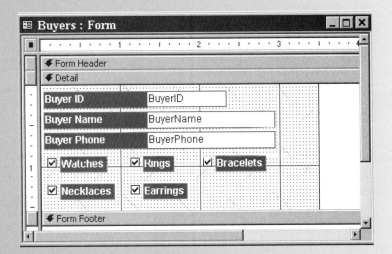

FIGURE 10.18

Modified Buyers Form in Design View

6 Change your view of the form to Form view.

7 Update each record from the Buyers form to indicate in what category each buyer specializes. Buyer 1 specializes in watches, necklaces, and earrings. After updating this record your Buyers form should look like Figure 10.19.

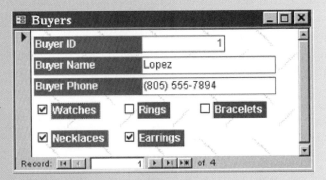

FIGURE 10.19

Updated Buyers Form

8 Continue your update. Buyer 3 specializes in necklaces and earrings. (*Note:* Buyer 2 was previously deleted.) Buyer 4 specializes in watches and rings. Buyer 5 specializes in watches only.

9 Save the modified form as Buyers A.

10 Close the form.

"I like using these new controls," comments Meagan. "But I still have a question on the combo box controls we did before. Is there a way to give our database users a choice of options which change as our company grows?"

"There sure is," Kyle responds. "I'll introduce you to special combo box controls next."

SPECIAL COMBO BOX CONTROL

An additional possible use of a combo box control would be to give the user a choice of options that change based upon other changes which may occur in the database. For instance, let's say you want to give the user the option of selecting a specific supplier for each product but you want that list not to be static, but dynamic. In other words, you'd like the choices available to the user to be limited to those suppliers currently in your Supplier table. Thus, when you add a supplier the list expands, and, of course, when you delete a supplier the list diminishes.

"That would be perfect for our product form," you suggest. "I can see using that form to add new products and choosing from a list of existing suppliers to provide the product."

"How is that different from what we just did with the state and country combo boxes?" Meagan asks.

"In those situations," Kyle explains, "we provided a list of choices for the combo list. However, the user could type in a different state or country from those we listed. Plus, the list never changes unless we physically rewrite the list in the control."

"So where do we create the list?" you ask.

"Actually, we just point the control to the Supplier table. As the table is added to or subtracted from, the combo box control changes," says Kyle. "Nathan, let me show you how it is done."

Kyle explains that Nathan's goal will be to modify the existing Product form so that the Supplier text box control is transformed to a combo box control with a list containing the supplier identification numbers and supplier names that exist in the Supplier table. To do so requires that the existing relationship between the Product table and the Supplier table be temporarily eliminated (since it currently enforces referential integrity) and that the SupplierID fields data type be changed.

To modify the Product table and change the SupplierID field's data type:

1 Click the **Relationships** tool 🔠 on the Database toolbar.

2 Right-click the relationship between the Product table and the Supplier table, then click **Delete** as shown in Figure 10.20.

3 Click **Yes** in the dialog box which appears next to confirm your deletion.

4 Close the Relationships window.

5 Open the Product table.

6 Change your view of the form to Design view.

7 Change the data type of the SupplierID field to **Lookup Wizard...**

8 Click in the first option button as shown in Figure 10.21, then click **Next.**

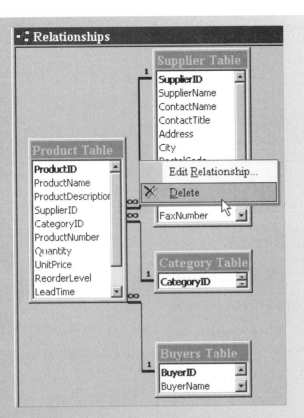

This wizard creates a lookup column, which displays a list of values you can choose from. How do you want your lookup column to get its values?

○ I want the lookup column to look up the values in a table or query.

○ I will type in the values that I want.

9 Click **Table: Supplier Table** from the next Lookup Wizard dialog box, then click **Next**.

10 Move the SupplierID and SupplierName fields from the list of Available Fields to the list of Selected Fields as shown in Figure 10.22, then click **Next**.

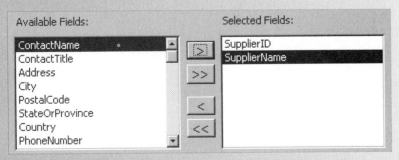

11 Uncheck the **Hide key column** check box and resize the column widths to look like Figure 10.23, then click **Next**.

FIGURE 10.23

Lookup Wizard Dialog Box for Columns

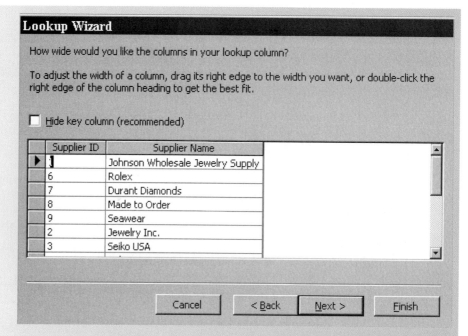

12 Click **Next** again to keep the SupplierID as the field being stored.

13 Click **Finish** to keep SupplierID as the label for your column.

14 Click **Yes** to save the table.

15 Close the modified Product table.

16 Once again, click the **Relationships** tool on the Database toolbar.

17 Double-click the relationship between the Product table and the Supplier table.

18 Click in the **Enforce Referential Integrity** check box, then click **OK**.

19 Close the Relationships window.

Kyle explains that now Nathan can modify the Products form to include the new and revised SupplierID field as a combo box control. But first, he cautions, Nathan will have to remove the old SupplierID text box control from the form.

To create a combo box control linked to the Supplier table:

1 Open the Products A form previously saved.

2 Change your view of the form to Design view.

3 Click the existing **SupplierID** text box control, then press the **Delete** key.

4 Click the Field List tool ▣ from the Form Design toolbar to open the Product table field list window if it is not already open.

5 Click and drag the **SupplierID** field to the Products A form as shown in Figure 10.24.

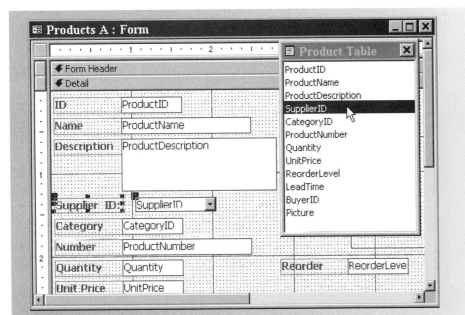

FIGURE 10.24

Adding the New SupplierID Field to the Products A Form

6 Close the Product Table field list window.

7 Change your view of the form to Form view.

8 Note that the SupplierID of record 1 in the Products A form is still specified at 4. Click on the drop-down list **arrow** of the SupplierID combo box control to see the options available as shown in Figure 10.25.

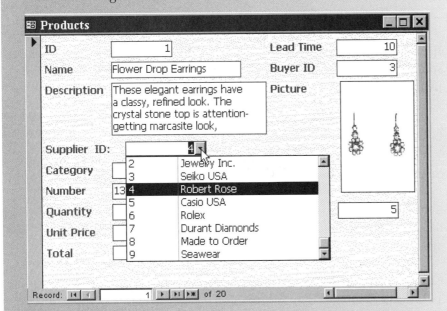

FIGURE 10.25

New SupplierID Combo Box

9 Save the revised form as Products B.

10 Go to record 7, the Diamond Heart Slide, and change the Supplier ID from 1 to **2** (Jewelry Inc.) as shown in Figure 10.26.

11 Now change the Supplier ID of the same record by typing **10** in the combo box control, then moving to the next record.

FIGURE 10.26

Changing the Supplier ID of Record 7

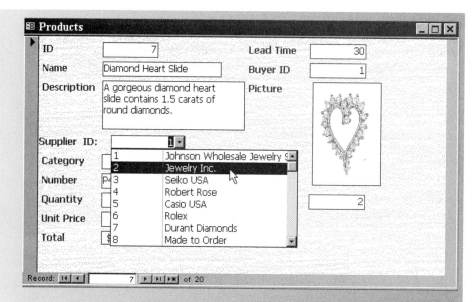

FIGURE 10.26

Changing the Supplier ID of Record 7

12 An alert dialog box should appear indicating that this choice is not acceptable since a related record is required in the Supplier table. Since there is no supplier with an ID of 10, the system rejects your change. Click **OK**.

13 Change the Supplier ID back to **2**.

14 Close the form.

In addition to form controls, subforms can be very helpful for situations where a one-to-many relationship exists. Kyle suggests that understanding subforms may in fact help solve some of their previously expressed inventory tracking concerns.

SUBFORMS

Subforms are simple forms within forms. To exist, the information from one form must have a one-to-many relationship with the information in another form. Kyle explains that many times users would like to see specific information on one form that has some common characteristic.

"For instance," says Kyle. "You have already established a relationship between the categories of your products and the products themselves. There exists a one-to-many relationship. One category, for example, includes many products."

"So we could create a form which shows all the products we have that fall within any of our categories?" asks Meagan.

"That's it!" Kyle responds. "Let's have you create this form within a form."

To create a form and subform of categories and products:

1 Select the **Forms** object then double-click **Create form by using wizard**.

2 Select **Table: Category Table** from the list of Tables/Queries.

3 Click **Category Name** from the list of Available Fields, then click the **>** button to move Category Name from the list of Available Fields to the list of Selected Fields.

4 Select **Table: Product Table** from the list of Tables/Queries.

5 Click **ProductName** from the list of Available Fields, then click the **>** button.

6 Click **Quantity** from the list of Available Fields, then click the **>** button.

7 Click **UnitPrice** from the list of Available Fields, then click the **>** button.

8 Click the **Next** button.

9 Click **by Category Table** to view data as shown in Figure 10.27.

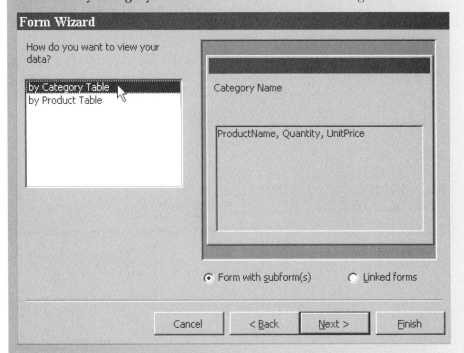

FIGURE 10.27

Form Wizard Data View Window

10 Click the **Form with subform(s)** option button, then click **Next**.

11 Click the **Datasheet layout** option button, then click **Next**.

12 Click the **Industrial style** option button, then click **Next**.

13 Click **Finish** to save the default titles for your new forms.

14 View the newly created form by clicking on the category record navigator at the bottom of the form. The Watches category should look similar to Figure 10.28 on page 210.

FIGURE 10.28

Category Form with Products Subform

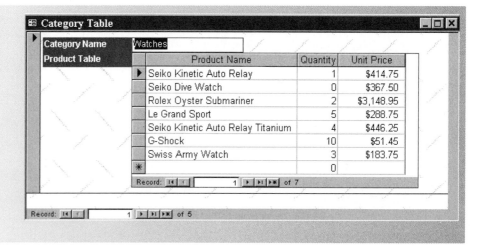

This newly created form and subform is very useful for viewing products by categories. Nathan is impressed.

END NOTE

· ·

In this chapter, you have learned how to modify a form's labels and text box controls, use list, combo box, calculated, and check box controls, and how to create a form with a subform. Feeling fairly confident, you're ready to finish up with variations on report creation.

practice

Chapter 10 Questions

1 What view of a form is used to edit an existing form?

2 What is the difference between bound and unbound controls?

3 Why are text box controls used on a form?

4 Why are list box controls used on a form?

5 Why are combo box controls used on a form?

6 Why are calculated controls used on a form?

7 Why are check box controls used on a form?

8 When is the Lookup Wizard used?

9 Why must an existing relationship be deleted to modify a field's data type?

10 What type of relationship must exist if a subform is used on a form?

Chapter 10 Assignments

Make the following changes for Coast Jewelers using the Ch10 - Coast.mdb file found on your student disk *after* you have completed all the changes specified in the chapter.

1 *Modify a form's labels and text box controls for Coast Jewelers*

  a Modify the existing Category form to look like this:

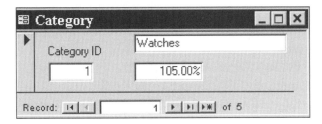

  b Save the new form as **Category A**.
  c Print the new form.

2 *Create a list box control for Coast Jewelers*

  a Modify the Category form (not Category A) by changing the sales markup text box control to a list box control listing the choices at 100%, 125%, 150%, 175%, and 200%.
  b Save the new form as **Category B**.
  c Print record 1 (Category ID1) using the new form. (*Hint:* To print a specific record, navigate to that record; select Print from the File menu, then select Selected record(s) as the print range.)

3 *Create a combo box control for Coast Jewelers*

  a Modify the Category form (not Category A or B) by changing the sales markup text box control to a combo box control listing the choices at 100%, 125%, 150%, 175%, and 200%.

  b Format the text box control to a percent format with decimal places = 0.

  c Save the new form as **Category C**.

  d Print record 1 using the new form.

4 *Create a special combo box control for Coast Jewelers*

  a Modify the Products form (not Products A or B) by changing the BuyerID text box control to a combo box control listing the choices of BuyerID and BuyerName from the Buyers table. (*Hint:* Be sure to remove the relationship between the Product and Buyer tables first, and then reestablish the relationship, and related referential integrity, after you've created the combo box control.

  b Save the new form as **Products C**.

  c Print record 1 (Flower Drop Earrings) using the new form. (*Hint:* To print a specific record, navigate to that record; select Print from the File menu, then select Selected record(s) as the print range.)

5 *Create a calculated control for Coast Jewelers*

  a Sales persons earn a 7 percent commission on the cost of each sale. Create a new unbound calculated control to compute the possible commission on each product. Modify the Products form (not Products A, B or C) by adding a calculated control called **Commission**. The expression created should multiply the unit price times .07. Format the control in a currency format.

  b Save the new form as **Products D**.

  c Print record 7 (Diamond Heart Slide) using the new form. (*Hint:* To print a specific record, navigate to that record; select Print from the File menu, then select Selected record(s) as the print range.)

6 *Create a check box control for Coast Jewelers*

  a Add a new field (Taxable) to the Products Table.

  b Make the field a Yes/No data type.

  c Add this new field to the Products form (not Products A, B, or C) under the label Reorder.

  d Save the new form as **Products E**.

  e Make record 4 (G-Shock) taxable.

  f Print record 4 using the new form. (*Hint:* To print a specific record, navigate to that record; select Print from the File menu, then select Selected record(s) as the print range.)

7 *Create a form and subform for Coast Jewelers*

    a Create a form for each buyer that contains the product name, quantity, and unit price of each product he or she is responsible for. Use the subform option with a datasheet layout, and Stone style.

    b Save the form as **Buyers B**, and the subform as **Products F Subform**.

    c Print record 2 (Fortier) using this form and subform. (*Hint:* To print a specific record, navigate to that record; select Print from the File menu, then select Selected record(s) as the print range.)

Chapter 10 Case Problem: Kelly's Boutique

In the last chapter you created some select and action queries for Kelly's Boutique. She would now like you to create and print some forms. Use the file labeled Ch 10 - Kelly.mdb on your student disk.

1 Modify the existing Book form to look like the form below. Print record 1 (*The Cat in the Hat*), then save the modified form as **Ch 10 Kelly Case 1**.

2 Create a list box control using the form created in item 1. This control should provide the user a list of departments as shown below. Move other controls around the form as shown. Print record 2 (*Hop on Pop*), then save the modified form as **Ch 10 Kelly Case 2**.

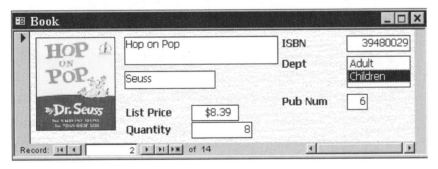

3   Create a combo box control using the form created in item 2. This control should provide the user a list of departments like in 2 above but with a combo box instead of a list box. See example below. Print record 3 (*Divine Secrets of the Ya-Ya Sisterhood*), then save the modified form as **Ch 10 Kelly Case 3**.

4   Create a special combo box control using the form created in item 3. This control should provide the user a dynamic list of publishers based on the publishers listed in the Publisher table. The combo box should list publisher number and name and referential integrity must be enforced. Label the combo box column **Publisher**. Print record 4 (*Betsy–Tacy*) then save the modified form as **Ch 10 Kelly Case 4**.

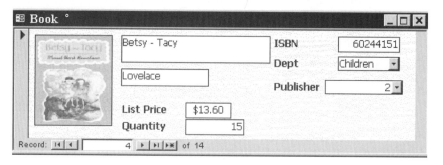

5   Create a calculated control to compute the total cost of each book in stock. Format the control in currency and label the control **Total Cost** as shown below. Print record 5 (*Deep End of the Ocean*) then save the modified form as **Ch 10 Kelly Case 5**.

6   Create a check box control to indicate if the text is a bestseller. Label the field and control **Best Seller** as shown below. Mark records 1, 2, 6, 8, 9, and 11 as bestsellers using your new form. Print record 6 (*Green Eggs and Ham*) then save the modified form as **Ch 10 Kelly Case 6**.

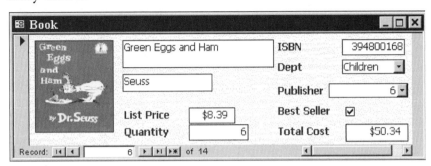

7   Create a form and subform which shows all books by each publisher. Move and resize all controls so that your form looks like that shown below. Print record 9 (Arthur A. Levine Books), then save the modified form with default names provided.

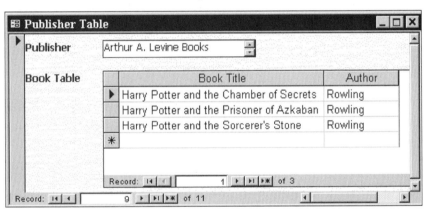

11

Reports

In this chapter you will learn to:

- Use a query to create a report
- Use grouping and summarizing in a report
- Modify an existing report design

CASE: COAST JEWELERS, INC.

You, Nathan, and Meagan are feeling rather confident in using Access. You've created and modified tables, queries, and forms in your database so far but are anxious to see some results of your work in a more formal presentation.

"How are reports different from queries and forms?" Meagan asks.

"Remember that forms are used to view and update information in the database," Kyle answers. "Queries are your means of asking questions about the data and reports are your means of expressing that information in a usable fashion."

He reminds you that when you explored queries you were able to use select, update, and delete queries to locate certain information as well as compute totals and statistics. However, when you printed those queries they weren't formatted very well. They could be sorted, but they didn't have the header, footer, grouping, or summarizing features of reports.

He suggests that you start with using a query as your basis for a report and learn more about reporting features available using Access.

USE A QUERY TO CREATE A REPORT

To demonstrate the use of queries in a report Kyle creates a simple select query which simply lists the category, product name, quantity, unit price, and total cost of all products in inventory with a unit price greater than $100.

We can now create a report using this query. The first question he asks is what information from this query needs to be displayed in a report.

"Well if you ask me," says Nathan, "I'd like to see a report of products we have which cost more that $100 sorted alphabetically by product name. I'd like to see each product's quantity, unit price, and total cost."

"Could we also add information to the report like the category name for each item?" Meagan asks.

"Sure," Kyle responds.

He then explains the process for creating such a report and offers to demonstrate it to you now.

To create a report using a query:

1 Start Access and open the file on your student disk titled Ch 11 - Coast. mdb.

2 Select the **Reports** object, and then double-click **Create a report by using wizard**.

3 Select **Query: Product Query** from the Tables/Queries drop-down list.

4 Double-click **ProductName** from the list of available fields as shown in Figure 11.1.

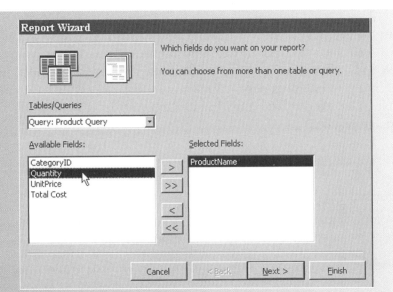

FIGURE 11.1

*Creating a Report
from a Query*

5 Double-click **Quantity**, **UnitPrice**, and **Total Cost** from the list of available fields.

6 Select **Table: Category Table** from the Tables/Queries drop-down list.

7 Double-click **Category Name** from the list of available fields, then click **Next**.

8 Click **Next** when asked a question about view and again when asked about grouping. We'll come back to this later.

9 Click **ProductName** in the Sort Order window, then click **Next**. By default the Ascending button should be active.

10 Select a **tabular** layout and **portrait** orientation.

11 Check the **Adjust the field width so that all fields fit on a page** check box, then click **Next**.

12 Select a **Corporate** style, then click **Next**.

13 Title your report **Product Query**, then click **Finish**. The top of your finished report, created from a query, should look like Figure 11.2. (*Note:* When you click Finish, Access automatically saves your report using the title you provided. Thus, there is no need to manually save the report.)

FIGURE 11.2

Product Query Report

Product Query

Product Name	Quantity	Unit Price	Total Cost	Category Name
Amethyst Pendant	8	$204.75	$1,638.00	Necklaces
Blue Topaz Ring	7	$261.45	$1,830.15	Rings
Diamond Earrings	2	$535.50	$1,071.00	Earrings
Diamond Heart Slide	4	$918.75	$3,675.00	Necklaces

14 Close the report.

"That's great that we can add a field from another table that is not a part of the query from which the report is created," you mention.

"Well that's not quite true," Kyle explains. "The only reason we were able to add the category name was because the category ID was a part of the query. That provides a link between the query and the category table. If we tried to add a field such as reorder level we would get some strange results."

"How so?" Nathan asks.

"Let me show you," Kyle answers.

To create a report using a query:

1 Select the **Reports** object, and then double-click **Create a report by using wizard**.

2 Select **Query: Product Query** from the Tables/Queries drop-down list.

3 Click the ⟫ button to include all the Available Fields in the Selected Fields window.

4 Select **Table: Product Table** from the Tables/Queries drop-down list.

5 Double-click **ReorderLevel** to include it as a Selected Field in the report.

6 Click **Next** five times, then click **Finish** to title the report **Product Query1**. The top of the report generated should look like Figure 11.3, which lists each product multiple times.

FIGURE 11.3

Product Query Report with Added Field

Product Query1

Category ID	Product Name	Quantity	Unit Price	Total Cost	Reorder Level
1	Seiko Kinetic Auto Rela	4	$446.25	$1,785.00	2
1	Seiko Kinetic Auto Rela	4	$446.25	$1,785.00	2
1	Seiko Kinetic Auto Rela	4	$446.25	$1,785.00	2
1	Seiko Kinetic Auto Rela	4	$446.25	$1,785.00	3

7 Close the report.

Kyle further explains that it is best to create a report from a query that has all the information you need. He demonstrates by going back to the Product Query query and adding the reorder level field to the query, saving it, and then recreating the report you just generated. The resulting report, shown in Figure 11.4 makes more sense.

"Should we do that now?" you ask.

"No," Kyle answers. "I just wanted you to know that it's important to create a report from a query that has all the information you need."

Kyle directs you to learn more about reports by working on grouping and summarizing information.

Product Query2

FIGURE 11.4

Revised Product Query Report after the Query Is Changed

Category ID	Product Name	Quantity	Unit Price	Total Cost	Reorder Level
1	Rolex Oyster Submari	2	$3,148.95	$6,297.90	2
1	Seiko Dive Watch	0	$367.50	$0.00	2
1	Swiss Army Watch	3	$183.75	$551.25	3
1	Le Grand Sport	5	$288.75	$1,443.75	2

USE GROUPING AND SUMMARIZING IN A REPORT

Kyle explains that grouping arranges the records in your report. When you group records, each group that shares a common characteristic is displayed together. You can group on one or several characteristics. Further, he explains that once a report has groups assigned, those groups can be summarized in many ways, including subtotals, grand totals, average, etc.

"Can I get a report that lists my inventory by category and subtotals each group?" Nathan asks.

"Sure," says Kyle. "But I suggest we learn how to group first and then worry about summarizing later."

Grouping

"Let's create a report similar to the one we just created but grouped by category name," suggests Kyle.

To create a report using grouping:

1 Select the **Reports** object, and then double-click **Create a report by using wizard.**

2 Select **Query: Product Query** from the Tables/Queries drop-down list.

3 Double-click **ProductName**, **Quantity**, **UnitPrice**, and **Total Cost** from the list of available fields.

4 Select **Table: Category Table** from the Tables/Queries drop-down list.

5 Double-click **Category Name** from the list of available fields, then click **Next.**

6 Select **Category Table** as your data view. See Figure 11.5.

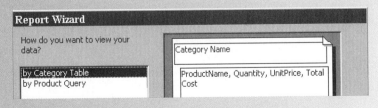

FIGURE 11.5

Part of the Report Wizard Data View Screen

7 Click **Next** two times.

8 Select **ProductName** as the sort order then click **Next** three times.

9 Name the report **Products by Category**, and then click **Finish**. See Figure 11.6.

FIGURE 11.6

Top of the Products by Category Report

Products by Category

Category Name	Product Name	Quantity	Unit Price	Total Cost
Watches				
	Le Grand Sport	5	$288.75	$1,443.75
	Rolex Oyster Submariner	2	$3,148.95	$6,297.90
	Seiko Dive Watch	0	$367.50	$0.00
	Seiko Kinetic Auto Relay	1	$414.75	$414.75
	Seiko Kinetic Auto Relay	4	$446.25	$1,785.00
	Swiss Army Watch	3	$183.75	$551.25
Rings				
	Blue Topaz Ring	7	$261.45	$1,830.15
	Diamond Wedding Ring	5	$682.50	$3,412.50
	Engagement Ring	12	$420.00	$5,040.00
	Tanzanite Ring	9	$467.25	$4,205.25

10 Close the report.

"Is it possible to group more than one time?" Meagan asks.

"Yes," explains Kyle. "Access will let you group on any number of categories."

He suggests you create a report listing the product name and quantity by category by supplier. That way you could see what products you have in each category and which suppliers provide them.

To create a report using grouping:

1 Select the **Reports** object, then double-click **Create a report by using wizard**.

2 Select **Table: Product Table** from the Tables/Queries drop-down list.

3 Double-click **ProductName** and **Quantity** from the list of available fields.

4 Select **Table: Category Table** from the Tables/Queries drop-down list.

5 Double-click **Category Name** from the list of available fields.

6 Select **Table: Supplier Table** from the Tables/Queries drop-down list.

7 Double-click **SupplierName** from the list of available fields, then click **Next**.

8 Select **Category Table** as your data view, then click **Next**.

9 Double-click **SupplierName** to add a grouping level, then click **Next** four times.

10 Name the report **Products by Category by Supplier**, then click **Finish**. See Figure 11.7.

FIGURE 11.7

Products by Category by Supplier

Products by Category by Supplier

Category Name	SupplierName	Product Name	Quantity
Watches			
	Casio USA		
		Swiss Army Watch	3
		G-Shock	10
	Rolex		
		Rolex Oyster Submariner	2
	Seiko USA		
		Seiko Dive Watch	0
		Seiko Kinetic Auto Relay	1
		Le Grand Sport	5
		Seiko Kinetic Auto Relay Titan	4
Rings			
	Johnson Wholesale Jewelry		
		Engagement Ring	12
		Diamond Wedding Ring	5
		Blue Topaz Ring	7
		Tanzanite Ring	9

11 Close the report.

"I can imagine all sorts of reports I would like to generate in our business," says Meagan. "But you said we could summarize as well, right?"

"Correct," Kyle responds. "Let me introduce you to the summarizing process."

SUMMARIZING

Kyle explains that Access will automatically provide summaries on numeric fields in your report if you use the report wizard and establish groups. Summary functions available include summation, average, minimum, and maximum. It will also calculate the percent of total for sums if you like.

"It's important to remember that Access won't let you sum text or other non-numeric fields for obvious reasons," says Kyle. "So if you accidentally set up a field in a table that contains numeric values but identify the field as a data type other than number, you won't be able to use the summary features."

He suggests creating a product cost by category report which sums the total cost of products in each category.

To create a report using grouping and summary options using the report wizard:

1 Select the **Reports** object, and then double-click **Create a report by using wizard**.

2 Select **Query: Product Query** from the Tables/Queries drop-down list.

3 Double-click **ProductName**, **Quantity**, **UnitPrice**, and **Total Cost** from the list of available fields.

4 Select **Table: Category Table** from the Tables/Queries drop-down list.

5 Double-click **Category Name** from the list of available fields, then click **Next**.

6 Select **Category Table** as your data view, then click **Next** two times.

7 Click the **Summary Options** button in the Report Wizard box.

8 Click **Sum** on the Total Cost row to direct Access to add the total cost of each product by group as shown in Figure 11.8.

9 Click **OK** in the Summary Options window, then click **Next** three times.

FIGURE 11.8

Summary Options

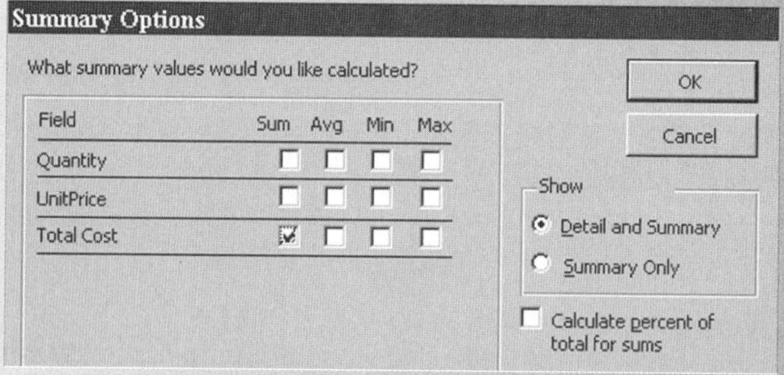

10 Name the report **Product Total Cost by Category**, then click **Finish**. The top part of the report is shown in Figure 11.9 on page 225.

11 Leave the Report window open.

Kyle further explains the nature of the report just generated. In addition to the total provided for each category, the report created a grand total cost of all products as shown in Figure 11.10.

"To help you understand how this summary was created I think it best to show you the Report Design view of this report," Kyle suggests. "Let's open up the report and look."

To examine the sum functions created in the previous report:

1 Switch to the **Design view** of the Product Total Cost by Category report. See Figure 11.11 on page 225.

2 Note the Sum label control and the =Sum([Total Cost]) formula in a text box control both located in the Category ID footer.

Product Total Cost by Category

Category Name	Product Name	Quantity	Unit Price	Total Cost
Watches				
	Seiko Dive Watch	0	$367.50	$0.00
	Rolex Oyster Submariner	2	$3,148.95	$6,297.90
	Le Grand Sport	5	$288.75	$1,443.75
	Seiko Kinetic Auto Relay Tita	4	$446.25	$1,785.00
	Swiss Army Watch	3	$183.75	$551.25
	Seiko Kinetic Auto Relay	1	$414.75	$414.75
Summary for 'CategoryID' = 1 (6 detail records)				
Sum				10492.65
Rings				
	Diamond Wedding Ring	5	$682.50	$3,412.50
	Tanzanite Ring	9	$467.25	$4,205.25
	Engagement Ring	12	$420.00	$5,040.00
	Blue Topaz Ring	7	$261.45	$1,830.15
Summary for 'CategoryID' = 2 (4 detail records)				
Sum				14487.9

FIGURE 11.9

Partial View of the Product Total Cost by Category Report

Earrings				
	Diamond Earrings	2	$535.50	$1,071.00
	Diamond Studs	3	$787.50	$2,362.50
	Diamond Solitare Earrings	3	$1,044.75	$3,134.25
Summary for 'CategoryID' = 4 (3 detail records)				
Sum				6567.75
Grand Total				41586.3

FIGURE 11.10

Bottom View of the Product Total Cost by Category Report

FIGURE 11.11

Design View of Product Total Cost by Category Report

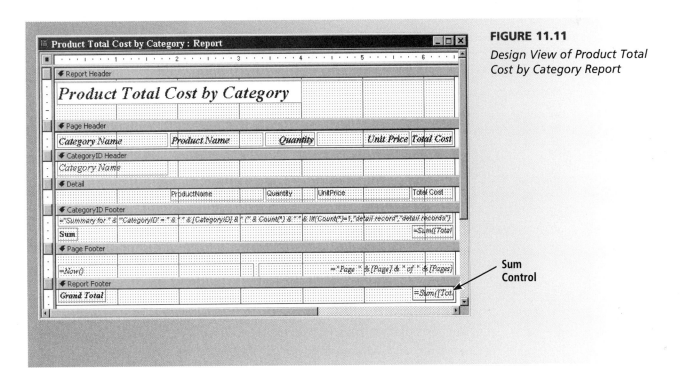

Sum Control

3 Also note the Grand Total label control and the =Sum([Total Cost]) formula in a text box control both located in the Report footer.

4 Right-click one of the **=Sum([Total Cost])** controls, then select **Properties** to reveal the Properties window as shown in Figure 11.12.

FIGURE 11.12
Properties Window

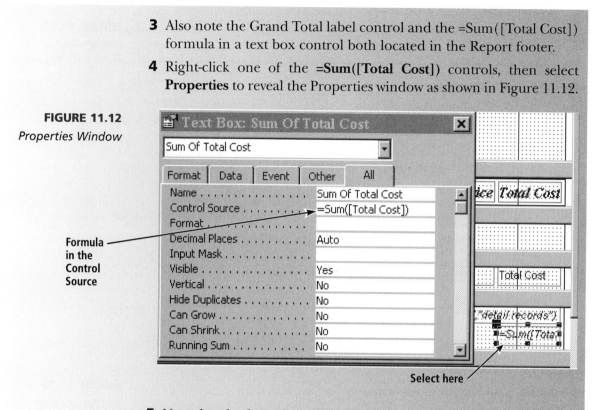

Formula in the Control Source

Select here

5 Note that the formula in the Control Source section of the Properties window contains the formula to sum the Total Cost field of the report.

6 Close the Properties and Report windows. Do not save the changes.

"Placement of these controls determines what gets summed," Kyle explains. "The first control, placed in the CategoryID footer sums the total cost for each category, while the second control, placed in the report footer, sums the total cost for the whole report."

"Why is Total Cost in brackets?" asks Meagan.

"The brackets indicate a field name is being used in a formula," explains Kyle. "The Sum function will sum all the fields named Total Cost located within the CategoryID detail section."

Kyle now advises you to learn more about reports by working on modifying reports.

MODIFY AN EXISTING REPORT

Not all reports you create with the report wizard will look and present the information you need. Thus it is important that you be able to modify an existing report. Kyle has explained how placement of controls in the various sections of a report dictate the information displayed. He suggests that you learn about each report section while creating controls to count and sum, and modifying those control's properties.

Counting and Summing in Report Sections

Kyle explains that all reports have a detail section, but a report can also include a report header, a page header, page footer, and a report footer section. Each section has a specific purpose and prints in a predictable order in the report.

In Design view, sections are represented as bands, and each section that the report contains is represented once. In a printed report, some sections might be repeated many times. You determine where information appears in every section by placing controls such as labels and text boxes. See Figure 11.13.

The Report header appears once at the beginning of a report. You can use it for items such as a logo, report title, or print date. The report header is printed before the Page header on the first page of the report.

The Page header appears at the top of every page in the report. You use it to display items such as column headings.

The Detail section contains the main body of a report's data. This section is repeated for each record in the report's underlying record source.

The Page footer appears at the bottom of every page in the report. You use it to display items such as page numbers.

The Report footer appears once at the end of the report. You use it to display items such as report totals. The Report footer is the last section in the report design but appears before the Page footer on the last page of the printed report.

Kyle explains that the CategoryID footer generated by the report wizard created a text box control for this report which specified which

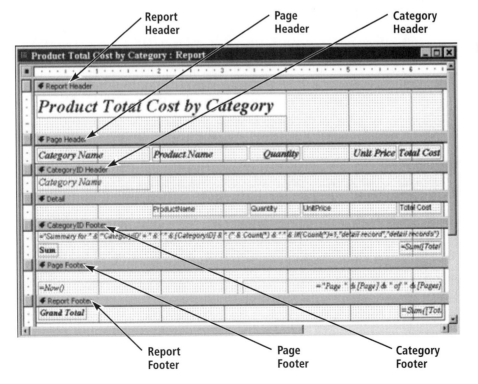

FIGURE 11.13

Report Sections

CategoryID was being totaled, and how many detail records were in the each category section. This was accomplished by using the field name in the control and by using the Count function to add up the number of detail records in each category section.

The formula used in the text box control was ="Summary for " & "'CategoryID' = " & " " & [CategoryID] & " (" & Count(*) & " " & IIf(Count(*)=1,"detail record","detail records") & ")".

In the report this text box control printed the following result for the first category—Summary for 'CategoryID' = 1 (6 detail records). The most important part of this formula was the function Count. To count records in a section the formula Count (*) was used. The **&** symbol is used to separate text from fields and the **IIf** function was to change the final text to either read record or records, depending on whether one or more records were counted.

The CategoryID footer also included a text box control to sum the total cost for each category. Also note that the Report footer also included the identical text box control. The placement of the control in the CategoryID footer caused the control to calculate the total cost for each category while the control placed in the Report footer caused that control to calculate the total cost for the entire report.

"Why don't you use the report you just created to experiment on modifying report sections by adding a control to sum the quantity of each category and adding a control to count all detail records in the entire report?" Kyle recommends.

To modify report sections to sum and count:

1 Open report Product Total Cost by Category in Design view.

2 Open the Toolbox by clicking ⚒ on the toolbar.

3 Select the Textbox button ⎡ab⎤ in the toolbox, then click and drag to create a new textbox control in the CategoryID footer like the one shown in Figure 11.14.

FIGURE 11.14

Creating a New Textbox Control to Sum Quantities

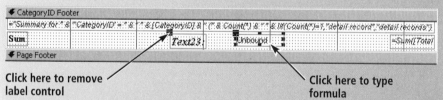

Click here to remove label control

Click here to type formula

4 Click inside the new textbox control and type **=Sum([Quantity])**.

5 Delete the new textbox control label by clicking in the upper left corner of the label, then press the **Delete** key.

6 Change to Layout view and compare your report to Figure 11.15.

7 Change back to Design view.

8 Move the Grand Total label control in the Report footer to the right and place it next to the Grand Total amount as shown in Figure 11.16.

9 Select the **Textbox** button in the toolbox again, then click and drag to create a new textbox control in the Report footer.

Category Name	Product Name	Quantity	Unit Price	Total Cost
Watches				
	Seiko Dive Watch	0	$367.50	$0.00
	Rolex Oyster Submariner	2	$3,148.95	$6,297.90
	Le Grand Sport	5	$288.75	$1,443.75
	Seiko Kinetic Auto Relay Tita	4	$446.25	$1,785.00
	Swiss Army Watch	3	$183.75	$551.25
	Seiko Kinetic Auto Relay	1	$414.75	$414.75
Summary for 'CategoryID' = 1 (6 detail records)				
Sum		15		10492.65

Total quantity for each category

FIGURE 11.15

Modified Report

10 Change the label of the new text box by typing **Total detail records =** in the Label box.

11 Create a formula in the textbox to count the number of records in the entire report by typing **=Count(*)** in the textbox itself. Resize the Label and Text box as shown in Figure 11.16.

Report Footer				
Total detail records -	=Count(*)		Grand Total	=Sum([TTot]

FIGURE 11.16

Modified Report for Counting All Records

12 Change to the Layout view. The bottom portion of your report should look like Figure 11.17.

Earrings				
	Diamond Earrings	2	$535.50	$1,071.00
	Diamond Studs	3	$787.50	$2,362.50
	Diamond Solitare Earrings	3	$1,044.75	$3,134.25
Summary for 'CategoryID' = 4 (3 detail records)				
Sum		8		6567.75
Total detail records -	17		Grand Total	41586.3

FIGURE 11.17

Partial View of Modified Report

13 Save the modified report as Product Total Cost by Category A. Leave the report open.

After adding controls to Count records and Sum different values it is time to modify various properties of those controls like borders, lines, fonts, etc.

Lines, Borders, and Formatting in Report Sections

Access allows you to modify reports by adding lines and modifying properties of existing controls like the font name, size, weight, etc. Kyle suggests that you and Nathan look over the report you just modified and determine what changes you think would add to its look and usefulness.

"I think it would be nice to better separate each category section with a line," Nathan comments, "and get rid of that border around the grand total."

"I agree," you respond. "We should also have a line above each total for the sum of watches, earrings, etc. Plus I would like to change the font style of the controls in the Report footer to Times New Roman, size 10, bold, and italicized."

"How about making the total cost of each category look like currency?" Meagan suggests.

"Go for it!" Kyle exclaims.

To add lines, modify borders, and change formatting:

1 Continue with the modified report you just completed above.

2 Change back to the Design view.

3 Select the **Line button** ⬚ in the toolbox.

4 Click and drag the mouse cursor from just under the label Sum in the CategoryID footer to just under the lower right corner of the =Sum([Total]) text box. A line should appear in the Layout view as shown in Figure 11.18.

5 Select the **Line button** in the toolbox again.

6 Add a short line just above the =Sum([Quantity]) control in the CategoryID footer. A line should appear in the Layout view as shown in Figure 11.18.

7 Change back to the Layout view. The top portion of your report should look like Figure 11.18

FIGURE 11.18

Lines Added to Report

Category Name	Product Name	Quantity	Unit Price	Total Cost
Watches				
	Seiko Dive Watch	0	$367.50	$0.00
	Rolex Oyster Submariner	2	$3,148.95	$6,297.90
	Le Grand Sport	5	$288.75	$1,443.75
	Seiko Kinetic Auto Relay Tita	4	$446.25	$1,785.00
	Swiss Army Watch	3	$183.75	$551.25
	Seiko Kinetic Auto Relay	1	$414.75	$414.75
Summary for 'CategoryID' = 1 (6 detail records)				
Sum		15		10492.65
Rings				

Lines Added

8 Change back to Design view.

9 Right-click the **=Sum([Total])** control in the Report footer section, then click **Properties**.

10 Click the drop-down arrow in the **Format property**, then scroll down the list of format alternatives.

11 Select **Currency** like in Figure 11.19.

12 Scroll down the properties listing until you see the Border Style property.

13 Click the drop-down arrow in the **Border Style property** (which currently says Solid) and select **Transparent**.

14 Scroll down the properties listing until you see the Font Weight property.

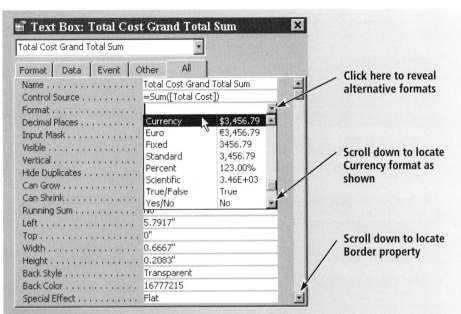

FIGURE 11.19

*Text Box Properties
Window*

15 Click the drop-down arrow in the **Font Weight property** (which currently says Normal) and select **Bold**, then close the Text Box Properties window.

16 Change the formatting for the =Sum([Total]) control in the CategoryID footer section to **Currency** following the same procedures, then close the Properties window.

17 Change the Font Name, Font Size, Font Weight, and Font Italic properties of all the Report Footer controls to Times New Roman, 10, Bold, and Italics. This can be done as described before using the Properties window or by using the toolbar. This time select all of the labels and text boxes located in the Report footer section by holding the **Shift** key down while you select each control.

18 Select **Times New Roman**, **10**, **Bold**, and **Italics** from the formatting toolbar as shown in Figure 11.20 on page 232.

19 Change back to the layout view. Your report should look like Figure 11.21 on page 233.

20 Close the report window saving all changes.

FIGURE 11.20

Changing Text Properties Using the Formatting Toolbar

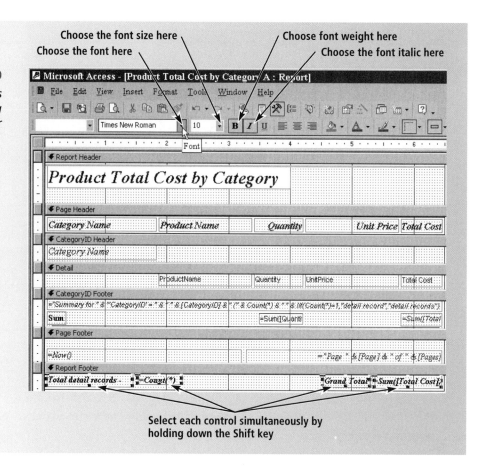

FIGURE 11.21

Final Revised Report

Product Total Cost by Category

Category Name	Product Name	Quantity	Unit Price	Total Cost
Watches				
	Seiko Dive Watch	0	$367.50	$0.00
	Rolex Oyster Submariner	2	$3,148.95	$6,297.90
	Le Grand Sport	5	$288.75	$1,443.75
	Seiko Kinetic Auto Relay Tita	4	$446.25	$1,785.00
	Swiss Army Watch	3	$183.75	$551.25
	Seiko Kinetic Auto Relay	1	$414.75	$414.75
Summary for 'CategoryID' = 1 (6 detail records)				
Sum		15		$10,492.65
Rings				
	Diamond Wedding Ring	5	$682.50	$3,412.50
	Tanzanite Ring	9	$467.25	$4,205.25
	Engagement Ring	12	$420.00	$5,040.00
	Blue Topaz Ring	7	$261.45	$1,830.15
Summary for 'CategoryID' = 2 (4 detail records)				
Sum		33		$14,487.90
Necklaces				
	Diamond Pendant	7	$393.75	$2,756.25
	Topaz Necklace	5	$393.75	$1,968.75
	Amethyst Pendant	8	$204.75	$1,638.00
	Diamond Heart Slide	4	$918.75	$3,675.00
Summary for 'CategoryID' = 3 (4 detail records)				
Sum		24		$10,038.00
Earrings				
	Diamond Earrings	2	$535.50	$1,071.00
	Diamond Studs	3	$787.50	$2,362.50
	Diamond Solitare Earrings	3	$1,044.75	$3,134.25
Summary for 'CategoryID' = 4 (3 detail records)				
Sum		8		$6,567.75
Total detail records -	17		Grand Total	$41,586.30

"Wow, that was a lot of work," Meagan complains. "Why can't the Report wizard do all this for us in the first place?"

"Good question," Kyle answers. "Reports have so many variations that the Report wizard can only begin to create reports. The rest is up to us!"

END NOTE
. . . .

In this chapter, you have learned how to use a query to create a report, use grouping and summarizing to enhance a report's usefulness, and modified a report generated by a report wizard to be more useful. Now you are ready to take on the world and create your own solutions to database organization and reporting problems.

practice

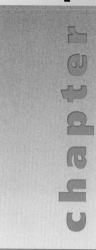

Chapter 11 Questions

1 Why create a report from a query? Why not just print your query results?

2 Can you always add a field from any table to a report based on a query?

3 When creating a report, what does grouping accomplish?

4 When creating a report, what does the summarization process accomplish?

5 Is it possible to group more than one item?

6 What do the [ ] (brackets) signify in an Access formula?

7 How do you determine where information appears in a report?

8 What type of control is used in a report to add values?

9 What function is used (and how is it written) to count records in a report?

10 Describe two separate means by which a control's font weight can be modified from normal to bold.

Chapter 11 Assignments

Make the following changes for Coast Jewelers using the Ch 11 - Coast.mdb file found on your student disk *after* you have completed all the changes specified in the chapter.

1 *Create a new report for Coast Jewelers using a query from the report wizard*

    a Create a report using all the fields present in the Buyer query. View the data by Buyers table with no grouping or summarization in a compact style.

    b Save the new report as **Buyers A**.

    c Print the new report.

2 *Create a new report for Coast Jewelers with grouping and summarization*

    a Create a report using the BuyerName, ProductName, Quantity, UnitPrice, and Total Cost fields present in the Buyer query. View the data by Buyers Table and group by BuyerName. Calculate the sum value for Total Cost showing detail and summary in a compact style.

    b Save the new report as **Buyers B**.

    c Print the new report.

3 *Modify a report for Coast Jewelers*

    a Open the report created in Assignment 2.

    b Change the name of the report to Products by Buyer.

    c Format the total cost controls in the BuyerID and Report footers to Currency.

    d Create new controls in the BuyerID and Report footers to sum the quantity field placing the new controls directly under the quantity column. Remove the labels associated with the new controls.

    e Move the Grand Total label in the Report footer to the right next to the Quantity control create above.

    f Create a new control to count the number of records in the entire report placing the control in the left-most part of the Report footer. Label the control Total Records:.

    g Change the font name and font size properties of the Count text box control and label to Arial and 10 respectively.

    h Add lines to separate each buyer.

    i Add a line above each quantity total.

    j Add a line above each total cost total.

    k Save the new report as **Buyers C**.

    l Print the new report.

Chapter 11 Case Problem: Kelly's Boutique

In the last chapter you created some forms for Kelly's Boutique. She would now like you to create and print some reports for her use in better understanding her inventory needs in the future. Use the file Ch 11 - Kelly.mdb on your student disk.

1 Kelly would like you to use an existing query (Book Query) to generate a report listing all of the field names provided in the query and viewed by department table with no grouping or summarizing in a formal style. Save the newly created report as **Ch 11 Kelly Case 1**, and then print it without any modifications.

2 Next, Kelly would like you to use an existing query (Publisher Query) to generate a report including the publisher, dept, booktitle, listprice, quantity, and retail value fields provided in the query and viewed by publisher table with no grouping or summarizing in a formal style. Save the newly created report as **Ch 11 Kelly Case 2**, and then print it without any modifications.

3 Next, Kelly would like you to use an existing query (Publisher Query) to generate a report including the publisher, dept, booktitle, listprice, quantity, and retail value fields provided in the query and viewed by publisher table grouped by publisher with a total retail value subtotal and total in a formal style. Include a total records text box control and label in the report footer and a total quantity of books text box control by publisher and in total with no label. Change the font size of the report title to 11 and the font weight to bold. Resize the report header so that the entire report prints on one page. Save the newly created report as **Ch 11 Kelly Case 3**, and then print it without any further modifications.

4 Modify the report you created in Item 3 above by moving column labels and fields around to make the report more presentable. Change the title to Ch 11 Kelly Case 4. Remove the text box control which totals the number or records for each publisher. Move the controls in the PubNum footer up and shrink the PubNum footer as well. Include lines to separate publishers and total quantity and retail values. Modify font names and sizes for consistency and format the retail value totals to currency. Save the newly created report as **Ch 11 Kelly Case 4**, and then print it.

Index

Excel Chapters (1–6)